Twayne's Filmmakers Series

Frank Beaver, Editor

David Lynch

David Lynch with Billy Wilder. Courtesy of *Women's Wear Daily* and Richard Bowditch. © Richard Bowditch 1991.

DAVID LYNCH

Kenneth C. Kaleta

TWAYNE PUBLISHERS • NEW YORK
MAXWELL MACMILLAN CANADA • TORONTO
MAXWELL MACMILLAN INTERNATIONAL
NEW YORK • OXFORD • SINGAPORE • SYDNEY

David Lynch
Kenneth C. Kaleta

Twayne Publishers
Macmillan Publishing Company
866 Third Avenue
New York, New York 10022

Maxwell Macmillan Canada, Inc.
1200 Eglinton Avenue East
Suite 200
Don Mills, Ontario M3C 3N1

Library of Congress Cataloging-in-Publication Data
Kaleta, Kenneth C.
David Lynch / Kenneth C. Kaleta.
p. cm. — (Twayne's filmmakers series)
Includes bibliographical references and index.
ISBN 0-8057-9317-8 — ISBN 0-8057-9323-2 (pbk.)
1. Lynch, David, 1946– — Criticism and interpretation.
I. Title. II. Series.
PN1998.3.L96K35 1992
791.43′0233′092—dc20 92-4794
CIP

The paper used in this publication meets the minimum requirements of American National Standard for Information Sciences—Permanence of Paper for Printed Library Materials. ANSI Z3948-1984. ♾™

10 9 8 7 6 5 4 3 2 1 (hc)
10 9 8 7 6 5 4 3 2 1 (pb)

Printed in the United States of America

CONTENTS

FOREWORD

Of all the contemporary arts, the motion picture is particularly timely and diverse as a popular culture enterprise. This lively art form cleverly combines storytelling with photography to achieve what has been a quintessential twentieth-century phenomenon. Individual as well as national and cultural interests have made the medium an unusually varied one for artistic expression and analysis. Films have been exploited for commercial gain, for political purposes, for experimentation, and for self-exploration. The various responses to the motion picture have given rise to different labels for both the fun and the seriousness with which this art form has been received, ranging from "the movies" to "cinema." These labels hint at both the theoretical and sociological parameters of the film medium.

A collective art, the motion picture has nevertheless allowed individual genius to flourish in all its artistic and technical areas: directing, screenwriting, cinematography, acting, editing. The medium also encompasses many genres beyond the narrative film, including documentary, animated, and avant-garde expression. The range and diversity of motion pictures suggest rich opportunities for appreciation and for study.

The Twayne Filmmakers Series examines the full panorama of motion picture history and art. Many studies are auteur-oriented and elucidate the work of individual directors whose ideas and cinematic styles make them authors of their films. Other studies examine film movements and genres or analyze cinema from a national perspective. The series seeks to illuminate all the many aspects of film for the film student, the scholar, and the general reader.

Frank Beaver

PREFACE

David Lynch has made his world part of the twentieth-century experience. Dialogue from his screenplays has become colloquial language; scenes from his films have become pop-culture Americana. People, locations, and events are described as "something out of David Lynch."

What is it in a shot from his films or a line of his dialogue that insinuates itself into the audience's imagination? Certainly audience members have not recently found a severed body part in a vacant lot, chased a deformed creature through London's streets, or invented a silent runner for drapes. That these scenes are Lynch's vision of his world is unquestionable; but more significant, the force of his images—their charge—uniquely and accurately describes our contemporary world. Lynch's cinematic shards reflect and create contemporary reality.

Bridging the eighteenth and nineteenth centuries, William Blake created a mythic world of Innocence and Experience in his poetry and copper-plate illustrations. His was a world of spiritualism, dreams and nightmares, inhabited by angels and devils. His literary and visual creation of a dual world may be a forerunner of David Lynch's evolving cinematic world. Lynch bridges the twentieth and twenty-first centuries with his dual world of beauty and violence, with dual evocations of wonder and terror. Lynch creates these physical and emotional worlds as screenwriter and director; he extends his artistic innovations with musical compositions and production work; he expands from his theater films to include television films. But make no mistake, David Lynch's masterstroke, regardless of the medium, is always a compelling invitation into Lynch's world. His world is focused on its very lack of core, a postmodernist rendering, oxymoronic and awesome, forcing us to watch while we think we would like to turn away.

Lynch's world is good and evil. Bad and good openly and plainly coexist. Under every façade lies an infected root; under every clean, middle American picture is some dark and hidden secret. But in Lynch, good and evil also commingle. Good may be evil or evil good.

"Job Troubled By Dreams." Engraving by William Blake. Courtesy of the Philadelphia Museum of Art.

It is left to the observer to make the value judgment. A woman is beautiful, then grotesque, as a shift in camera angle changes her clean good looks to a common harshness. In Lynch's world, "Nothing is good or bad but *viewing* makes it so." Lynch does not write his story in words and tell it with pictures; he is a filmmaker who creates objective duality, so suitable to the world of the motion picture.

Lynch films life as it passes before the camera; Lynch gives us montage without superimposing an edit. Evaluation and narration, therefore, become a joint task of filmmaker and audience. Lynch presents his world, but we need to understand it as ours. Thus, Lynch's films are genuine images; they demand input from the viewer, they demand perspective. Lynch invites us into his world and finally demands our evaluation.

In this way, Lynch's films recall the films of Luis Buñuel, particularly early works like *Un Chien Andalou.* Lynch begins his work with pictures and a series of scenes. "You want to make a feature film, you get ideas for 70 scenes. Put them on three-by-five cards. As soon as you have 70, you have a feature film."[1]

As in *Un Chien Andalou,* Lynch grafts singular visual episodes into a fluid film narrative. Each of the shots is a visualization of Lynch's world. Yet each in context is a part of the film's flow. The scenes of the beautiful and the ugly pass before the viewer without directorial definition. The camera makes an aesthetic but amoral choice. Images are often grotesque, always spellbinding: the bloated, floating, orange-haired Baron Vladimir Harkonnen in *Dune,* the rotted teeth of Bobby Peru in *Wild at Heart,* the sanguine chicken on Henry's dinner plate in *Eraserhead.* Frightening shots, ironically often beautiful, are juxtaposed with lyric, pastoral shots and sounds of innocence: the stained-glass windows of a Lumberton church in *Blue Velvet,* the scenic beauty of Washington's "Twin Peaks," the blue sky framing castle spires in *Dune.* Lynch, beyond the scope of Buñuel's early films, adds sound to the visual message. He uses the sounds of machinery and wind and glorious music, sometimes with lyrics of his own creation. He also uses the sounds of silence—in Lynch often the loudest sound of all.

Duality exists as well in Lynch's pacing. Time often passes too quickly at a moment of complicated dialogue. "Did we miss the explanation of the water of life? Who did they say is mining the spice?" Other scenes seem to hold too long and hang too static in a motion picture. A mother's pitiful grief becomes grotesque as the camera holds a shot of her wailing face. Of course, time is a personal measure of passing events; moments lazing after the alarm clock sounds do not equal moments in the dentist's chair. The audience makes an evaluation of too much or too little time spent on a scene; Lynch's camera does not editorialize.

Lynch's world is violent and hilarious, bizarre and banal. The deformed creature in *Elephant Man* makes a brilliant speech to defend his life and his humanity while cowering in the public urinals in London's Liverpool Station. The mise-en-scène earlier gave us a lyrical parade in a shot of circus freaks lantern-lighted in the foreground, their escape reflected in dark waters of the open Belgian countryside. Lula's frenzied thrashing on cotton balls on a bed in *Wild at Heart* gives way to Sailor's rock-and-roll posing on a dance floor. Dancing couples in *Twin Peaks* don't care that a man is going mad on the floor; in fact, the impassioned forehead-slapping of the madman—a murdered girl's father and murderer—starts a dance fad. The dog that carries away a severed hand in *Wild at Heart* is no more extraordinary than the boy who finds a severed ear in a field in *Blue Velvet*. Life is desperate, and life is desperately funny.

Lynch is an innovator in cinema. Yet Lynch is an imitator in cinema. He is a filmmaker who knows, loves, and uses film history and its conventions. In *Blue Velvet,* the long, panning shot from the picket fence and neon-bright flowers down to the maggots that live beneath our backyards is as much Lynch innovation as the shot of the frenzied, oxygen-snorting drug dealer. Rossellini's rendition of the title song in close-up suggests Ingrid Bergman's face and evokes a screen icon. In another scene, Jeffrey Beaumont watches Dorothy Vallens through wardrobe doors in a sadomasochistic sexual encounter that recalls Hitchcock's famous heroes and their voyeuristic hanky-panky in some of our most treasured film classics.

As his style evolves, Lynch assimilates idiosyncrasies of his latest medium, TV. A Summer's Eve or Fruit of the Loom commercial seems not to intrude on *Twin Peaks,* but to extend the surreal implications of Lynch on film. Lynch is involved in directing commercials and in merchandising his TV film. Lynch's merchandising ideas enhance this contemporary motion-picture/business phenomenon and illustrate that Lynch is not the *aloof artist.*

Thus, too, Lynch's artistic creations include Lynch himself. He continues beyond precedent to extend, to satirize, and to display his contemporary aesthetic. Somewhere of course a line may be crossed and his balance disrupted. Here, over the border, the artist wakes up to be merely a celebrity. Will it be another projected TV sitcom? Another battery of perfume ads? Will the new music video do it? Or can David Lynch continue to explore this technical, electronic frontier, finding some new-world, next-century post-postmodernism?

In fact, Lynch consistently keeps an ear to the tempo of the times, scores ratings successes and starts trends. He continues to achieve critical success—including Oscar nominations for writing and directing, awards from the New York and Los Angeles critics, and the Golden Palm Award for Best Film at the Cannes Film Festival—while continuing to create cult classics. Lynch turns his films simultaneously into homage, parody, joke, and guessing game. But most important, he creates riveting movies. You don't take your eyes off Lynch—although you may want to. You marvel at the technical expertise, the twists, the references to history and culture, the nuances, the jokes. You turn away from the horror; you hide your face—from terror? from laughing? But you don't take your eyes off Lynch.

David Lynch is a filmmaker. He knows movies and movie making. The world he presents is his own. Yet, in its dark and hilarious peculiarities, we see universal human reflections through his severe camera lens. To watch Lynch's films is to study motion pictures. To enter Lynch's world is to see our own.

ACKNOWLEDGMENTS

This project has been realized with contributions from family, friends, and professionals in the art and academic communities. I note with particular gratitude Jane, my wife, for her continuing support and for her research skills and Kevin Pawley for his tireless rhetorical and electronic assistance. I also acknowledge: in New Jersey, extenders Casey and Rudy, faculty and staff of the communications department of Rowan College of New Jersey, and my mother; in Philadelphia, Anthony and Joan D'Antonio, Rodger La Pelle, and, at the Pennsylvania Academy of the Fine Arts, Sharon Skeel; in New York, Richard Bowditch, Mary Corliss at the film archives of the Museum of Modern Art, Diane Jones at *W,* and Mark Zadrozny at Twayne; in Wilmington, N.C., Thurston Edwards, and, at the New Hanover Library, Daniel C. Horne; in California, Dr. Ronald N. Burkoff, College Library, University of Southern California; in Japan, Rumi Miura, Preparing Office, Touku Museum; and in England, David Nunn, Director, London Hospital Medical College Museum; my dad; and, of course, all my past, present, and future students. Thank you.

CHRONOLOGY

1946	David Keith Lynch born on 20 January in Missoula, Montana.
1963–1964	Attends the Corcoran School of Art in Washington, D.C.
1964–1965	Attends the Boston Museum School.
1966	Enters the Pennsylvania Academy of the Fine Arts in Philadelphia.
1967	*Six Men Getting Sick* filmed and awarded the second annual Dr. William S. Biddle Cadwalader Memorial Prize, Pennsylvania Academy of the Fine Arts. *The Alphabet* filmed and awarded an American Film Institute Grant.
1968	Participates in a group exhibition at the William Barnett Gallery in Philadelphia.
1969	Solo exhibition at the Paley Library Gallery in Philadelphia.
1970	*The Grandmother.* Attends the American Film Institute's Center for Advanced Film Studies in Los Angeles.
1972	Begins shooting *Eraserhead,* his first full-length film.
1977	*Eraserhead* premieres in Los Angeles.
1979	Participates in a group exhibition at the Washington International Art Fair, Washington, D.C.
1980	*The Elephant Man.*
1982	Launches his weekly cartoon, "The Angriest Dog in the World."
1984	*Dune.*

1986 *Blue Velvet* premieres and is voted best film of 1986 by the National Society of Film Critics. *Blue Velvet* is also nominated for Academy Awards for best film and best director.

1987 Solo exhibition at the Rodger La Pelle Galleries in Philadelphia. Awarded the first annual Rossellini Award for Film Direction. Lynch also designs the statuette for the Rossellini Award (a crystal egg hatching a filmstrip).

1988 Appears as an actor in Tina Rathborne's *Zelly and Me*.

1989 Solo exhibition at the Leo Castelli Gallery in New York. Participates in a group exhibition at the University of Hawaii in Honolulu and in the "Revelations" exhibition at the Espace Lamartine in Paris. With Angelo Badalamenti, coproduces a videotape, *Industrial Symphony No. 1,* and a concert at the New Wave Festival, Brooklyn Academy of Music.

1990 "American Chronicles" airs on television. First season of "Twin Peaks." Appears in *Hollywood Mavericks: Top Directors Talk about Filmmaking*. *Wild at Heart* opens and is awarded the Golden Palm for best film at the 43d International Film Festival in Cannes.

1991 "Twin Peaks" is canceled during its second season on television. Solo exhibition at the Payne Galleries, Moravian College, Bethlehem, Pennsylvania. The Touku Museum of Contemporary Art in Tokyo mounts an exhibition of Lynch's paintings. Recipient of the American Film Institute's first Franklin J. Schaffner Alumni Medal.

1992 Television debut of "On the Air." *Twin Peaks: Fire Walk with Me* (feature film).

Early Lynch—*Eraserhead*

> Suppose yourself in a large cinema, sitting at first in the back row, and gradually moving up . . . until your nose is almost pressed against the screen. Gradually the stars' faces dissolve into dancing grain; tiny details assume grotesque proportions . . . it becomes clear that the illusion itself is reality.
>
> —Salman Rushdie

David Keith Lynch seems to have been the all-American Boy. He was born in Missoula, Montana, 20 January 1946. Lynch remembers a rural childhood: "My father was a research scientist for the Department of Agriculture in Washington. We were in the woods all the time. I'd sorta had enough of the woods by the time I left, but still, lumber and lumberjacks, all this kinda thing, that's America to me."[1] Lynch grew up in the Pacific Northwest, in small towns in Montana, Idaho, and Washington and lived for a time in North Carolina. The first of three children, he was a Boy Scout and an usher at John F. Kennedy's presidential inauguration.

During his high-school years "he ran for class treasurer; his slogan was Save with Dave. He lost."[2] Lynch attended Hammond High School in Alexandria, Virginia. "'As a teenager, I was really trying to have fun 24 hours a day,' says Lynch. 'I didn't start thinking until I was 20 or 21. I was doing regular goofball stuff.' According to the director Jack Fisk, who went to high school with him, Lynch and his girlfriend were voted 'cutest couple' and are pictured in the yearbook aboard a bicycle built for two" (Woodward, 30).

Lynch shares the maturation process of the U.S. baby boomers' first wave. A child of the affluent, promising fifties, he grew up in the turbulent sixties. He was a member of a youth culture that sought a world of mind-expanding experimentation and uninhibited exuberance; he witnessed the national idealism assassinated with JFK in Dallas. "In the official biography prepared for *Wild at Heart,* Mr. Lynch divulges only two pieces of information: that he is a native of Missoula, Mont., and that he is an Eagle Scout. 'Those two things are not a joke; they are there because they are the most important,' he said earnestly, explaining factors that have formed his values and his outlook in life."[3]

From his childhood years, Lynch recalls having had fantasies and dark thoughts. Neither stereotypically all-American nor always resulting in artistic issue, Lynch's adolescent brooding is, nonetheless, identifiable to most of his audience. Heightened by his fascination with the forbidden, a sensitivity to hypocrisy tinged with melancholy pervades his films. "Lynch brings this canny naivete, this promiscuous curiosity, to every aspect of his life and work."[4]

Lynch attended the Corcoran School of Art in Washington, D.C., from 1963 to 1964. He studied at the Boston Museum School in that city from 1964 to 1965, where he was attracted to works by artists ranging from Francis Bacon to James Hopper. He was drawn to the expressionists, who seek an objective representation of inner feelings. Enthusiastically, the student artist abandoned the confines of the dusty classroom and "set off for Europe to study with the expressionist painter Oskar Kokoschka" (Woodward, 30).

Kokoschka (1869–1980) generated his style in central Europe at the beginning of the century. The artist was influenced by Hodler, Klimt, Munch, and his own graphic works, particularly illustrations from his story "The Dreaming Boys." Kokoschka further related his painting to architecture. The canvas of *The Tempest,* for example, is more than seven feet long, dominating the largest rooms in museums; his composition enhances the relationship. His influence is felt in early silent German mood films, including Wiene's expressionistic masterpiece, *The Cabinet of Dr. Caligari* (1919). Obviously, the larger-than-life movie screen is an idealized province for making bold, expressionistic statements.

Dismissed from art school because of his works' exoticism, Kokoschka joined the avant-garde. Kokoschka developed a multifaceted career; his interests spread far beyond painting to include writing, lecturing, and some dabbling as an art theorist. Kokoschka's larger-than-life history epitomizes that of the classic "artist." His flamboyant convictions about art often made his personal life a drama. Incidents in his biography exemplify the confrontation of the artist with conventional authority. Like this multimedia master before him, Lynch is a dynamic personality, a recognizable figure in art. "Like Kokoschka—who out of his profound obsession with the woman who rejected him, made a clumsy life-size replica of her, complete with genitals—Lynch has cultivated an unusual fondness for dolls. In art school Lynch made a pinball machine in the figure of a woman—lights flashed and the figure screamed if the ball went in its mouth."[5]

Lynch's first trip to Europe in 1965 was made with boyhood friend Jack Fisk. His experience as an expatriate fell apart after only 15 days. Lynch returned to the U.S. to continue his study of painting, and in January 1966, entered the Pennsylvania Academy of the Fine Arts in Philadelphia (PAFA). The young student painter studied, acquired urban experiences, and experimented in filmmaking. "After two short years there, he started making short films, 'but only because I wanted my paintings to move,' he said."[6]

Lynch's monumental nightmare world on screen cell-by-cell suggests moving studies for an idealized cinematic canvas. A painterly point of view is fundamental to Lynch's filmmaking. Like Theodore Géricault's studies of corpses for his massive painting *The Raft of the Medusa,* Lynch experiments with mice and other animals to investigate tones and textures. This connection to training in the plastic arts is also a conduit in the work of other avant-garde filmmakers of our time. The evolving painter's perspective in contemporary cinema makes the influence of the plastic arts formative for Lynch and for an emerging film aesthetic.

In his art study, Lynch read theorists and "discovered a book called *The Art Spirit,*" written by American turn-of-the-century artist and teacher Robert Henri."[7] Like Lynch, Henri (1865–1929) moved from rural America (Ohio) to an urban, cultural center (New York City). A distinctively American artist, Henri was an urban realist painter and a leader of the Ash Can School. He legitimized everyday city life as a subject of painting. Henri, like Lynch, studied at PAFA in Philadelphia. Henri too bridges changing centuries, crossing over with America from the agricultural nineteenth into the industrial twentieth century.

Henri's aesthetics recognize the beautiful and the ugly as Art's province. The artist too is seen to have a double perspective. "A work of art in itself is a gesture and it may be warm or cold, inviting or repellent."[8] Henri teaches that the dual intention of the artist is to evoke

"The Sick Man." Painting by David Lynch. Courtesy of Rodger La Pelle and Christine McGinnis.

pleasure or abhorrence of his work. Both responses to art are desirable, as long as response is achieved.

Consequently, an artist must turn his eye toward everything and find his subject in all things. He must recognize that his world encompasses everything everywhere. "Nature is sometimes seen through very obscure evidences," he wrote, suggesting that the truth is often found by unconventional methods and in unusual places as well as in the most obvious (Henri, 186). The mundane and the extraordinary are presented without moralizing. Henri's theory seems to have claimed a niche in Lynch's developing artistic philosophy. Lynch encompasses vomiting, maiming, and violence in his world of giants, children, and cockroaches.

"If you look past the model at the background," Henri wrote more than once, "it responds to your appeal and comes forward. It is no longer a background" (Henri, 58). Lynch seems to have adopted this theory as well. *Eraserhead* is overtly a film in which background is indiscernible from foreground; subconscious and fantasy are indistinguishable, nightmare ebbs into reality. Lynch is a filmmaker who sees each shot as a composition, not as a step in a narrative process. He refuses to define; he creates pattern. And throughout all of Lynch's works, his details, nuances, complicated minor characters, dense texture, elliptical structure, and fluidity of thoughts and actions illustrate the evolution of the philosophy Lynch determined in art school.

Lynch's passionate style is the constant in a plethora of seemingly contradictory interests he pursues from the most esoteric to the most shamelessly commercial. It is impossible to miss Lynch's connection as artist and celebrity to Henri's exhortation: "Do whatever you do intensely" (Henri, 262). David Lynch becomes increasingly difficult to separate from his art. Lynch is the pop icon, "The Wizard of Weird" of a *Time* cover story (Corliss 1990, 84–86). From filmmaking to furniture design, David Lynch is an artist continuing to explore. Lynch today is his own creation, in part the incarnation of the artistic philosophy of Robert Henri.

While an art student Lynch also assimilated urban life in the old East Coast city of Philadelphia. This city has been a target of abuse in American films ever since it was the butt of W. C. Fields's comic epitaph in *Vanity Fair*: "Here Lies W. C. Fields. I Would Rather Be in Philadelphia."[9] Later, in the golden decade of the 1930s, Ginger Rogers and Una Merkel play musical-comedy actresses who loathe trying out *42nd Street*'s "Pretty Lady" at the Arch Street Theater in Philadelphia and change the postal abbreviation of the Keystone State to a state of mind: "Philadelphia, PA, and on Sunday it's PU." But perhaps the city's greatest motion-picture notoriety to date—second only to the *Rocky* films—is its effect on the young David Lynch. Lynch's traumatic experiences in Philadelphia are ironically credited by him with igniting his artistic philosophy.

Lynch lived in Philadelphia from 1966 through 1970, collecting "dead things including mice, weeds, bugs, and even a moldy sandwich. They were arranged on a window sill."[10] While studying at

PAFA and beginning his painting career, "he lived for much of that time in an industrial district at 13th and Wood Streets, across from the old city morgue."[11] Violence and danger lurked around every corner. Renting catercorner from Philadelphia's city morgue exposed Lynch to urban brutality. He knew firsthand the fear of decaying urban order. Yet he studied art daily—true and beautiful representations of truth and beauty. His perception became dual: he saw both the surface and its rotten underbelly. Philadelphia sparks the artist's epiphany.

Lynch's center-city resume also includes residing near a murder scene and being home on several occasions during burglaries. "Lynch told writer Gary Indiana in 1978, '. . . There was racial tension and just . . . violence and fear. I said to someone, all that separated me from the outside world was this brick wall, and they started laughing, like, "What more do you want?" you know? But that brick wall was like paper.' "[12] David Lynch acknowledges Philadelphia as the impetus that fascinated and frightened him into his philosophy. Almost fifteen years later, Lynch appraised his response to the city: "I've said many, many, many unkind things about Philadelphia, and I meant every one" (Gary Thompson, 33).

This connection to Philadelphia suggests Lynch's artistic development outside of the studio classroom. Assimilating new places is part of the youthful experience, but Philadelphia's impact on Lynch is quite dramatic. The seediness of the city repels and ignites a fuse: Philadelphia coerces Lynch into an artistic catharsis. "In an interview with the *Inquirer* in September 1986, Lynch called Philadelphia 'the sickest, most corrupt, decaying city filled with fear I ever set foot in in my life. I saw horrible things, horrible, horrible things while I lived there.' He said, 'It was a strange life. For the first time I really lived beneath the surface. I was never aware of anything normal. I was only aware of this world of fear and art. I lived inside this cocoon of fear.' He has said, 'I never had an original idea until I came to Philadelphia.' "[13]

Lynch began making films while in art school in Philadelphia, where his talent was immediately recognized. Already given honorable mention in the faculty prize selection the first year for his sculpture, David Lynch was awarded the second annual Dr. William S. Biddle Cadwalader Memorial Prize from PAFA in May 1967. The prize awarded the sum of $250, according to its description in the school catalogue, and the award-winning work was exhibited. "The prize was divided this year, and the two winners were David Lynch, who did an experimental motion picture combined with sculpture;

and Nikolai Sibiriakoff, who did a painting. Honorable mentions were awarded to Bruce Samuelson and Nicolas Feher."[14]

Memory of the reaction to the film project's exhibition still surfaces more than twenty years later in Philadelphia. Stylistically and thematically forerunner of *Eraserhead* and later works of Lynch, his first film also attests to Lynch's ability to shock and cause audience sensation. "His PAFA file shows a rectangular screen with three gape-mouthed face fragments staring out while a fuller bust, jaw pressed to palm, leers disapprovingly. Onto the three-dimensional screen, Lynch projected a short film that, as then fellow student Bruce Samuelson recalls, was wound around long arms extended on each side of his secondhand 8mm camera, so the film literally ran in a loop on the squeaking, rattling contraption. Samuelson remembers images of burning canvases and, prominently, vomiting heads; the crowd loved it, he says. Lynch, never one to describe his work literally, characterizes *Six Men Getting Sick* as '57 minutes of growth and fire, and three seconds of vomit.' "[15]

The animated color painting runs only one minute. It was produced at a cost of $200. As a continuous loop, it ran over and over again. Lynch described it: "It started off with six heads and then arms and stomachs grew in. The heads caught fire and then all of the heads got violently sick and then it started all over again" (Robertson, 1). Lynch's sculpture screen for the project suggests his later style in both plastic and cinematic art. The use of a projector and the inclusion of the operating machine as part of the sculpture introduces an industrial element present in many subsequent Lynch works. The project also initiates Lynch's interest in vomiting, which will be graphically and frequently represented in his paintings as well as in his full-length films from *Eraserhead* to *Wild at Heart*.

Most important, *Six Men Getting Sick* involves the young student painter in making film. The first film minute also triggers several significant events of Lynch's next years. H. Barton Wasserman and Rodger La Pelle, painter and center-city gallery owner, hire Lynch after seeing his prize-winning exhibition at PAFA. After leaving the academy, David Lynch works at the La Pelle Printers in Philadelphia's Germantown. He learns printing at La Pelle's while working on his second film, a project commissioned by H. Barton Wasserman. Wasserman asks Lynch to make another moving painting like *Six Men Getting Sick* for his home. The film Lynch creates is something quite different.

The Alphabet, four times the length of Lynch's previous film, is a 16-millimeter color film without a conventional storyline. It includes animation. The animation is infectious. Celluloid kinesis, the film generates and assimilates letters of the alphabet. The cells are boldly colored. Movement is unexpected and fascinating.

The drawings are accompanied by the *Alphabet Song,* changing from the rote children's jingle to the operatic to the ominous. The letters appear as characters, designs, and decorations, even animated into shapes suggesting moving symbols. These include life-cycle symbols: phallic symbols, tubes, and a birth-canal of the letter *A* giving life to a litter of *a*'s, letters in full bloom, and letters submerged back into the screen. A woman (Peggy Lynch), in white kabuki-like makeup and large, dark sunglasses is cut live into the animation. The live action of the film includes shots of an exaggerated rendering of sultry lips, a prominent iron bed, and assorted body parts. "Remember you are dealing with the human form" is enunciated by the woman in a tight close-up, breaking into the repetition of the alphabet. Tension in the film is heightened by the dual structure of black-and-white photography with color animation. As animated figures decay, wither, and die, the black-and-white reality of the stylized dreamer is increasingly disturbed by the animation's darkening tone. Finally, live action becomes as disturbing. Red dots from the animation become blood spots splattering onto the sheets of the writhing woman in the bed. The pelting from the animation results in her vomiting blood.

By the time *The Alphabet* is completed, Lynch has moved from a rental near 24th and Aspen streets to his own center-city home at Ringold and Poplar streets, near the Philadelphia Museum of Art, with first wife, Peggy Lynch (nee Lentz) and their infant daughter. He is a working man, no longer an art student. Moreover, with this second film David Lynch has begun to get his film footing. Lynch's first film project was a motion-picture sculpture. *The Alphabet* is already a film. His cinematic work earns Lynch an American Film Institute grant to continue filmmaking.

Printing small animals, including owls, with Christine McGinnis, Lynch continues his work for La Pelle, sometimes "diverting himself watching the TV soap opera, *Another World.* He expresses an environmentally sound interest—with heavy commercial overtones—in painting "the inside of candy-wrappers like leaves so that when discarded, they would still be visually acceptable."[16] His time is also spent creating his own black paintings with names like *Pollution Man.* But his interest also continues in filmmaking, and so he next writes, animates, and films *The Grandmother,* about a disturbed boy nurturing a grandmother he plants from a seed bag.

This film starred Lynch's coworker, La Pelle's mother-in-law, Dorothy McGinnis. First financed by a production grant from the American Film Institute, the film would be another 16-millimeter color, combination live action–animation. Its intense nine-week shoot paired Lynch for the first time with Alan Splet for sound work. As Lynch experienced money delays with his film, it became a more complicated and demanding project.

In the film a young boy escapes his abusive parental environment by planting a loving grandmother of his own. The black-and-white live action has the look of early silent films: grainy shots, stylized makeup, exaggerated acting techniques, erratic pacing, diversity of lighting, and unassuming costumes. This similarity in look reinforces the feel in Lynch's early experimental films of Luis Buñuel's surrealistic film work with Salvador Dali.

The film already has the look, and more particularly the sound, of Lynch's later works. For example, a growing yellow spot on the boy's sheets mirrors the animated yellow orb of the sun and flows into a yellow shot of the boy's idealized grandmother. Lynch spins the webs of his visual fabric. The boy's elongated, pathetic screams of both ecstasy and misery, the thunderous downpour, and the parents' exaggerated enunciation and ominous clipped dialogue aurally reinforce the film's disquieting mood.

The misery of the boy's colorless existence is pathetic in dark, static shots. The seed bag, boldly labeled "seeds," stands out in the murky setting of the boy's home, as do the vivid colors of the boy's animated dreams. The grandmother dies choking in her own chirping sounds, fluttering madly around the room like a captured bird smashing itself against the confines of its cage. Generated and undone by a birdsong heard throughout the film, the grandmother is only a momentary flight of fancy in the little boy's painful existence. As the figures and colors of the animation become darker and more portentous, black-and-white shots look softer, grayer, and more muted. Therefore, the look and sound of the film technically mirror what they represent, and techniques describe and overlap as do the incidents of the story they relate.

For example, the grandmother's appearance and disappearance mesh. The young boy's pressed tuxedo suggests a tiny maestro, a magician, and an apprentice undertaker. His masturbatory spill on the bed is simultaneously his shame and the fertilization of his illusion of salvation. This is a dual world of sex and death, love and pain, reality and wish, that Lynch will continue to explore. His exploration is of particular importance in his next and first full-length film, *Eraserhead.*

The combination of cartoon animation and live-action fantasy, the not-so-happy resolution and its setting in the local Knights of Pithius cemetery, ties the film to Lynch's previous work. So too does the film's feeling of bittersweet. *The Grandmother* blends romantic strokes, heightened by bizarre fantasies, with realistic tones anchored in the inescapable cruelty of naturalism. Thus the film hints at Lynch's emerging dual perspective not only in narrative content, but also in the cinematic context of merging techniques: black and white, color, animation, images, and sounds.

The Grandmother illustrates a geometric progression from *The Alphabet* in technical sophistication of filming and animation. The whimsical mood of the animation and its assimilation into the film are excellent. Lynch's early admiration of comic genius Jacques Tati is evident in his lyric, comic touch in the film. Running over thirty minutes, nine times the length of its predecessor, Lynch's film is a further evolution of his technique. Visually, the film is cohesive and provocative. The soundtrack, which cost Lynch and Alan Splet weeks of work, is first rate. Distinctive to Lynch films, sight and sound images not only carry but also create the film. Aesthetically, Lynch's sense of uninhibited fun blends with a hard-hitting depiction of the darker side.

Only three years after his art-school film project, Lynch's film work already includes moving sculpture, animation, animation/live action mix, color and black-and-white photography, and running times ranging from a minute to over half an hour. And by his third film, student experimentation has evolved into the confident work of a filmmaker. "In 1970, a 35-minute live-action–animated feature called *The Grandmother* about a lonely, abused boy whose deceased grandmother sprouts back to life from a seed planted in his bed—earned Lynch a place at the American Film Institute's Center for Advanced Film Studies in LA. He spent the next five years making *Eraserhead.*"[17] *The Grandmother*'s awards, international showings, and a Boston TV airing moved Lynch from the City of Brotherly Love to Hollywood.

He spent a great deal of his first year in LA working on an unproduced screenplay, "Gardenback." Lynch had difficulty padding the film to great-enough length. He also studied for a time with Czech filmmaker Frank Daniel. He even worked delivering the *Wall Street Journal* for extra income.

David Lynch spent most of the next five years realizing his first full-length film, *Eraserhead*. Lynch began shooting *Eraserhead* on 29 May 1972. The black-and-white, live-action film runs 100 minutes according to its original credits, but as later edited by Lynch (now running 89 minutes) is still more than twice the length of its predecessor, *The Grandmother*. In fact, *Eraserhead* is more than double the length of all of Lynch's previous films run together.

Several of Lynch's inner circle were involved in the project. Jack Fisk, Lynch's longtime friend, who later married actress Sissy Spacek, plays the man in the planet who handles the cosmic throttle. Jack (John) Nance, at one time Lynch's brother-in-law, portrays Henry Spencer on the screen in the first of many performances for Lynch. Cinematographer Frederick Elmes first works on a Lynch film crew with cinematography, while Alan Splet continues his sound work with Lynch. These men will have continuing screen credits in Lynch's film productions. *Eraserhead* premiered 19 March 1977 at Filmex in LA, and opened at the Cinema Village in New York that fall, after Lynch had spent months in New York to get a good 35-millimeter print.

There is something defiant and excellent about a first work. It hints at a glimpse of the precious metal veined under its gritty surface. It implies entry into a new canon of works. It insinuates an emerging style. Grandest perhaps is its very existence. Such a work is one of potential—of raw energy. At first the audience abandons itself to the film without expectation; in retrospect, they forgive it in the context of later works.

Eraserhead is such a motion picture. Viewing it, the audience enters irrevocably into Lynch's world. Viewing the film again, they recognize the world's convolutions. Next they appreciate that world's conventions. In repeated viewings, they become complacent and familiar with the images. Familiarity diminishes, even tarnishes, some of the charge of the film; *Eraserhead*'s power is in its initial impact. But familiarity also prompts an awareness of the strength of the film's techniques.

This film is the work of an American visionary. It positioned Lynch in the first echelon of avant-garde filmmakers. The screenplay introduces several themes that haunt his scenarios. The film is permeated by the galvanic flashes of humor that will become emblematic of Lynch's style. Henry's character is forerunner of Lynch's distinctive, dark figures. In the first of Lynch's two full-length films shot in black and white, Lynch and Frederick Elmes hint boldly at their later cinematography style.

Eraserhead introduces the images that will continue to appear and evolve in Lynch's visual universe. It also reveals the sounds that will define his auditory world. His idiosyncratic pacing is here. Most significant, this first film both separates Lynch's efforts as writer and director from motion-picture history and surely guarantees him a place in it. Here, in the grainy, brute use of the camera, the force of the Hollywood B movie unfolds: cheap sets, cardboard acting, deadpan delivery of clipped dialogue, slashes of black comedy, a lack of glamour caused by the stark reality of the budget—and, of course, a suggestion that this independent film is poised to take flight unencumbered by the commercial conventions of bigger budgets.

What the frames of the film lose in subsequent viewings of *Eraserhead* may be balanced by a knowledge of the context of Lynch's next ten years of work. *Eraserhead* introduces many of the same qualities that the later, larger Lynch films create. It presents Lynch's themes and techniques overtly. Lynch's growing distance from a film, as his films become necessarily more collaborative, lessens his self-consciousness. More sophisticated production values make Lynch's ties to future films less personal than his ties to *Eraserhead.* In later films Lynch delegates some of the hands-on intensity that makes *Eraserhead* so personal a project. But Lynch's mastery of multiple themes and contexts evolves. Lynch has more production know-how and better funding. Allusions in both form and content increase ambiguity in later works, making them less self-indulgent. Artistically and technically, if later films lose intensity, Lynch's growing mastery of filmmaking enhances their ability to suggest.

A first for Lynch, the universe explored in *Eraserhead* is certainly not new to motion pictures. Georges Méliès had already taken the camera out of the mirror world of physical replication and into the fantastic in the 1890s, the motion picture's first decade, before the turn to the twentieth century. *The Cabinet of Dr. Caligari* expanded film's entry into neurotic delusions and madness with its artificial sets, dream frame, exaggerated lighting, fades and shadows, and expressionistic style. Wiene visually compelled the viewer into the inner world of feelings and ambiguous symbols and meanings. Luis Buñuel's first silent film, *Un Chien Andalou* (1926), best described as symbolically surreal, completely released the camera from the constraints of picturing slice-of-life reality. In collaboration with Salvador Dali, Buñuel opened the audience's eyes to nether reality as dreamily as the moon and as brutally as the eye sliced in the opening shots.

Lynch films express no dedication to Méliès's or Wiene's work. He makes no claim to Buñuel as an influence—in fact, he denies the bond. "I never saw, I still haven't seen a lot of Buñuel. I saw 'An Andalusian Dog' a lot later. I don't even know that much about surrealism—I guess it's just my take on what's floating by" (Breskin, 62). But these filmmakers are the first explorers of this dark world in cinema's earliest history. Their masterpieces define, as exceptions often will, the "classic" film tradition. They were the cinematic forerunners of Lynch.

A later forerunner of Lynch's aesthetics was director Billy Wilder. Several of Wilder's directorial characteristics come to mind, including his sly sense of humor. *Sunset Boulevard* (1950) smoothed the way for Lynch's work. Lynch knows his movie history, and his "Twin Peaks" casting of himself as Gordon Cole, a Wilder character name, suggests the tie. A more obvious connection is the decay and wreckage of the Wilder film, as seen in the rooms of Desmond's mausoleum/mansion, her flamboyant costumes and exaggerated makeup, the props, like her stately car with telephone and her mechanical, almost medical-looking cigarette holder. Throughout the film, in settings, props, and costumes, Wilder too crosses between reality and illusion; he blurs distinctions between the characters and the role of "the movies" in the characters' real lives: Wilder casts real directors, silent-comedy stars, and a silent-film beauty to play his butlers and card players and faded legends. Wilder overlaps comedy and the macabre. He beautifully shoots the ugliness, as in the death of Norma's pet: the lying in state, and a midnight, murky 1930s movie sequence of the chimp's funeral—or the New Year's party: the ancient orchestra, the fabulous catering, and gloriously romantic dancing of Joe in formal attire, and Norma in the deserted caverns of her resplendent, cryptlike ballroom.

The film is one of excess in story and technique. The extreme close-ups of murderess Desmond, sensuously tingling before the newsreel cameras, mix her hideousness and her delight at returning to the spotlight. Lynch will use this same mixture of reality and illusion throughout his career. Norma Desmond is pathetic, ridiculous, and repulsive as she descends step by step right into the lens in the conclusion of Wilder's film. Henry Spencer's overlighted extreme close-up concludes Lynch's *Eraserhead. Eraserhead* evokes Wilder's severe black-and-white composition. Moreover, *Sunset Boulevard* is "hard boiled" in its feel and tone in a way Lynch duplicates in both black-and-white and color cinematography. Most important, Wilder, like Lynch, creates a film point of view. The lurid, surreal shot that opens *Sunset Boulevard,* of Joe Ginnis floating dead above the camera, is oddly narrated by the corpse. This breaks a literary convention as surely as it creates a cinematic point of view.

Along with John Waters—whose "work was so outrageous," says David Lynch, who credits Waters with creating a new bizarre genre, "that I think he carved out a lot of space for other film makers to go into"[18]—Lynch becomes one of a group of filmmakers with a strong, personal style. Lynch's placement in this group may not be intentional, but it is certainly undeniable. Today, however, these unconventional scenarist/directors do not operate in a splinter genre. Sometimes trained in painting, or working in fiction, poetry, or music, or involved commercially in advertising and video, filmmakers like Waters, Lynch, Peter Greenaway, Tim Burton, Peter Medak, Stephen Frears, and Philip Ridley have become a powerful force in contemporary cinema.

These filmmakers define a direction of film in our times. They are not merely a tangent to it. Their influences, like the influences upon them, are multi-media, multi-genre, and multi–art form. Their films must be reckoned with, not as exceptions to a Hollywood system, but as quintessential works of cinematic art. These new filmmakers generate aesthetics for film's second century. In *Eraserhead,* Lynch's contribution to the emerging renaissance of modern cinema begins its own evolution.

It is far easier in this film than in any other Lynch motion picture to see the hand of the man himself. During the production of the film, Lynch was a young father, and reading his apprehension into the film is irresistible. *Eraserhead* was a film that took years of his life and more than all of his money. Living for some time in the Doheny Mansion—AFI headquarters and the LA location on which he filmed *Eraserhead*—Lynch was at this time neither supported nor burdened by the reputation he was soon to achieve.

Lynch not only had to be—he was free to be—more unguardedly himself. First efforts are often more obviously attached to their creators' biographies. This is true in painting, music, and literature. *Eraserhead* reflects its truth in film as well. Lynch's involvement in every aspect of the film is underscored in the credits, including lists of friends and family to whom Lynch is personally grateful.

Of course, more sophisticated filmmaking expands the need for collaboration. Lynch began to select other artists and technicians with whom to work. As film is a collaborative art and an industry, one man's stamp is inevitably and increasingly filtered through the extended filmmaking process.

However, if Lynch's stamp in more collaborative films is filtered, it never becomes cloudy. David Lynch is multi-talented and multi-involved in each of his films as director and writer, sometimes in additional roles as producer, composer, technician, and actor. Nonetheless, prior to *Eraserhead,* Lynch's three films were short, almost single-handed outlets of his artistic effort. Obviously, the early film must more overtly evidence Lynch than can his later, larger, more commercial works. The years spent on *Eraserhead* and Lynch's daily, hands-on, almost exclusive involvement with it remain unique in his filmmaking experience. In that way, the film is another kind of first for Lynch: *Eraserhead* simultaneously begins Lynch's full-length feature work and culminates his experimental, independent work.

Lynch's personal rendering, however, should not be confused with a rendering of person. Personal ties do affect *Eraserhead.* But no matter how biographically instigated or personally wrought, film is not merely biographical record—film is artistic creation. Analysis and criticism, like appreciation of film, should seek not only to identify source facts but to evaluate their function as artistic elements of film. Therefore, analysis of *Eraserhead* lies not in isolating replication of biography but rather in criticizing the creation as art. Critics already recognize the power of Lynch's artistic perspective in this small-budgeted first film. "What's amazing is how Lynch transmuted such painful autobiographical material into such pure traumatic poetry, utterly free of self-pity" (Ansen, April 1990, 71).

It is of particular significance to note Lynch's objective rather than subjective use of his material. He shows without editorializing, prioritizing, or moralizing. It is his mastery of the presentation—not the evaluation—of a shot that underlies the richness of his images. The aesthetic philosophy to organize the images—sounds, incidents, characters, plot, and words—not into a scripted virtual reality, but into a cohesive world of film, is fundamental to Lynch's artistic process. Even in *Eraserhead,* his most personal film, he achieves distance from memory; Lynch creates a film vision of artistic intensity.

"David Lynch presents *Eraserhead*" reads the lettering across the screen as a prone man with an orb attached to his head stares over the cavernous whistling of the soundtrack. So the cult classic opens. "Lynch has created with *Eraserhead* an insane comedy adventure of the subconscious mind in a hostile environment. The film's nightmare logic is a total experience of densely-layered morbid images and sound that took Lynch five years to finish with his meager funds . . . Filmed in black and white. A man's head. Dreaming with eyes open? A globe. Pimpled and pockmarked. Vibrating sound track. Camera glides over globe. The man's face again, a silent scream. He wears a suit, shirt, tie. Another man, in tatters, flesh decaying, watching through a cobwebby window. A roaring sound. Deep blacks and whites, ominous. A snakelike thing, a huge spermatozoa, or an umbilical cord, issues from the dreamer's mouth. The other man, the watcher at the window, pulls one of several levers. Like a cosmic switchman. The snakelike thing goes hurtling off to splash into water. Giving birth to Eraserhead?"[19]

The film's opening shots immediately fill the screen with a menagerie of Freudian symbols—female and male, disgusting and disquieting, horrific and hilarious. No patina from a second, more literal level of narrative burnishes the picture of this symbolic world. Personal symbols are almost too obviously trotted before the camera to perform their tricks. Thus the seams in the fashioning of Lynch's subconscious nightmare world are exposed.

Eraserhead is a trek into the subconscious. A detailed summary of plot actions neither replicates nor illuminates the film. Images from the subconscious are not merely tied to the plot; in *Eraserhead,* images from the subconscious are the plot. The images fall into distinct if related areas, and an investigation into the film's image network reveals a visual cohesion.

The film illustrates Henry's state of mind, and Lynch uses personal as well as universal symbols. *Eraserhead* gains its force from presenting images that somehow affect the viewers. Appropriately, they are affected by the sometimes unknown and often unexplained images on a subconscious level. They need not understand or analyze the images.

How does Lynch get the audience to respond to his nightmare vision? What are the types of cinematic images Lynch uses to give *Eraserhead* its impact? Lynch's images are categorized in a criticism of the film. "It's effect stems from three sources: questions without answers being given (as so often in life), unreasonable horror, and images of extraordinary impact."[20] These three sources are a key to the appreciation of the film.

Eraserhead asks a number of questions; reducing *Eraserhead* to its ultimate question is self-defeating. The film's basic question translates into phrases like "Why was I born?" or "Why am I living?" This is at best a rhetorical question. Attempts to answer it resound in the teachings of Jesus Christ in the New Testament and the lyrics of Jerome Kern in musical comedy, from William Shakespeare's soliloquies in iambic pentameter to the scrawling of a desperate suicide note as accounted in a local newspaper.

Henry is trying to put his life into order, trying to gain control of fantasy and reality, trying to master his own destiny—Henry questions existence. Human experience suggests both that his pursuit will be a lifelong query and that in human context, because death is inevitable, the question is a vain one. Thus, within all human experience, *Eraserhead* asks *the* unanswerable question.

Therefore, images that visualize the question are often left unresolved and unfinished. The question "Who's in charge?" translates visually into the abrupt, unexplained appearance of the man at the controls in the film's opening shots. He is just there. But it is more important—and more maddening—that the image in the film fades just as easily as it has come, without exposition, without development, without context. Lynch asks the visual question, then dismisses it without rationale and without an answer. The question thus finds its true cinematic equivalent; a rhetorical question becomes an unfinished image. And the image is just as disquieting.

The audience wants to make the man a symbol. They know he is a symbol; they've seen Renoir, they've read *Cahiers du cinéma*—in French. But the image is not developed on the screen to permit the viewers—whatever personal experiences they contribute—to resolve with any satisfaction what the symbol means in the film. They only see, as does Henry, what the symbol is. The audience strains, determined to make sense of it.

In this way, Lynch's audience must actively involve itself in Henry's process of wondering, frantically wondering. They are forced by Lynch to join in Henry's futile pursuit. As with images in poetry, Lynch's visual and auditory images and their interaction do not merely allow, they demand that his audience take an active role. Lynch presents *Eraserhead* with a visual, aural, and narrative context. The audience is sent a message in none of these contexts, but rather must image all of them through personal experience. Lynch remains, like the movie camera, the presenter: he shows, he sounds, he focuses, he looks and eavesdrops—but Lynch does not construct the message. He leaves that part of the film experience—interpretation—to the audience. Thus his viewer/listener, Lynch's audience, is a cinematic respondent.

In *Eraserhead,* images drawn from the subconscious assault the audience into becoming actively involved. But the film cushions nothing with a narrative resolve. Like Henry, the viewers seek explanations which they may already know do not exist. *Eraserhead* selects and arranges questions, but takes no steps toward answering them, or even toward understanding them. *Eraserhead* illustrates human confusion. The film does not answer. The film asks. The film shows. The film refuses to explain. *Eraserhead* is.

The audience is buried by Lynch's avalanche of repugnant images. A blonde Kewpie with cheeks swollen like hamster pouches dances on an astral plane, an assembly line fashions human heads into erasers, a radiator opens into a nether world. Images and incidents challenge the film's depiction of any obvious place in a *virtual reality.*

"A place, in this non-geographical sense, is a created thing, an ethnic domain made visible, tangible, sensible. As such it is, of course, an illusion. Like any other plastic symbol, it is primarily an illusion of self-contained, self-sufficient, perceptual space. But the principle of organization is its own: for it is organized as a functional realm made visible—the center of a virtual world, the 'ethnic domain' and itself a geographical semblance."[21] If, as Langer sees it, sculpture makes actual three-dimensional material into virtual kinetic volume, and architecture articulates virtual place by treating actual place, virtual reality is the world created by the motion picture, the artistic universe that exists on film.

Lynch forgoes constructing a world that merely reflects slice-of-life reality to be viewed in the time elapsed between the beginning and end of a film. His virtual reality is intense. It is film-conscious, aware of conventions and history. It presents and varies visual, aural, and narrative contexts and their relationship. It demands the audience's response, a contribution of personal experiences, to enter the virtual reality on the screen. Lynch immerses the audience in his film world, a cinematically generated virtual reality not unlike the computer-generated artificial worlds of scientific experimentation in its powerful creation of a new dimension.[22] Without need of the hat or gloves of the computer-generated experience, *Eraserhead* forces the audience to become part of its world, to enter its virtual reality.

The world is frightening: *Eraserhead* exists in images from the subconscious. This is unfamiliar terrain. But even when later films make audiences more accepting of Lynch innovations, *Eraserhead*'s world remains an unsettling reality. Without answering who, why, or where, a blonde dances away over the radiator while squashing spermlike creatures under her feet. The image neither answers nor continues an interest in the question of the previous frame; the shot shrieks a new one. The image annihilates the search for answers to any previous question. And frame by frame *Eraserhead* asks questions, assaults with images, then jumps to the next question, next uncomfortable shot, next disquieting image.

Unanswered questions might find resolution in plot actions. Henry finds out that Mary gives premature birth, ostensibly to a child. Henry and Mary attempt to rear what may very well be his illegitimate and deformed offspring. Mary walks out and Henry has a liaison with the sultry woman across the hall. Henry destroys the baby after unwrapping its swaddling clothes and then loses his head. After being run through a pencil-making assembly line, the recapitated Henry finds solace in the arms of a singing and dancing blonde on the other side of his radiator.

There is no conventional storyline. Like Henry, the audience is zapped into the world without a clue as to how they got there. They go through radiators awash in song, steam, and sperm. They see dinners bleed and some kind of infant creature's bloody obliteration by its peculiar father. And the audience is sure they are traveling, if flabbergasted by the distance.

This feeling, of course, reaffirms the existence of artistic organization in the surreal representation of the film's world. Random and dreamlike as the sequence of these images feel, erratic as the plot actions seem, Lynch has determined order and sequence. Somehow the subconscious world of the film is cohesive. But how?

The organization of *Eraserhead*'s subconscious world revolves around Lynch's musings on conception and decay, through imagery depicting the beginning and end of life. The film's realm extends both before life in some cosmic control room and after death to the galaxy behind Henry's radiator. Although *Eraserhead*'s images hint at the spiritual, they are mired in a sexual quagmire of inseparable pleasure and pain. Intercourse and death are welded, as are conception and guilt.

Thus the unanswered question is imaged both physically and spiritually. The film asks: *Why?*

Contradictions run parallel and crash into each other, drowning the viewer in the maelstrom of Henry's subconscious. The power to compel further ingress into the film is generated *image-to-image,* not by an artificial superimposition of narrative order. Here is *Eraserhead*'s force, coherence, and cohesion. "The inexorable, skewed logic of 'Eraserhead,' [*Blue Velvet* and the new *Wild at Heart* also] seems to be derived from conscious access to what are properly unconscious states of mind. The imagery alone bespeaks the sheer ingenuity of dream reality, in which several psychological imperatives are satisfied in single gestures."[23]

The subconscious world is where Lynch's film operates. And *Eraserhead* suggests the powerful pairing of the filmmaker's subject and techniques. What the film asks and how it asks are synonymous. The audience is responding not to questions on film but to film questions in *Eraserhead.* The filmmaker employs the viewers' collective point of view as the focus for his camera. "We aren't swept along by Lynch's camera; we're caught by his images, our memory of his works is likely to be a series of mysterious, iconographic compositions—as if we had been looking at an exhibition of paintings rather than a film."[24]

Interviewer David Breskin quotes Lynch to Lynch to confirm meanings in Lynch's films. "One of the confusions seems to be over whether art has to mean anything. Let me quote you: 'I don't know why people expect art to make sense when they accept the fact that life doesn't make sense.' First off, I don't think people accept the fact that life doesn't make sense. I think it makes people terribly uncomfortable. It seems like religion and myth were invented against that, trying to make some sense out of it. Don't you think that's where art comes from, too?"

Lynch responds to his own question, "Maybe some of it does. But for me, I'm of the Western Union school. If you want to send a message, go to Western Union. It's even a problem with responsibility. You have to be free to think up things. They come along, these ideas, and they hook themselves together, and the unifying thing is the euphoria they give you or the repulsion they give you—and you throw those ideas away. You have to just trust yourself."

"So you don't resist the idea that your films mean something?" Breskin continues. "Not a bit," clarifies Lynch. "But they mean different things to different people. Some mean more or less the same things to a large number of people. It's okay. Just as long as there's not one message, spoon-fed. That's what films by committee end up being, and it's a real bummer to me . . . Life is very, very complicated, and so films should be allowed to be, too" (Breskin, 63).

Pigeonholing art is a futile endeavor. And pigeonholing Lynch looks like the stuff lifetime pursuits are made of. But an awareness, or perhaps an understanding, of elements composing a film is a useful analytical tool. Lynch's condemning a single, correct reading of any film as tremendously restrictive to the myriad interpretations of art is well taken. More important, information about the artist never explains the artist's intentions. Even if, and this is a big *if,* the artist knows some single message that he intends in a work, the art work still will and must be addressed as "it speaks for itself." Again, members of the audience play a role in creating the film's meaning for themselves.

Seeing not a film, but Film as cultural evidence is a possible investigation; however interesting, film in and as a context of its time is not the subject here. Works of art, creators, and audiences of an era are related. This is the case with film noir, a genre of interest in looking at Lynch's films. The definite techniques, attitudes, and themes of the genre reflect culture, just as collected interpretations, criticisms, and responses to them illuminate the culture. "Meaning in film is perhaps best left to observers, and much of what we learn about our collective contemporary consciousness comes from an analysis of groups of films rather than individual masterworks. This is the coral theory of mythopoeia. The mythic reef builds up slowly but inexorably through the accretion of thousands of mythogenic bits and mini-mythic pieces."[25] Film both reflects and influences twentieth-century culture.

More to the point, and without attempting to categorize films with any sweeping generalization, as Lynch's films are "very complicated" and "allowed to be, too," investigation and careful analysis of his aesthetics in a film develop the ability of viewers to approach each film as informed critics. The capability of realizing more of the possibilities of the art work is thereby increased. The viewers can appreciate more than a single line carrying some ordained celluloid message; they better understand the faceted universe of the filmmaker. Active investigation shouldn't dull the work of art by filing it under some preordained formula, but rather intensify an awareness of the changing dynamics of the film-and-audience continuum.

Eraserhead is a film pervaded by a feeling of unreasonable horror. The unanswered questions that are the film and the look and tone of the shots create the feeling of foreboding and apprehension. The setting is not only ugly, it is ominous. The lighting is dark and erratic; the viewers are suspicious and anxious about what may be shown. Sounds too are grating and surprising—coming and going with their own sense of rhythm—intruding, dominating, even overpowering scenes.

Throughout the film the audience never knows what to expect next. There is no sense of surety in narrative conventions. The technical setup of the scenes is suspenseful. Hideous sights occur frequently and abruptly. The frames' composition and tone are disquieting. The audience is in constant fear of what atrocity is around the corner.

Lynch's experiments with animals to better understand textures and patterns are seen here. *Eraserhead* has a feel of the laboratory and clinical experimentation. More than in any other Lynch film, his interest in biology surfaces here, as fetal deformity is graphically added to a visual mix already rife with allusions to phallic symbols and ejaculation, female genitalia and menstruation.

Eraserhead poses a quantitative imagery question. And it is characteristically a question of excess. Who would have thought that a world could have so many bodily fluids in it? Even when Henry crosses from his sexually suggestive world of machinery, pipelines, tubing, and churning appliances into the astral plane of his flamenco placenta-dancer, the spermatozoa abound. No wonder the audience fears the long, dark walk down the theater aisle. No wonder they dread that sticky feeling in the theater under their feet.

In a sequence of bright daylight—practically overlighted daylight—Lynch's gnawing film style begins to take root. Henry, his coiffure suggesting a state of constant arousal or surprise, stands before gigantic warehouse doors. The color, or lack of color, and the composition of the shot remind the audience, as is so often the case in Lynch, of Lynch's training as a painter. Here Lynch achieves a spellbinding, monochromatic mise-en-scène in his shot. The shot's visual charge telegraphs frustration, futility, loneliness, and paranoia.

Among Lynch's network of images of unfounded terror are factory shots, massive machinery, and industrial mechanisms. *Eraserhead*'s first shot of the factory doors boldly reinforces the audience's awareness of the lack of control over modern inventions, progress run wild, twentieth-century paranoia. Unable to program contemporary machinery, the audience doesn't even pretend to comprehend how it operates. The audience who realized only yesterday it could not survive without the personal computer is in panic today without a car phone and is doomed to dread a tomorrow without a home fax machine. In the industrial age the inclusion of the factory landscape and the film's cruel, blatant photography of machines plays on the audience's constant irritation and shame that they live as the captives of the very world they have created: computers go down, paralyzing offices; vast phone-line systems fail, holding whole cities captive; machines mute rows of clerks unable to count change without digital instructions.

It is the terrifying universe of Kafka. In fact Lynch proclaims an interest in reading/adapting Kafka (Campbell, 34). The audience sees the large, blank doors to unknown industrial caverns and mechanical fears. The shot triggers the nightmare of being lost in the state's Motor Vehicles Department. The audience remembers drop-and-add snafus in labyrinthine college-registration lines. The machinery evokes numbers: warranty numbers, insurance-policy numbers, health-plan identification numbers, phone numbers with area codes, expanded zip codes, touch-tone numbers demanded by electronic voices in order to talk endlessly to other computer voices about account numbers. Henry is living life on the edge of the mechanical abyss that the audience fears every time they can't remember their Social Security number or produce two photo IDs on demand before facing number upon number of standard duplicate forms.

Film played in this arena of dehumanizing technology as early as Fritz Lang's *Metropolis* (1926), with its industrial-production design. Henry's world has evolved from Bauhaus to urban decay. Cinematically, opening shots of *Eraserhead*'s doors decry, as did opening shots of Fritz Lang's doors, the cannibalistic mouths of futuristic industry swallowing workers into the machinery. The viewers see themselves, like Henry, being devoured by industry, somehow dragged through senseless situations without the power to extricate themselves.

Strong industrial images continue to be used in *Eraserhead* and throughout Lynch's film work. These mechanically conscious shots not only evoke the film's mood, but also gain in context as the audience remembers previous film associations. They not only suggest aversion to the sterile modern wasteland depicted in this film—in which the audience also lives—but they also awaken the collective imaging of the wasteland depicted by other motion pictures. Shots evoke shots, ironically supported by the movies, the technological art form of our electronic century.

The factory images are dense and frequent. Beyond the plants and industrial parks that are the setting of Henry's mechanical world is a factory assembly line that turns heads into pencils. The production stages move along briskly, unencumbered and at a modern industrial clip. The machines here buzz with a tone no more ominous than that of any other recycling process. Modern technology finds a use for everything and finds everything for which it has a use. Detached heads gain pragmatic value as pencils. Here too the film intensifies the viewers' underlying anxiety about what more-horrific violence may be the product of the next-depicted factory.

On the everyday side of the radiator, Lynch envisions a mechanical world. There are recognizable elements, like the record player, lamp, and other household appliances in Henry's apartment, to add to the gruesome and the whimsical outside his door. The machinery is also sometimes used as a visual and auditory element of the film. For example, Lynch uses the record player to rationalize music in the film. The soundtrack is more often noise, sound effects, or silence than either music or dialogue. So the record player first serves a technical use. It is how Henry and the audience hear the soundtrack music.

The record player, an antiquated machine, also is an image as an appliance: it evokes the past. The image works ironically. Music, almost classical at times, ranges to the strange pop ditty of Henry's radiator tune. Music is Henry's escape from industrial routine. And music carries Henry from the squalor of his everyday room. Real beauty, like real chickens, is a thing of the past. But Henry's music is provided by a machine: music is not real, but is actually technological reproduction.

A torcher lamp stands sentinel in Henry's room, almost a spindly character in its distinctive styling. The room becomes an abstraction of frightening shapes and shadows in its irregular lighting. It lights the blank wall in some shots, while it casts the rest of the room in darkness. The nomenclature of Henry's room has no consistency or familiarity. The room suddenly looks threatening and bizarre in the crackling lamp light, then institutional and barren. Thus neither Henry nor the audience feels any security in the setting. The shorting out of the lamp redefines reality with a speed and random brutality that extinguishes any sense of comfortable familiarity in the scenes. The audience constantly fears that something is going to happen with the light, with the lighting, perhaps even with the torcher lamp itself.

The apprehension is about mechanics: Henry's lamp and Lynch's technology.

The viewer is also apprehensive attempting to decipher the meaning of the transports or lack of transports from Henry's room. For example, the camera passes without penalty through the bars of Henry's iron headboard and back again. The bed's iron bars are more translucent than the room's window. The dirty windowpanes look outside, but straight into brick walls. Cabinet doors and drawers open into all sorts of other worlds and unknown chambers. There is no bottom or end when expected; there is infinite extension of other areas.

Confusion is relentlessly evoked in the banal, both outside and inside Henry's room. Henry drowns in his own bed during a promiscuous sexual encounter with the woman across the hall. Henry makes guilty examination of microscopic collectibles secreted in a cabinet in his room. Shots offer other realities. The mundane heating appliance is also illusion's gate, and there is an entire world, the other component of his dual reality, somewhere over Henry's radiator. He uses the radiator's metal bars, like the music, as a door from the industrial landscape to an astral one. The vista is the itinerary of a trip through the radiator.

The blonde sings and stamps on spermlike, umbilical-cord creatures. She dances to a song promising other realities, suggesting the solace of a world beyond the cycle of sex-conception-decay. The singing woman finally welcomes Henry to her breast. Her abrupt appearances are disquieting. Another unsolicited cut to her stage show heightens the feeling of unrest engendered in the viewers. Thus every reality in the film, both in what it depicts and in how it depicts, compels the audience's anxiety.

Another pivotal element of *Eraserhead* is a woven network of provocative images. Henry's dinner at his prospective in-laws' provides an example of the dynamics of Lynch's extraordinary imagery throughout the film. The depressing neighborhood, the house's decor, cooking preparations, and the oppressive conversation of the horrific visit are themselves quite disquieting. Perhaps the most celebrated, repellent, and disturbing image in *Eraserhead* is the chicken dinner. Throughout the sequence Lynch creates tone and tempo, setting up the fowl on the plate as a grotesque climax to the crescendo of jarring atonal notes.

Summoned by a repeated telephone message, Henry seeks an address in an industrial neighborhood filled with ominous noises. His quest takes him beyond the warehouse through desolate fields.

He rounds urban crevices, passing streets tucked under shadows of bridges and factories. Windows look onto trash and trash containers, parking lots, and brick walls. The viewer feels as claustrophobic as Henry looks on his stealthy walk. Henry walks into smoke and steam until he is spotted by Mary through the filthy windowpanes of the Xs' back door. He enters the house.

Mary's father, Mr. X, is responsible for the pipes running through his home—for the whole neighborhood, he suggests—and the viewer fears for the whole pipe-infested world. The house is magnificently lighted. Prominent lamps, looking like industrial refuse, illuminate blank walls in eerie and disconcerting shots of ugly, dark rooms suddenly sparked into ominous brightness. And the X household resembles the shots; nearly comatose, mute, and moaning in static small talk, they abruptly launch into shouting tirades.

The mother makes a mockery of parental concern in her stilted conversation. She ferrets out that Henry is gainfully employed, if currently "on vacation" from his printing job at La Pelle's. The inquisition prompts Mary's seizure, but Mrs. X continues her interrogation of Henry. Mary becomes hysterical when her mother insinuates that Henry is having sexual relations with her daughter. Mrs. X calms Mary's spasm with some motherly hair brushing, transporting Mary from her anxiety and guilt at being exposed to the security of her innocent childhood.

Mary's father, Bill, is at his most convivial when in his zombie trance. His more verbose if equally lethargic description of tonight's dinner fare is harder to endure. So too is his lackluster shop talk about his damaged knees and his melodramatic demonstration of his crippled arm earlier in the evening. His first workman's soliloquy, nostalgically recalling his moment of glory when he piped the neighborhood, is only silenced by Mrs. X's taking him to the kitchen. His tale of physical maiming is upstaged by a chicken's hemorrhage.

Bill takes an active interest in describing the dinner menu. He even assists in its cooking, by basting the chickens in one of the two ovens in the kitchen. The rationale he uses to get Henry to carve the meat includes a circular verbal history of the affliction, cure, and decay of his arm, with emphatic arm slapping to demonstrate. Bill continues to eat, even as the other characters become embroiled in accusation and suspicion. He is oblivious to the sexual intrigue around him and is concerned only about the dinner getting cold.

Mrs. X's fit brings her near to poultry orgasm as she watches the chicken bleeding on Henry's plate. She calms herself by leaving the dinner table with Mary. She returns to accuse Henry of seducing her daughter, going after him and making him the victim of her sexual aggression. Her earlier fit at the dinner table is introductory to her smothering Henry with a burst of kisses during their altercation. Her hunting Henry as prey and attempting to mount him after dinner make the pathetic bird he carved a more offensive foreshadowing.

Granny (that *is* Granny, isn't it?) doesn't join the dinner party. She sits either in the final stages of very quiet or in the first stages of rather dead in the kitchen. She sits with the other appliances near the two stoves side by side by side. A cigarette is dangled from her mouth, and her arms are guided to mix the salad. She is not the most inviting prep chef. Her presence is felt at the table, but she is not allowed to join the meal.

Bill labels dinner a *faux* chicken, a synthetic just like the real thing in every way. Except it is minute, a pygmy bird, crunching pathetically under what appears to be a gigantic carving blade. Because Mr. X is injured, Henry is asked to stand in as host and do the carving for Mary's father. Tentatively, Henry obliges.

Once on his plate the diminutive bird begins to spread its legs. Then it bleeds—a stream of blood first, then deep, rich, turgid dollops of blood—finally expelling its bloody issue. It evokes the pose of sexual intercourse, the blood of the menstrual cycle interrupted by Henry's copulation, the resultant conception of Henry's passion, as it lies spread-legged before Henry, chicken legs flailing. Among other things, one wonders, like guilty Lady Macbeth fresh from Duncan's bedchamber, that so frail a bird could have so much blood in it. And guilt and eroticism are coupled here as in Henry's mind.

Mrs. X gasps as Henry carves with the sharp blade Mr. X has given him, and the surreal experience drives Henry from the table to terror. Bad as those nights with a lover's family can be, this one goes more than usually haywire. But what is confusing in plot is clear in meaning. And the incidents of the night are understandable as Henry's subconscious.

Regardless of the actions, images mesh into a texture. The violent upheavals and eclectic sights of the scene have rhythm and composition. The cuckoo's spasms are timed to shatter the silence of the room on the hour, every hour, and to be still—like clockwork. The flashes of the lamps dim and fade, erratic, but in measured sequence. Loud machine sounds erupt and quiet again to silence. Actions intrude and pass into the still, lifeless frame. As does the passing passion of sex; the several seconds of Henry's ejaculation now tie him to Mary and the Xs for a lifetime. The audience is given a cohesive film scene balanced in optical and aural elements, if not a developed narrative episode.

This is the strength of *Eraserhead*. As in later Lynch films, not everything in his first film works. Lynch's techniques are more hard sell than in later films. *Eraserhead* has a greater tendency to the glib, and it certainly lacks subtlety. The whole movie world has changed, so *Eraserhead* no longer seems as revolutionary and shocking. But the extent of the film's reach is impressive. *Eraserhead* succeeds in freeing itself of a story line. It often soars as film. And whenever *Eraserhead* falters as a story, it manages to keep struggling as a film. If it doesn't always work, it never sells out. It already has the cinematic veracity of Lynch's evolving film style. And *Eraserhead* is one of the reasons the whole movie world has changed: it is the quintessential midnight movie.

Even if on a subconscious level, everything the viewer sees has a visual context on the movie screen. Departing from so many of film's conventions, Lynch is amazingly fluid in his style. Lynch exhibits a painter's talent to create compelling images shot by shot. The screenplay indicates a writer's mastery of how films operate. The director's unique ability to evoke audience input into understanding his films is already present. This bravura makes Lynch a powerful filmmaker.

Eraserhead is cinema that includes illusion as a part of its reality. Entering subconscious reality is a tenet of *Eraserhead*. The meshing of subconscious and conscious images as elements of film galvanizes Lynch's style. He flaunts the ambiguity of reality and illusion, blurring the lines between them throughout his film. Lynch in the movies, like the youthful King Arthur in legend, frees the double-edged blade from eons of captivity in granite and boldly thrusts forward his new film style.

The images in *Eraserhead* are important because Lynch expands the filmmaker's options of figurative representation. His film extends the world explored by Luis Buñuel and film surrealists. Lynch's style is personal; it isn't yet evolved or defined. The film's visual and auditory contexts aren't refined, because Lynch still operates solely in the subconscious. Thus the images operate as representations or as symbols. The images do not yet function as metaphors. The further duality develops when Lynch runs several realities simultaneously, as in his later films. Later films retain *Eraserhead*'s mental terrain, but add another film reality to Lynch's film texture.

Nonetheless, in this film Lynch makes clear that texture—the tactile, sensual feel—of filmmaking will be significant to his style. "Lynch thinks like a painter, not like a writer: he never talks about themes and messages; what interests him are textures, moods, contrasts, silences" (Ansen, April 1990, 71). *Eraserhead* is a film that defines the fabric of Lynch's film world. Lynch's presentation of this world will be developed, but the world will remain intact.

As he promises in *Eraserhead,* Lynch will not adapt his aesthetic to viewer expectations. He will develop his style so that viewer demands and expectations will change. Lynch's first film reveals the world the filmmaker intends to pursue. "I like things that go into hidden, mysterious places, places I want to explore that are very disturbing," the filmmaker says. "In that disturbing thing, there is sometimes tremendous poetry and truth" (Jerome, 82).

He will change modes to suit the aesthetic. Lynch satiates, sardonically even titillates, the growing audience that appreciates the complexity of his films as an art form. Moreover, his later works challenge a growing film audience to develop that appreciation. Thus his films achieve a commercial release without pandering to conventional mainstream expectations. Lynch's vision of the *Eraserhead* world remains clear.

Even after Lynch becomes a recognizable film director, he attempts to sustain *Eraserhead*'s independent spirit. Everything about the trappings of the filmmaker has changed since *Eraserhead*—but not the filmmaker's philosophy. Lynch remains himself in work from cartoons to commercials. He makes himself the constant in the world he enters. *Wild at Heart,* far from a midnight show, is a summer release in 1990. General release makes different demands and reveals different critical expectations. The sequels, action stories, and teen movies that customarily abound in the summer are a different kind of box-office competition. Lynch has changed the movie conventions, the business, and the audience. *Wild at Heart* is *Eraserhead*'s kin.

Eraserhead suggests that Lynch's philosophy includes the extension of his brand of aesthetics into the mainstream. Lynch continues to redefine film's province as he continues to assess that his audience is to be approached without a bias as to their limitations. His demands on a general-release audience mirror his expectations of a response to *Eraserhead.*

A reliance on metaphor and simile to describe Lynch's accomplishments is appropriate because he forces film into a new vocabulary and a new century. Like Luther's bold nailing of his philosophy on the doors of Wittenberg, Lynch has in *Eraserhead* remolded the cinematic conventions: blasting, redirecting, reforming, glorifying, and inventing. In this rough, bold film, the cinematic innovations of Lynch surface. He defines the province of contemporary film as the creation of images *and* metaphor.

Eraserhead is a tentative, soaring early step in that direction.

2

Lynch and History—*The Elephant Man*

> A work of art is the trace of a magnificent struggle.
>
> —Robert Henri, *The Art Spirit*

There is a connection and a separation between history and art. A comparative analysis of David's source and his vision as expressed in *The Coronation of Napoleon* is a productive way of understanding the painting's place in art history, as well as the creative process and philosophy of its creator, and therefore its dynamics as a work of art. A comparative analysis of Homer's epic poem and the facts surrounding the Greek navy's pursuit of Helen of Troy clarifies the poet's use of figurative language as a literary technique and gives specific indication of his artistic philosophy.

Similarly, a filmmaker who presents historical information must make choices among incidents and ways of portraying those incidents on film. He must adapt fact to film. But he may choose to alter reality so that it best transfers to film and agrees with his artistic interpretation. His freedom as an artist cannot be inhibited by a necessity to record events that have actually transpired. Film is not a history chapter on celluloid; film is a work of art.

This study is not, therefore, an investigation of events, dates, and characters in the history of Joseph Merrick, known as the Elephant Man, but rather of how those facts have been treated as elements in David Lynch's film *The Elephant Man*. The duplication, alteration, and translation of the historical record provide an insight into Lynch's processes. A comparative analysis of fact and film identifies Lynch's choices in presenting history on film and illuminates his aesthetics.

Filmmakers, like other artists, may choose to replicate actual historical experience. The motion picture has perhaps the greatest possibility of any art form to create a virtual reality. Primary authorities are sought; sometimes firsthand observers of events are hired as technical advisors to the film to ensure accuracy. The events may be carefully researched to create verisimilitude. Places may be brought before the camera as like those in history as possible. Either they are reconstructed according to factual plans of the original or shot on a location as much like the setting as is possible—sometimes shot in the actual place where the events transpired. Characters may be researched to be presented on film as close to the actual people as possible in their appearance, manner, speech, and dress. In short, care may be taken—more and more *is* taken—to make the story on film as close as possible to reality.

Even when changes or interpretations are used to translate the facts, the filmmaker may make these adaptations to achieve the same charge on film as the incident had in history. History is to be represented as an element on film. However, regardless of the filmmaker's orientation or interpretation, historical error and anachronism are not options. History may be interpreted, but historical carelessness is not accepted. Coiffures from the 1950s on characters in a film about the Spanish Inquisition is historical carelessness; Stanley Kubrick's choice to light *Barry Lyndon* so as to translate the subtlety of the candlelight of eighteenth-century Britain is a way of conveying historical fact.

Consequently, it becomes most interesting to compare the life of Joseph Merrick, the Elephant Man, in history and Lynch's John Merrick, *The Elephant Man*. Lynch investigated the facts of his story at the Royal London Hospital. Additional nonfiction sources for the screenplay include *The Elephant Man and Other Reminiscences* by Sir Frederick Treves and *The Elephant Man: A Study in Human Dignity* by Ashley Montagu.

Joseph Carey Merrick was born in a house at 50 Lee Street in Leicester on 5 August 1862. He was named after his father, Joseph Rockley Merrick, and after a prominent Baptist minister, Carey. His mother, Mary Jane, who may herself have been a cripple, died of bronchopneumonia when Merrick was about 10 years of age, shortly after his younger brother, William, had died of scarlet fever. Like his baby sister, Marion Eliza, Joseph Merrick was crippled. Unlike his sister, who was a registered cripple from birth, Merrick found life unbearable at home after his father's remarriage. Merrick failed as well to find a home with an uncle, and his ever-increasing ailments and deformities made work impossible. Joseph put himself in a workhouse. Failing to find a refuge, Joseph chose to leave Leicester and attempt to support himself. Merrick exhibited himself as a freak to maintain himself with an income.

Sir Frederick Treves was a lecturer and demonstrator in anatomy, and a noted surgeon. In November of 1884, Treves found Merrick on exhibition in a freak show across Whitechapel from his hospital. He arranged for Merrick to be studied at the medical college of the teaching hospital. As Merrick attracted considerable public attention, Treves gave him an admission ticket to the hospital, his costume, and a cab across the street.

Grotesquely deformed, Merrick looked heinous. His repulsive looks necessitated that he appear on the streets in a cloak and black cap shrouded in brown flannel from the brim, with a horizontal slit through which to see without being seen. He was afflicted with neurofibromatosis, a running case present from 21 months of age—severe and pitiless. His head was deformed beyond normal proportions to almost 36 inches around, his right arm was enormous, his spine curved, and most of his body (except for his left hand, parts of his face, eyelids, ears, and his genitals) was covered with tumors, bony masses, and papillomata. Portions of his skin drooped and hung; a scar remained where a workhouse amputation had altered the trunk-like growth above his puffy lips. It was with great physical effort that the Elephant Man survived. For example, his head was so large and breathing made such a demand on his weakened system that lying down would suffocate him. Thus he needed to sleep sitting propped up. His speech was tremendously impaired by his misshapen cheeks, swollen enough to move his hard palate up and forward. Treves called his specimen a most miserable one.

After the sessions of medical study, in fact, Merrick's exhibition was soon stopped by the police as an outrage. His unhappy attempt to return to the life of an exhibited freak drove him farther and farther from London and the police. His freak career ended after two years when he fled Brussels, where he had been displayed on a continental tour, and returned to England. He arrived on a train at Liverpool Station in London. Chased by taunting crowds, the battered Merrick's grunting was judged to be Arabic. Fortunately the admission ticket Treves had given Merrick was found in his pocket. This led to his being taken to the hospital.

During his years at the Royal London Hospital he was given rooms for life. Merrick made theater visits to a Christmas pantomime at the

Theater Royal Drury Lane in the box of the Baroness Burdett-Coutts and perhaps to other shows. He was visited by notables, most particularly the Prince and Princess of Wales, which made him a cause célèbre in Victorian society. He collected gifts from and photographs of the famous who supported his cause. He visited Treves's home. In the summer of 1889 he made a six-week excursion into the countryside to Fawsley Park in Northampton, where he collected wild flowers, observed trout and other wildlife, and befriended a dog, one of his happiest relationships.

Joseph Merrick returned to live out his days at the hospital in his ground-floor rooms on Bedstead Square. By the last year of his life, he was tremendously deteriorated, only exercising one hour a day. His death was nonetheless more rapid than his physicians had expected. He had taken his customary walk in Bedstead Square on a spring Thursday evening. After waking around noon the next day, which was his custom, his needs were attended to by his nurse. Lunch was delivered to him in his rooms on a tray at around half past one on that Friday, 11 April 1890. When the dishes and his uneaten lunch were collected several hours later, he was found dead. He had resided at the Royal London Hospital for over three years.

There are discrepancies in the facts of his story, including the date of his death, many stemming from a pamphlet published by Merrick himself, but he was by best account 27 years old. Mr. Carr Gomm wrote a public letter as Merrick's epitaph. Statements to the public did not mention his dissection, perhaps because of Treves's sensitivity to Merrick's family and supporters. Merrick's skeleton is in the London Hospital Medical College Museum; "His other (flesh) remains were buried in an unmarked grave in 1890. More recently members of the Merrick family applied to the Ecclesiastical Council to have Joseph's skeletal remains cremated and buried near Treves's grave."[1]

Other historical evidence of the story remains visible today in the Royal London Hospital and its environs. The Royal London Hospital presides over Whitechapel in London like a great lady pouring at a gypsy tea. All around, the busy neighborhood still scurries, now with street stalls almost like a market of Delhi. An integral part of the bustling community, the hospital is recognized for its contemporary medical care. It is, as it has always been, a center for medical treatment and teaching. The Royal London Hospital is also an integral part of London's history.

The Royal London Hospital. Merrick was first kept in a room behind the large clock. Photo courtesy of the author.

The neighborhood evokes Joseph Merrick. Coming up from the tube stop on Whitechapel, one passes Smith's butcher shop, said to be the location of the freak show where Merrick met Sir Frederick Treves, the surgeon who would change Merrick's life. Behind a statue of Queen Victoria on an island in the traffic, looms the hospital itself. Merrick had first been kept in a room behind the large clock over the since-altered entrance portico.

Inside the main building the bell that called students to surgery stands still. Near it is the dumbwaiter Treves used to get quickly from his office upstairs to the lecture hall. The nursing building Princess Alexandra dedicated on 21 May 1887, when she and her husband, the future King Edward VII, met Merrick, is still part of the hospital complex. And St. Philip's church is now a part of the hospital's library system. Bedstead Square, Merrick's patch of green garden, named for the bedding once placed in the sun there, is now an urban parking lot crammed with trash, deliveries, and ambulance and lorry traffic. The location of the door to Merrick's rooms on Bedstead Square, where

Merrick's hat and mask in the London Hospital Medical Museum. Photo courtesy of the author.

Merrick made a model of a church for Mrs. Madge Kendal. In the London Hospital Medical Museum. Photo courtesy of the author.

he lived his last years at the hospital, can be identified, although now much altered by time and the Blitz.

The London Hospital Medical College houses a museum that contains a collection of medical exhibits and archives. The archives include important photos, papers, letters, and other documents. The coroner's report of Merrick's death, however, is not here. Secured at the inquest following his death and not to be opened for 100 years, the certificate was disposed of in a bookkeeping scheme some 50 years later. But museum records do include original illustrations from a nineteenth-century children's book about the Elephant Man. The posters advertising his exhibition as a freak are also collected here.

The church model made by Merrick for Mrs. Madge Kendal is here. This gift of Mrs. Kendal represents the six or seven children's cardboard kits Merrick painstakingly constructed while at the hospital. Most notably Merrick's mask and hat are also here. The museum is negotiating to restore the brim at the London College of Art. 100 years have taken a toll on this draped hat, particularly on its brim. The blunt slit in the heavy brown veiling gives mute testament to the man who hid beneath it in order to camouflage his painful deformities. Somehow Merrick's skeleton nearby seems a less human artifact.

When Merrick was a patient at the Royal London Hospital, the area behind the hospital was open all the way to the Thames. The approach to the formidable hospital building was a much greener, open route. The hospital façade at that time (it was remodeled in 1891) was more imposing with its pillars and porters.

But Whitechapel even then was a teeming neighborhood of shops, pubs, homes, and thriving businesses. New citizens of London often made this river section their first home. In the 1880s crowds of Jewish immigrants from eastern Europe joined the working-class Londoners and filled the streets. In the heart of the industrial docklands, an unsavory element of streetwalkers and drunks, con artists and criminals also made this neighborhood home. The victims of Jack the Ripper were found nearby at local Whitechapel addresses. In fact, in the first years of the Ripper murders, before Merrick became increasingly debilitated, he was himself suspected by some students and members of the hospital staff. Merrick, the Elephant Man, was often the object of scorn, always the object of curiosity.

This basis in historical fact appears to make *The Elephant Man* unlike other Lynch films. Nevertheless, although it seems an exception, *The Elephant Man* crystallizes the consistency of theme and aesthetics in Lynch's work. And like other of his works, it provokes a customary range of responses, from critical praise as a classic to critical vilification. It is dismissed as a failure, even called Lynch's biggest commercial sellout. But it finally proves to be more a Lynch film than it first appears.

While Lynch's first film had exhibited his singular vision, it had been a single-handed project as well. But in his second film Lynch had neither complete control nor complete responsibility. He faced deadlines, but he enjoyed established funding. He worked with as celebrated a cast as he ever has: Anthony Hopkins, John Hurt, Anne Bancroft, Sir John Gielgud, and Dame Wendy Hiller.

This time Lynch was not working with his own invented story line but with facts of history and reality as his source. He had factual sources, including hospital records, memoirs and biographies, and literary sources, from a nineteenth-century children's book to a contemporary drama produced on stage from London's West End to Broadway. The differences in budget, cast, and crew on the film, as well as these differences in source materials, would produce a different kind of film, triggering critical response and popular acclaim. Suddenly, this former art student with only school films and one full-length feature to his credit was an Academy Award nominee for the Best Film Oscar of 1980. Directing *The Elephant Man* gave Lynch a different set of challenges from his previous work, including the burden of becoming Hollywood's reigning enfant terrible.

Of course Lynch would never again face the film industry as a novice. He would never again be in transition from a first-time filmmaker to a major celebrity. And celebrity is inherent in Lynch. The flamboyant man of the nineties, then, is rooted in this opportunity to undertake a conventional multimillion-dollar project. Now Lynch could bring his "midnight show" techniques of *Eraserhead* to the multi-screened theaters of general release. Now Lynch could juggle several careers at one time. For example, Lynch was nominated for the Oscar the same season that an exhibition of his paintings was mounted and opened at a gallery in Philadelphia.

At first view, changes in both Lynch's reputation and his film techniques seem to separate *The Elephant Man* from *Eraserhead*. This second film also appears to be as distinct from the Lynch films that are to follow. No other Lynch film has historical fact as a basis; no other Lynch film is set in an identifiable year or in the definite past; no other film, with the exception of *Dune,* is set other than in the United States. After *The Elephant Man* Lynch would not again (through 1992) work in black-and-white photography. Although Lynch's crew was beginning to congeal—Splet in sound design from *Eraserhead,* De Vore and Bergren, who would work on the script of *Dune,* Patricia Norris, who would do the costumes for *Blue Velvet*—Lynch works in this second film without his customary repertory of actors.

As the narrative and other differences in *The Elephant Man* separate it from Lynch's other works, his technical, aesthetic, and thematic philosophy can be seen in the film. Thus *The Elephant Man* is a cohesive phase in Lynch's evolution as an artist.

And beyond the visible differences, the first two films by Lynch were connected, and critics in 1980 already began to note strong artistic ties between them. The Lynch painting *Sick Man* (1967), according to friend Rodger La Pelle, seems to foreshadow Lynch's interest in Joseph Merrick, the Elephant Man. This connection was recognized by Lynch himself. "In many of its details *The Elephant Man* is like a commercial remake of *Eraserhead.* Lynch told me recently," writes David Steritt, "that he was attracted to *The Elephant Man* by its title alone, even before he knew the story. 'It suggested so many things,' he said during a conversation not long ago. 'And it seemed right down my alley, though I'm not sure just what that alley is.'"[2]

Elements of this film show Lynch's style emerging from the earlier *Eraserhead.* Critical response recognized Lynch's style of direction. "Lynch revitalizes Expressionist techniques through the subjective use of cinema."[3] And the film's reviews cite as already present the distinct style of a significant filmmaker. "Every time the director does something risky and new or reinterprets something very old, you know you're watching real moviemaking."[4] The *New Yorker* goes further in identifying the cinematic energy and in exalting Lynch's painterly style of filmmaking. "But this young director (he's thirty-four) has extraordinary taste; it's not the kind of taste that enervates artists—it's closer to grace" (Kael 1987, 178).

Lynch's concern with the actual events rather than with the dramatized fiction sometimes finds its way into his choices in creating the film. For instance, Merrick is shown as a diseased man, a character drawn from his medical records. The depiction of the Elephant Man as a physically deformed creature is a change from his presentation as a symbolically deformed character in the play. Lynch opts to show

Merrick's neurofibromatosis graphically rather than symbolically, the way the clinical sources would have annotated their diagnosis of this physical deformity.

The film depicts a diseased human body; the screenplay is the record of the body perverted (perhaps as an allegory of the captured soul). Although the narrative works on an allegorical level—the plight of one man holding out to salvage his humanity in the brutal, industrialized world—the film depicts Merrick graphically, not in muted abstraction—he is hideous. The choice to show explicitly the physical ugliness of the character and his mangled voice juxtaposes Merrick's looks with his humanity and his voice with the clarity of his message. Similarly, the freak shows, teeming squalor, industrial hell holes, and hospital wards of London are also explicitly depicted. This choice frees the film to operate visually and aurally, if it is still sometimes cumbersome or sentimental in its dialogue.

Like a hospital chart, the film's structure presents scenes as notes, episodes, incidents from a tortured life rather than as dramatically cohesive plot actions in a drama. The look and pace of the film are charged. This cinematic power is noted in the film's initial critical reception. "Even when its psychology becomes simplisitic . . . *The Elephant Man* is explosively bold in its audiovisual style. Credit for this goes entirely to the young director, David Lynch. Curiously, he has made only one feature before now, a piece of unprecedented surrealism called *Eraserhead*" (Steritt, 28).

Lynch's attitude toward history is probably no better illustrated than in his use of black-and-white cinematography. And there are few better examples of his inherent "grace" as a filmmaker than this choice of black-and-white photography in *The Elephant Man*. Here is a particularly effective blending of the film's narrative events and its feeling. Although he is working without Frederick Elmes, a powerhouse in the cinematography of other Lynch films, Freddie Francis captures the look of nineteenth-century London, and more important, the feel of Merrick's nineteenth-century London world.

The statistical, clinical rendering of Merrick's medical plight and the barrenness of his psychological universe are captured in the gray camera shots. Historically, here is the cruel, monochromatic world of Merrick, part freak, part lab animal. Artistically, the lack of color in the film and Lynch's characteristic pacing transcend the factual details of the scene, moving Merrick into the world of dream-nightmare with the fluidity of murky water in the Thames. There are myriad tones in the black and white of the film as in the hues of history—mode is message.

Thus Lynch elevates his entire film to a level beyond the more obvious technicolor reality of Merrick's history. The film is capable of evoking Merrick's life in London, but is in Lynch's world on screen. Here is Lynch's mastery as creator of his own universe: the battleground of pain and pleasure, good and evil, the seething duality of beautiful and ugly—the world in black and white. "Yet, as in his cult film *Eraserhead,* Lynch is determined to impose his personality and distinctive visual style on his elephant-man material. The decision to shoot in black and white, thus abstracting the all too literal subject matter, was unquestionably right. And from a purely aesthetic point of view, his stylized short scenes, gracefully poised between the real and the surreal and tapering into fade-outs, are a pleasure to watch."[5]

Another of the most effective elements of *The Elephant Man* is the casting. Actors of established talent flesh out even the small roles and contribute much to the "grace" of the film. John Hurt, whose performance is somehow not obliterated by the grisly makeup, portrays Merrick. In the film Merrick's first name is John, when in fact his name was Joseph. There is historical confusion about his Christian name. He may have been misheard to mutter, "John," when attempting to say his own name, Joseph, because of his difficulty speaking with his oral deformities. A contemporary newspaper article continued the use of the wrong name by mistakenly calling him John. Treves calls Merrick John in the film as he did in history.

Hurt's performance as John Merrick was well received and Oscar nominated (losing Best Actor of 1980 to Robert De Niro in *Raging Bull*). In criticism of Lynch's view of Merrick, there is little criticism of Hurt's performance. "Even the industry's top directors seem to hold him in awe."[6] The article quotes Jim Sheridan who thinks Hurt is "like a snooker player—deadly accurate" (Norman, 55). Director David Puttnam recognizes the contribution of Hurt's physical acting techniques in his performance as the grotesquely made-up Merrick. "John's got a tremendous sadness in his eyes . . . And that may be the actor's greatest asset because he can convey pain" (Norman, 55). Lynch himself values Hurt with enthusiasm. "John Hurt is simply the greatest actor in the world, says David Lynch who directed *The Elephant Man*" (Norman, 55). This is casting gold, because as written, even with all that vile bodily imperfection, Merrick comes a bit too close to sainthood. He is certainly in nobility as far from most Lynch characters as he is close to them in plain physical repugnancy.

Anthony Hopkins has the authority to portray Sir Frederick Treves, the surgeon of considerable reputation who was connected to British royalty. Alexandra, Princess of Wales (Helen Ryan), a mentor of John Merrick during his stay at the hospital (1866–1890), knew Treves; the Prince of Wales was his patient. In fact Treves is celebrated for removing the infection in the appendix of the future king. Treves also served as director of the London Hospital Medical College Museum.

Hopkins's casting is particularly effective because of his powerful voice and his diction. His voice provides a striking contrast to the painful, halting delivery of Hurt, suggesting both the distance between the men and the efforts to bridge that chasm by doctor and patient. This stressful communication is evidenced in the dialogue they speak, but more important to the film, it is heard in the very way they sound—even their pauses and silences—because of the casting.

Anne Bancroft's performance as Mrs. Madge Kendal is also noteworthy. She exposes how one-dimensional the character is. This is usually not a flaw in Lynch, who presents most characters in his films with more complicated humanizing shading. But in *The Elephant Man* he seems to be hampered by his too-inspirational script. Her glorification makes the film's Mrs. Kendal stiff; she is a bit too good, a bit too fine.

Some have wondered if she would have been cast if she were not the producer's wife. Still others wonder if so celebrated a film star would have taken so small a role if not married to the producer. Regardless of the doubters, the part is a pivotal one to the film and this casting most important. Not only is the actress up to the role, but she is a notable star playing the notable star who befriends Merrick. Along with her considerable talents, Bancroft brings the recognition of her own celebrity to the role.

Sir John Gielgud's and Dame Wendy Hiller's portrayals are the casting coup. He is conservatively considered to be in the front rank of actors of our century; she has been revered for some fifty years on stage, in film, and on TV. Sir John brings his unique ability to be both acerbic and loveable to his role of Carr Gomm, humanizing and vastly extending the range of the characterization. Thus in the scene where he controls the hospital board's vote and defends Merrick by appealing to their reverence for the Royal Family, the audience is pleased, impressed, and a bit amused. Sir John suggests all of the nuances of the medical, financial, and national complications of the hospital's involvement. Dame Wendy, in her small role as Mothershead, establishes the humanity and affection under the starchy professionalism. She does this without approaching the sentimentality of the old "heart of gold" stereotype.

Mrs. Treves (Hannah Gordon) is another such character in her brief scene. Even Freddie Jones Bytes—in the film's most exaggerated role, as a villain without hope of redemption—prevents the part from becoming a complete caricature. Again, even in reviews which question the simplistic characterizations or plot actions, bemoaning Lynch's tendency to sentimentalism, these performances and Lynch's direction of them are critically regarded. These portrayals manage to maintain the balance in Lynch's black-and-white world. "Many moments in the script could lend themselves to gross sentimentality, but Lynch manipulates the dual nature of most of the film so gracefully that the sentiment is muted and distilled through an original sensibility" (Baker, 254).

The plot of the film both mirrors and varies from fact as Lynch structures it. After an opening dream sequence that conveys all of the anguish of Merrick's youth without detailing any of the facts of his childhood, Lynch's film begins its treatment of history by focusing on Treves, already an ambitious surgeon, in search of the Elephant Man, a deformed freak-show exhibit notorious in London. Merrick is not found at the first fair. Treves continues his pursuit, and upon a paid spy's advice, takes the long walk from his hospital operating room through London and finds Merrick, the Elephant Man. It is gray and rainy. The doctor walks a darkening road ever downward through neighborhoods becoming increasingly squalid. He leaves the Victorian upper-crust comfort of his world behind and descends into the bowels of brute poverty. This is another of Lynch's choices to alter fact, as the freak show was historically on Whitechapel just across the street from London Hospital. After exhibiting him at a meeting, Treves intimidates Merrick's drunken, abusive keeper, Bytes, into leaving the Elephant Man with him for further study.

The alarming realization that Merrick is not an imbecile but a man of some intelligence is made during this study. Mothershead and her hospital nursing staff begin to see the real worth in Merrick beyond his gargoyle countenance and twisted body. After tea at Treves's home, the surgeon begins to see Merrick as human rather than specimen. A newspaper article interests grande dame Mrs. Kendal in visiting Merrick. The actress's presentation of her autographed photo launches Merrick as the social cause of London society. After Mothershead's admonition Treves has to question if science has been his rationale to further exploit Merrick. The hospital board with an appeal to the Princess of Wales engineered by its director, the shrewdly politic Carr Gomm, votes to give Merrick permanent refuge.

Greed has given a night porter the idea to exhibit Merrick for money during his shift. Merrick is still abused by bands of drunken and obnoxious revelers in his hospital room after dark. His plight is obvious when his primping in his new finery is shattered by the intruders. After one of these cruel ordeals, Merrick is kidnapped by Bytes and again forced to perform in public freak shows. This time he performs on the Continent, as the British police are on their trail to close them down.

Mercifully, the beaten Merrick is freed from his cage by the other freaks. After an arduous boat trip, Merrick's train brings him home to an altercation leading to a painful chase, as he is hunted into the urinals in Liverpool Station. The police return him to his rooms at Royal London Hospital on Bedstead Square. Aware that he is dying, Mrs. Kendal arranges for him to go to the theater. Sitting in the royal box among all of his friends, Merrick is mesmerized by the pantomime and even introduced from the stage by Mrs. Kendal to the warm applause of the audience.

When he goes home he confides to Treves that he is utterly happy because he is loved. He has often expressed his wish to sleep like the "normal," although he knows his tremendous deformity will kill him if he tries. Merrick stares at the sketches that people his walls: contented children innocently sleeping. After working on his model church, the weary Merrick lies down. At peace, the Elephant Man sleeps. Lynch then returns to the dream and an after-death journey through the stars.

There is probably no stylistic device more generally analyzed than the film's frame. The history of Merrick is bordered by opening and closing sequences suggesting his birth and death—perhaps more cosmically, Birth and Death. In Roger Ebert's opinion, "The direction by David (*Eraserhead*) Lynch is competent, although he gives us an inexcusable opening scene in which Merrick's mother is trampled or scared by elephants or raped—who knows?—and an equally idiotic closing scene in which Merrick becomes the star child from *2001*, or something."[7] Ironically, Lynch expresses respect for Kubrick's films.

And Ebert offers but one critical view. Henry Baker, on the other hand, finds this opening frame effective. "The dream attack on Merrick's mother not only suggests a brutal accident, but also implies both rape and the pains of a difficult childbirth. Thus, subconsciously, one can associate the monotonous boom of the elephant feet with a queasy feeling of sexuality" (Baker, 254).

The opening dream is balanced by another dream sequence that frames the film as its conclusion. The opening sequence suggests the memory or the nightmare of a thrashing atrocity, the elephant-trampling conception of the deformed Merrick. In Lynch's world this opening conveys life's pain and pleasure, stressing both mystery and mysterious eroticism. Here, as in *Eraserhead,* is a fascination with the bloody ordeal of childbirth. Conception becomes a murky, almost primeval collective memory, even an archetypal act of remembered sexual violence. This act simultaneously repels and sustains. We are aware it gives us energy and shame, life and guilt. It feeds and feeds upon itself.

The film's opening grafts and electrifies the medical and legendary origins of the Elephant Man's deformities. Mary Jane Merrick did attend a parade of elephants at a fair three months before Joseph's birth. Although there is no record of her being frightened by elephants, the episode goes back to Merrick himself as a source. It is offered, according to Treves, as an explanation of the deformities at his first meeting with Merrick. The opening doesn't attempt to present medical accuracy; on the contrary, it makes Merrick's neurofibromatosis a mysterious and unique affliction. Currently diagnosed in about 22,000 of the 55,000,000 British subjects, in the 1880s this disease, if incurable, was diagnosable.

The ordeal of Merrick's idealized mother meshes myth and history. The film frame further blurs the line between symbolic and factual. It assimilates dream and delusion into medical history, fluidly meshing sights and sounds. Lynch sets the tone for an expressionistic, not historic, rendering of his story. He selects the historical and medical facts he is going to present as well as the mode of their presentation. Lynch's distinctive perspective expands the film from a retelling of Joseph Merrick's life by setting up a narrative and expressionistic seesaw of fact and dream. This setup makes factual and mythic perspectives of the story interchangeable, even sometimes indistinguishable.

Some limitations of the frame surface in the film's closing. Merrick lies down to sleep and to die. Merrick's mother's photograph begins a trip to the stars. A voice-over accompanies the shot. Too abrupt to stand as a conclusion, too romantic to stand as a metaphor, the sequence becomes cumbersome and simplistic. Unlike the opening frame, which brilliantly questioned without attempting to explain, the closing frame seeks answer rather than resolution on the mythic plane.

This is the kind of image that Lynch will learn to trade on in his post–*Elephant Man* career as a surrealist icon. But here the exaggerated sequence is simply—if sincerely—overdone. Its shots are attractive, but too pedestrian to answer the complex questions posed by the narrative and too visually and aurally obvious to enhance the cinematic suggestions of the movie. There is in early Lynch films a gnawing sense that some of the bloated images, like this starry ride, may be naively sincere. Later in the Lynch oeuvre, they are cushioned by his reputation and become complicated, "artsy," perhaps even camp. But here, without the trappings of genius, as early as 1980, the conclusion is more easily seen as self-indulgent; it doesn't entirely work.

However, the film's frame does serve as a stylistic device of the filmmaker. It enables the black-and-white rendering of the story and the blatant depiction of the cruel and grotesque to be measured against their romantic frame. The visual properties of the film on its allegoric level are so blatantly introduced in its opening and so bluntly stated at the conclusion that the audience ironically sees the mythic implications in every deplorable-action shot in the realistic film.

Thus the audience is consistently made to feel pain. The film makes the audience empathize with Merrick's plight, although they also comprehend his pain as allegoric. Because they must respond dually to the film, allegorically and factually, they learn by watching the film to recognize Merrick's duality. "What we do believe, and what Lynch's uncannily seductive images underscore, is that Merrick is a normal man in freak's armor" (Jacobs, 171). The film presents the horror of the incidents as history, as well as the beauty of these incidents as tale. The deft use of symbolic and biographic narrative blurs any tension created by the film's dreamy and static frames of Merrick's ordeal.

In short, this framing structure sets Lynch's premise and his conclusion. Lynch gives us a reality which can only be reality in the movies. Because the opening is dream, the film continues to be seen and heard as metaphor, regardless of its dialogue or its subject. The communication is in the music, silences, focus, and composition of every shot. As illustration, the black-and-white cinematography is more real than real color on screen; it's quasi-documentary—"factual photography."

And as the film continues through the factual incidents of Merrick's life on screen, we become increasingly and ironically involved with them as elements of film. We become increasingly drawn to them, even comfortable with them, as evocations of film history. "The humanism of *The Elephant Man* is conveyed not through its script so much as through its deliberate echoes of such compassionate horror films as *The Island of Lost Souls* ("Are we not men!"), *The Bride of Frankenstein, Freaks,* and *The Hunchback of Notre Dame*; the spirit of Lon Chaney Sr. is particularly felt, not just in the eloquently vulnerable performance of John Hurt as Merrick, but in the tone of the entire project."[8]

This premise to an interpretation of *The Elephant Man* can be used as the key to unlock Lynch's style. The power of Lynch's style—even in a film otherwise so far from Lynch's familiar terrain—is his film consciousness. Early in his career, before his images become so recognizably or so self-consciously those of David Lynch, it is quite fascinating to see how naturally his films operate as an evolution of our previous film experience. One marvels at how Lynch knows, evokes, and uses film history and conventions.

Along with his personal arsenal of images and his painter's eye, this film consciousness was already present in *Eraserhead*. But here in *The Elephant Man* he develops movie images not only as an integral part of the film but as a tool to communicate his film to the audience. Moreover, enhanced by many other of the film's most haunting effects, these images generate a network of understanding, mutually determined through the creation of the filmmaker and the contribution of the filmgoer. These images are reinforced by Lynch's filming techniques, casting, editing, sound, and cinematography. Thus, as his facility to build film on film conventions is foundational to his style, Lynch's ability to create images and metaphor through this style is his major contribution to cinema as it enters its second century.

When critics of the film review *The Elephant Man,* they appreciate Lynch's singular style but bemoan the film's apparent distance from Lynch. "David Lynch is a real original and a unique talent; he should be given the opportunity to work on his own concepts, his own material, his own technique."[9] Ironically, John Merrick's biography includes disease, hypocrisy, misery, industrial pollution, and is peppered with controversy—prime Lynch source material. But because the factual history of *The Elephant Man* is an entity in itself, it is different from the sources for other Lynch films. Yet through a comparison of the facts with their adaptation on film, this difference ultimately provides a blueprint for better analyzing many of Lynch's techniques in any of his films.

When the audience watches Merrick's historical biography on film, they see Lynch's cinematic vision of the Elephant Man's life. Identifying the facts of history and recognizing those elements on film, they see how Lynch adapts incidents to the language of film. As Lynch operates in images, inviting the audience to participate in his films in order to view them, Lynch compels the audience to face its own world in order to gain entry into his. "Lynch and his cowriters are very much in evidence as the creators of a structure in which the film addresses its own potential and guides the audience to examine its own quality of vision" (Kawin, 258).

Lynch balances real source incidents and surreal film images from his first shots. For example, the film's stark credits note the basis in historical fact. Yet the historical citation is underscored by a haunting melody insinuating itself into the film, nostalgically recalling the lost innocence of childhood in the circus music. The first shot of large eyes proves to be a photograph of Merrick's mother's gaze, expanding to the dreamlike elephant assault, phalluslike trunks, sounds of frenzied moaning, the flailing Mary Jane, and a resultant smoky explosion accompanying the sounds of a crying infant. Thus the film's opening does not merely document factual incidents; it is melancholy in mood, suggestive in imagery, and mythic in tone.

After the surreal dream frame, the film cuts to a second shot of eyes, Treve's eyes, then to gas-jet flames and spinning wheels and other sideshow gimmicks as the camera follows the top-hatted Treves through the tents of a circus. He seeks the advertised Elephant Man in the sideshow. The audience sees bobbies already on the prowl, garish signs and slogans, printed reference to the "fruit of original sin" (this reference to carnal knowledge recalls the lurid images of the preceding dream sequence), a specimen in a jar, fire-eaters, freaks in cages, and spectators, one lady leaving the show on the verge of vomiting; we hear sounds of an eerie conch shell being played, barkers, and a hurdy-gurdy.

These sequences blur the distinction between subjective and factual reality. They move fluidly from the illusion of the frame to the incidents of plot in the first scene. A concentration in both these dense, busy sequences on close-ups, particularly of eyes, supports this meshing of realities.

We enter the first world through Merrick's photograph of his mother's eyes. The elephant assault is seen by her and by her son as reality, whether the assault did or did not happen in history. The second episode we are shown—the film's Victorian sideshow—is seen by Treves as a maze that he must conquer to pursue scientific research. Both episodes are presented as they are seen. They are both real, therefore, whether or not either is factual.

The opening concentrates on reactions. In the film's early sequences, this is done to add to the suspense, building to Merrick's first appearance. The audience sees that the Elephant Man is seen as the world's greatest freak, seen as vile enough to be the object of police inquiry, seen as deformed enough to be studied by earnest scientists, and seen as grotesque enough to make genteel ladies sick to their stomachs. But we do not see Merrick. What we do see is how Merrick is seen.

More important, this device continues after Merrick is revealed to the camera. The film continues to show how others see Merrick, how Merrick is made to see himself. Lynch's *The Elephant Man* focuses not on what is, but on how it is seen. The film's structure, characterization, plot, and techniques unmask the subjectivity of what is or is not beautiful, what is or is not real. Consequently, in questioning how society views—and thus creates—the beautiful and ugly, the film culminates in questioning how each of us, arbitrarily, determines what is "normal."

The camera presents looking or being looked at almost continually. Merrick's deformities are illuminated behind a curtain to be studied by the assembled doctors. Merrick is seen as a hero in a theater box by the refined audience. Merrick is seen with compassion by the monkeys with whom he's caged in France. He is seen as a buffoon by drunks watching him through his hospital window. He is seen as a meal ticket by the guard. A treasure by Bytes. An experiment, and perhaps an opportunity, by Treves. Merrick sees his reflection in a mirror, in the window, in his gleaming silver toiletries, and in a young nurse's screaming face.

Other characters are also presented as they see themselves and as they are seen by others. Professional actress Mrs. Kendal, for instance, sees herself in the greatest, most noble role of her career as Juliet, the beauty to the beast. Mothershead sees herself beneath the cold professionalism she projects as a loving, maternal figure. After Mothershead's accusations, Treves sees himself as an exploiter.

This theme of contrasting appearance and reality is further illustrated in the photographs that play so meaningful a part in Merrick's life. In fact it is a deified photograph that comforts him at death and welcomes him into eternity. The film itself begins not with the character but with a photograph of Mary Jane Merrick. "The face of an angel." Merrick treasures this photograph as his mother. He collects photographs as proof of his place in society. The Treveses display ancestors' photos, which Merrick sees as "noble." And when Merrick holds his mother's photo out to Mrs. Treves later at tea, the audience sees that he is offering her his reality, just as they see that Mrs. Treves sees in the gesture not Merrick and his mother, but herself and her children. In *The Elephant Man,* photographs often have a different reality than pictured.

Other incidents in the film further blur the lines between appearance and its reality. A grotesquely barbaric composition—the bloodied body of a maimed worker on a table, under a knife held by a man in a butcher's apron—is identified as a medical operation. Bloodied harpies battling in the hospital waiting room look and sound like the sequence of the savage elephants—but this later scene depicts reality, waiting-room routine, not savage nightmare. Nothing has more charge than the large printed word FREAK—a static message—focused on by the camera in the film's fluid opening scenes at the fair among the visual hodgepodge and the cacophony. "Normal" characters are seen as acting aberrantly, while the deformed look quite "normal." Cruel exploitation and worthy investigation straddle a thin line. The film scene mirrors the subjective standards of normalcy. Or beauty. Or propriety. Or value. Or morality. And as the film continues to focus on society's arbitrary designations based on superficial judgments, one remembers this signboard and wonders if the label is best suited to Merrick or to Treves, his society or the film viewers.

The ascribing of value not to what we see but by how we see permeates the film. The twisting streets, smoke, fog, and haze are beautiful in the cinematography; the London hell of the Elephant Man is seen as tintypes and postcards. Like illustrations from a Dickens novel, teeming sweatshops are shown in shots of burnished nostalgia. We see the same shots differently as history. We see Merrick as a beautiful creature, physical atrocity that he is. For want of a more appropriate if less worn phrase, the film proves by its aesthetics that "you can't judge a book by its cover." For want of a more perceptive if no less hackneyed phrase, *The Elephant Man* proves by assault that "beauty is in the eye of the beholder."

In Lynch good and evil are not polar entities but rather a duality. They are both there to be observed. Thus Treves is shown in the film as suspicious of his own motives in studying Merrick. When he realizes that Merrick thinks, he is pictured as genuinely moved to pity, if not to affection or empathy. He is an ambitious man, and as such he is reprimanded as self-serving by a member of the hospital board. Vulnerable to Mothershead's accusations of misusing Merrick, he also sees the possibility that advancing his reputation, not Merrick's exploitation, is his real concern. Wholely appropriate to Lynch, these are the contradictory musings of the thinking man.

The film needs a character to externalize the duality. Tom Norman, the factual exhibitor of Merrick, was by no means an unadulterated villain. Consider the historical incidents relating Merrick to Norman. Merrick chose to exhibit himself. Norman was an exhibitor in what was at that time a tradition of entertainment. If exploitative, there is no record that Norman had a cruel or abusive hold on Merrick. On the contrary, in history Merrick terminated his relationship with Norman, while Norman continued his career.

Thus Lynch opts to fictionalize a keeper for Merrick. Bytes (Freddie Jones) is based not on history, but rather on the historical impressions of Sir Frederick Treves in his memoirs. In fact it is Treves who pinned the label of fiend on Tom Norman. Norman, no illiterate bully, retaliated in a book of his own. Lynch decided that a character drawn for film rather than from fact more effectively conveys his theme.

Rather than merely fashioning a nemesis for Merrick, the filmmaker rightly creates in Bytes a mirror image of Treves. Because Bytes is a fictionalized character he can be more evil than is historically accurate. Making him drunken, violent, and mercenary heightens the tension in his relationship with Treves for the camera. In history Merrick, according to Treves, was treated as an animal by Norman. Merrick, according to Norman, felt more a freak when on display in the lecture hall for Treves than when he was a paid freak in Norman's employ.

In the film these historical perceptions are exaggerated, even altered, for greater effect. Depicting the two sides is irresistible to Lynch, and it is an incendiary device for visualizing the movie's theme of subjective realities. Lynch has the loathsome Bytes directly accost Treves on the hospital stairs to Merrick's clock room. "You wanted a freak, I gave you the freak." Bytes instinctively recognizes his kinship with Treves: "We understand each other—completely." Later the audience sees Treves shaken with the fear that he and Bytes might be alike. But showing the characters defiantly face to face on film is what drives the audience's imagination: Bytes's assessment is a threat with ominous possibilities.

Lynch's choices in characterization and his alteration of fact make a blatant, visualized statement. Admitting good and evil in each character, he nonetheless elevates Treves's good actions and damns Bytes's evil motives in the film. This simplification strengthens their force as images in the film, if at the expense of developing their characterizations. Lynch makes a choice for visual and dramatic effect despite the cost.

Other changes in source facts are made in the film. Mrs. Kendal was central in history for gaining Merrick support in society. Among many other gifts, she gave the Elephant Man an autographed picture. He made a church model now in the museum as a gift for her. The film makes Merrick's visit with Mrs. Kendal cinematically epiphanic, crystallizing the Elephant Man's spirit of humanity. However, this pivotal encounter in the film has no basis in fact. Mrs. Kendal never met Merrick in his rooms on Bedstead Square. Merrick wrote Mrs. Kendal letters (now lost) and was visited by her husband.

Historically, realizing Merrick was so pleased visiting his home for tea, Dr. Treves arranged for Merrick to meet a young woman as a test case. Sir Frederick writes that a young, dark-haired widow was his choice in making this gentle gesture to Merrick. The meeting in his ground-floor rooms on Bedstead Square is recorded to have gone well; Merrick was quite taken with feminine beauty. This led to visits by many celebrated persons.

Lynch sees and interprets the facts differently. Merrick did meet and was enchanted by women. But showing more women, showing more successful visits with the glamorous or with royalty, would detract. Kings and queens set a political tone—the wrong tone. But an actress is someone who lives in illusions. This sets the right tone. Mrs. Kendal becomes a composite of all the women introduced to Merrick.

However, this alteration generates a bloated film scene. Because Lynch keeps the character of Mrs. Kendal historically accurate, he ties the film character to facts. Unlike the ahistorical Bytes, who can function freely in the film, Mrs. Kendal becomes tiresome, looking like either the world's biggest "goody two-shoes" or a fraud. The film neither transfers the history nor adapts it, but lets it lie there. And this character casts a shadow on the romantic simplicity of other Lynch characters. Lynch's Mrs. Kendal is simply too good—cardboard and one-dimensional.

On the other hand, Lynch's night porter (Michael Elphick) is pure cinematic invention. Although the London Hospital employed night porters, there is certainly no historical record of a hospital worker with access to Merrick's room who arranged private freak shows. There was no night porter who facilitated the keeper's kidnapping of Merrick from London Hospital, returning him to his degrading existence as a freak; in history there was no kidnapping of Merrick. No historic object on whom Treves can focus his angered defense of Merrick. No bully to be hit on the head by Mothershead. No villain to torment Merrick by pouring liquor down his throat, selling tickets and pandering to old men who get sexually aroused by watching Merrick's deformity, or pushing Merrick into the chilling abyss of seeing his own reflection in a looking glass.

In fact, Merrick went back to perform again as a freak immediately after he had been observed that November day by Treves. As his shows were closed down or moved on by the British police, Merrick hoped to find a better living on the Continent. No one kidnapped him. He never left the hospital, once he was in residence there, until he died. So there was no perpetrator for Treves to fire. Although Carr Gomm is a character in the film based on a historical source, and historically Merrick did have a nurse, Mothershead's character is the cinematic composite of the nursing staff that treated Merrick, so in history there was neither a night porter to hit nor a nurse to be hit by. What is Lynch's purpose in these cinematic inventions?

Lynch's ahistorical inventions make movie scenes. The night porter's character is telescoped from all of the brutal users who took advantage of Merrick. The night porter is a character who epitomizes Lynch's theme: costumed as a protector of Merrick, a man paid to serve the sick, he is the vilest abuser in the film.

The atrocities shown in the two-hour film translate the myriad dehumanizing incidents of Merrick's lifetime. Rearranging the dates of Merrick's return to freak-show exhibition and inventing his kidnapping destroy Merrick in the film just as his humanity begins to be recognized. How often real setbacks devastated the Elephant Man in the same way will never be known.

Merrick's setbacks are condensed by Lynch into the movie scene. But the translation doesn't change their effects; it actually adapts them to the elements of film. The alterations and additions convey facts from history in cinematic equivalents. They gain the same shattering effect as film that they held in reality. Lynch is a master at visualizing the facts of Merrick's life as metaphor in film terms.

Lynch also alters the timing of events involving Merrick. Although Mrs. Kendal did arrange Merrick's excursion to the Christmas pantomime, probably in 1887, the film makes this an outing on the night of his death. In fact Merrick died in April 1890. Merrick also made a six-week country visit arranged by Mrs. Kendal to Fawsley Park in Northampton the summer before his death. The film deletes this holiday just as it dismisses probable other trips to the theater and to the country.

Again Lynch's decision is an aesthetic one: showing a trip to the country is a move to open spaces and freedom. Merrick's prison of deformed bones and organs is better mirrored in the film's confinement to hospital rooms. Long shots of rolling landscape would drastically dilute the tense, caged feeling created by the relentless shots of dark rooms inside London buildings. One night of glory is much more dramatic on film than a career as a theatergoer. Death on that night—especially suicide, is devastatingly effective on film.

The list of Lynch's deviations from the facts goes on, but the changes on film are universally found to be "better to show." Analysis of the adaptations identifies Lynch's visual reinforcement, whenever and however possible, of his themes of deformity and beauty, of illusions and reality. Whether he alters, deletes, or replicates, he concentrates the film into a more powerful, cohesive work, while subtracting historical tangents and dismissing minor factual incidents and characters. History is the source, but the film is a work of art.

In some cases this comparison creates difficulties or limitations in the film. Specifically, some of Lynch's characters tend to caricature, the result of treating a character as half character and half historical personage. Princess Alex is an undoubted royal. The film's presentation of Mrs. Kendal is an oversimplification sharing a tendency with the film's conclusion to get too romantic, making her scenes in the film sentimental and a bit silly. Overlapping and contradictions that Lynch sees elsewhere do not shade the adaptation of these characters.

The fact-and-film conduit then generates how the film works. David Lynch chooses to transfer some facts and change others to create his movie. Whether successfully or unsuccessfully, his choices establish the film reality. Clarifying the concentration, development, and repetition of these choices helps illuminate how and why the choices were made.

Comparing history and its cinematic treatment is only one way, albeit a productive one, to approach *The Elephant Man* as a film. Lynch is also dealing here with an archetypal story of investigation gone haywire. Mining this legendary dilemma provides Lynch with other interesting film possibilities and gives his film greater impact. First, the roots in legend can be traced back to mythology and a tale like that of Prometheus exceeding the boundaries of Olympus. Second, this film has a literary forerunner in Mary Shelley's masterpiece, *Frankenstein*; her novel's subtitle, *A Modern Prometheus,* invokes again this mythic tale while adding a distrust of modernity and science. Third, and perhaps most important in looking at Lynch's film, *The Elephant Man* evokes cinematic masterpieces like *Frankenstein, The Invisible Man,* or *The Body Snatchers* in the rich genre of the horror film.

The old adage that it's a curse to get what you prayed for is as present in Prometheus's plight as in Treves's. The freak that Treves brings into society, the Elephant Man, is grotesque enough to launch Treves's career. Here the ugliest, rather than the most magical of experiments—fire—Merrick is a "treasure," the perfect medical specimen, the doctor's dream. Treves sees in him unlimited possibilities for scientific progress.

When Treves brings the Elephant Man from the freak show of Whitechapel into the hospital, he achieves what has heretofore been his medical dream, the ultimate case to treat. Dark enough already because it is covered with running sores and festering wounds, Lynch's film cuts on the much deeper level of its archetypal source. The audience knows dreams don't work out for Prometheus and is quite suspicious that bringing Merrick to light will provide no happy endings for Treves, the Elephant Man, or society.

Treves dares to interfere with the gods. He brings Merrick from Merrick's world to advance himself. Treves, a medical researcher, also intends to advance the world through the knowledge he will gain. The ends sought by Treves are thwarted.

Respected by the medical community, he finds himself in doubt as to his own motives. Seen in a state of agitation after his confrontation with Mothershead, Treves needs his wife's consolation. The accusation that he is using Merrick as an exhibit in his more civilized but equally self-serving version of Bytes's freak show gnaws at him. This doubt has become and will remain part of his punishment for bringing Merrick across the street and into a different world.

What has gone wrong with the experiment conducted by this medical Prometheus? Merrick is not an object, a gnarled specimen; he is a man. When Treves egotistically tells Carr Gomm that he certainly can understand what Merrick's life as a thinking man has been, the irony is complete; the inability to comprehend this is Treves's problem. His experiment is not as antiseptic as is he. Merrick, the laboratory subject, thinks and feels. What Treves has done to him, regardless of its scientific rationale, grows more inhumane with every halting human word Merrick mutters.

More significant, Merrick, a pitiful, lame creature, is capable of human sympathy and warmth: Merrick has feelings for the lofty Treves. These are feelings that Treves finds painfully difficult, perhaps impossible, to return. Infuriated by the night porter's atrocity, Merrick uncharacteristically loses his temper. Overjoyed to see Merrick return, Treves uncharacteristically embraces the battered cripple. Yet on the last night of Merrick's life, Treves is incapable of returning any of the warmth and affection of Merrick's loving remarks. We see, and the brilliant doctor recognizes, that he has more difficulty with speech than his subject. He is a cripple of another sort. What he has seen in the firelight of his egotistical scrutiny is the dark, damaged side of himself.

The last and most painful failure seen by Treves in the glow of Merrick's humanity is the failure of Treves's greatest rationalization—science, the bright glory of medicine. And most chilling for the film, Treves realizes the boundaries of science he cannot cross, the limitations of medical inquiry. With the memoirs of Treves as a historical source, Lynch creates an extremely understated scene. Calmly, Merrick asks if Treves can cure him. Treves responds that he can provide treatment but no cure. Merrick dismisses the conversation; this is what he had expected. But what of Treves, the scientist in this modern age of experimentation? He must swallow his pride and admit that, observer or exploiter, he is limited with all his knowledge and skill and can do nothing to change what he is given.

It is not coincidental that the visual medium of film and Lynch as a visionary with the painter/sculptor's eye conjure up in *The Elephant Man* the gigantic canvas of Reubens depicting the myth of Prometheus. The perfect, larger-than-life nude strapped to a rock suits the brilliant, learned Dr. Treves. Both men appear godlike but are tortured by the remnants of their egocntric kidnapping to elevate the human condition. Each of these giants has something eating away his insides. Thus Treves is the thinking man's Prometheus.

Daring to call him the modern man's Prometheus takes us to a different level—and another powerfully suggestive one—of the Lynch film. When Mary Shelley investigated the responsibilities of the creator to his creature in her novel, she also investigated the human price demanded in the name of scientific advancement. This literary theme too finds expression in Lynch's film.

Treves is anxious to provide the solution to the Elephant Man's affliction. When he becomes aware that he cannot cure the Elephant Man, he must also face the fact that he is ill-equipped to be his savior. Treves is human enough to realize his failures, caring enough to understand that he cannot care enough to salvage Merrick, will never know enough to cure him. This melancholy impasse is most effectively handled by Lynch in the Treveses' tea, "the key sequence in the movie."[10]

Watching Merrick costumed like a gentleman, his profane visage now identified as human by the cut of his proper attire, Treves sees the splendor of the actual man. His mixed reaction of repulsion and pity, pride and guilt, telegraphs passages of Shelley's language, pages of Treves's memoirs, into a series of images: the guilty exchange of Treves with his wife about how they have hidden their children from exposure to this freak; Treves's rush to communicate with the Elephant Man by displaying his collected photos; the paws of Merrick holding his fragile tea cup, like a circus dog trained to simulate refinement; the tears that Merrick sheds, that Mrs. Treves fights, and the doctor tries rationally to find; Lynch visually presents here what our reading of the classics has asked and what is echoed in the debate on current medical and ethical issues like cloning, genetic engineering, and euthanasia. Treves is now forced to anguish—what is the medical responsibility to human life? His experiment has crossed medical, ethical, and moral lines—and both he and the audience know it.

Recalling the great motion pictures of film history is *The Elephant Man*'s other masterful thematic stroke. Shot in black and white, set in nineteenth-century London, acted by a cast with meticulous diction, the film revives one after another of the frightening horror classics. Many of its devices are recognizably from these movies. Many of the scenes are bittersweet in their composition, making the Elephant

Man's case more effectively by their movie tones than by conventional appeals as reality.

Certainly ties to *Frankenstein* surface as the story progresses in laboratories and hospitals. Merrick's gigantic hands clutching a child's photo recall Frankenstein's deadly, powerful hold in a tragic game with a little village girl. Like the earlier child-monster encounter, which was edited from the 1931 film, Lynch also suggests but edits such an encounter here.

The examination scene in Treves's office in the London Hospital Medical College recalls the pursuit of another victim of scientific experimentation, *The Invisible Man* (1933). It is hard not to recall *Freaks* (1932), in which the deformed and ostracized bond to make their own society. Merrick's cry for understanding echoes the pitiful cry of *Island of Lost Souls* (1933).

Strongly present is the cinematic *Hunchback of Notre Dame* (1939). The repellent rabble and the heroine who recognizes the beauty in the disfigured beast's soul are mirrored not only in this story but in the very shots of the film. One feels the panic of Lon Chaney being chased to the Seine in *The Phantom of the Opera* (1925). Lynch's characteristic use of machinery as both abstract set decor and villainous foe has the feel of similar industrial shots in Fritz Lang's *Metropolis* (1925). One feels again the madness of the fair which opens Wiene's *The Cabinet of Dr. Caligari* (1919).

In fact Lynch's close shots of the hospital, the superiority of Merrick over supposedly normal people seen as disfigured in odd camera angles, and the use of a frame around the story questioning the narrative level with allegoric allusions reaffirm Lynch's ties to all of these older movies. The themes are not original in his 1980 film. Moreover, Lynch's film is enhanced in the context of the previous films. Lynch purposely and brilliantly replicates, plays against, and evokes the older films. Lynch again adapts facts from history—now from movie history—to create *The Elephant Man*'s world.

Additionally, few screenwriters have Lynch's ear for idiom. Like Orton in his plays, Lynch finds nuance and duality in the simplest of statements. He changes meanings through repeated verbal barrages of simple statements. He verbalizes obvious feelings in deadpan, declarative sentences, giving the observations entirely new meanings. He combines unlikely topics in conversations. In both dialogue and silence, Lynch's knack of conveying humor in the grotesque or eroticism in the unthinkable is consistently cinematic.

John Hurt portrays John Merrick in *The Elephant Man*. Courtesy of the Museum of Modern Art/Film Stills Archives.

Difficulty arises with the oversimplication. The inherent issue here seems to be one of the screenplay's lack of subtlety. For example, Madge Kendal is really very, very grand. Mrs. Treves is simply lovely. Merrick himself goes too quickly from dumb creature to pithy raconteur.

Here is the center of a critical argument. The "one-dimensional" characters are judgments based on literary expectations and comparison to elements of life. But the Lynch characters don't act as people really do, they act as movie characters do. Lynch the film director balances the shortcomings of his script. Ultimately, Lynch does not develop the characters, scenes, or the film solely in language. He develops them on the screen in a cinematic context. He chooses to present his story within the frame of the dreams of a character as he is born and as he dies, beyond the facts of his life and history.

Actually, it's a matter of seeing Lynch on film in other than a narrative line. It is a matter of seeing Lynch as we do dreams—no questions asked. As we do with poetry's figurative language, dismissing the unlikes in a metaphoric image and reading only the bridging bond. To watch—to listen—to feel as the movie glides by.

The audience can't superimpose expectations of story onto Lynch. His film doesn't operate within narrative conventions. It investigates, sometimes originates, film conventions. "Rudolf Arnheim said in *Film As Art* that film's limitations make its art possible, but it is further true that to grapple with the dialectic of such limits is to advance the form as well as its canon of possibilities, and the task in this particular film is to assert if not define the quality of what cannot be publicly seen" (Kawin, 258).

David Lynch is a filmmaker who consistently pokes at film's limitations. He dabbles in all of its elements. He did research and preproduction work on location in London. In addition to directing, Lynch takes screen credit for collaborating on the screenplay and the sound design.

Film sound is one of the limitations of film that Lynch redefines. *Eraserhead* was also an interesting film in sound, but *The Elephant Man,* as a larger-budgeted, more conventionally oriented film, more clearly illustrates Lynch's aesthetic in sound design. Film sound is a combination of dialogue, music, sound effects, and silence. The arrangement as well as the emphasis of these sound components in *The Elephant Man* are both distinctive and impressive.

Because the soundtrack is so effectively integrated, it is possible to respond to it without isolating its force. Film critics take note of the film's auditory elements in the film's atmosphere, tone, and story. "*The Elephant Man* has the power and some of the dream logic of a silent film, yet there are also wrenching pulsating sounds—the hissing steam and the pounding start of the industrial age" (Kael 1987, 179). From the first strains of the circus music that open the film, to the voice-over which brings it to its close, sound design is an integral component of *The Elephant Man*. Sound design operates in two ways: in the development of the film as a network of communication, and then by emphasis as a part of the total film.

Probably the most obvious element of the soundtrack is the words the audience hears. Lynch is credited as a screenwriter. The choice to treat the film as historically as possible, to frame it in a surreal dream, and to telescope characters and events has been discussed earlier. It is these choices that result in a streamlined film about the cruelty, the hypocrisy—even the stupidity—of labeling superficially.

Episodic and succinct, the screenplay uses historical facts which, aside from the frame, chronicle Merrick's years at the hospital. While there is some interesting dialogue between minor characters, the film's main points in dialogue are between Merrick and Treves. However, this visual film's main thrust is not made in spoken language. Even in its soundtrack, words are not the major device used to communicate the mode or the message of the film.

Music is illustrative here in setting the mood and in conveying the film's themes. Lynch is a filmmaker who uses music, although his later collaboration with Badalamenti will have many more dramatic effects than those of the scoring in *The Elephant Man*. Subtlety is this film score's musical success. John Morris has fashioned a companion to the black-and-white visuals. Three qualities of his musical score are especially noteworthy: appropriateness, placement, and repetition.

First, the music sounds appropriate to the chronological period pictured, and the score supports the film in mood. This is probably most significant in the Christmas panto episode. Here Merrick is lost in the world of beauty and illusion. Thus, as the film gives us a montage of the images on stage taking flight in Merrick's imagination, the music soars without the interruption of any other sound. Here too the music—played by the house orchestra—has reality in the narrative rather than being a grafted cinematic device. The score benefits from that tie to the pictured scene, as does the circus music played at the freak shows.

Music in *The Elephant Man* also insinuates itself. How it is inserted is more important than what type the music is. The music begins nearly inaudibly and creeps into the actions and into the audience's minds—like suppressed memories. The haunting musical strains invading the straightforward credits come to mind. The music that seeps into the wafting of the wind in the Belgian countryside is also subtly assimilated into its scene.

Finally, the music is repetitive, making connections between incidents in the movie without the need of dialogue to draw attention to the bridge. For example, the music first heard during the elephant assault during the opening dream is heard again when the night porter creeps the quiet hospital halls stalking Merrick as his prey. Heard again, it becomes increasingly louder, displacing words and stressing musically its message as Merrick is thrown about in his room by the night porter and his paying customers in their assault on the Elephant Man at his kidnapping. The music triggers the feeling of exploitation, forced entry, and rape and carries the scenes to powerful—and collective—impact.

It is, however, in the noises and the absolute absence of any noises as soundtrack that Lynch is most distinctively present in *The Elephant Man*. As with the music, there is a network of appropriate, assimilated noises in the film. These noises are accompanied by their negation—absolute silence. And they operate in combination with dialogue and the visuals of a scene. Noises convey the film's theme; noises set the film's mood.

First, these are the sounds of Victorian London: industrial, modern, and urban. They are entirely appropriate in bringing the sounds of the era to mind. The noises convey London's East End: the cheap chatter of a pub, the dripping of draining water, the blast of factory flames, the lighting of gas lamps in the hospital wards. These are also the sounds of *The Elephant Man*: the trumpeting of the beasts, the shrieking of the newborn child, the labored breathing of the deformed cripple as he hobbles through the hospital. The sounds portray Merrick's surroundings. They are the sounds of his experience: the noiseless void of his cage, the exaggerated applause of his friends at the Drury Lane, the elongated, piercing peals of ridicule and disgust. Thus sounds give us Merrick's world.

Sounds are exaggerated, distorted, and suspended. Noises of the hospital clock and Merrick's frightened breathing as he climbs to his room overpower the scene. At other times sound becomes almost inaudible: Merrick's last words are a muttered whisper. Scenes are silent pictures. Lynch and Splet make the silence painfully noisy. As the camera goes into the slit cut in Merrick's mask, there is the sound of a tremendous gush of wind. The soundtrack sucks out the air, the breath, and then swallows us up into Merrick's silent mental world. There is the noiselessness of an abyss.

Communicating through sounds is also accomplished in their rhythm and occurrence. For example, that tremendous pounding. Bytes knocks for Merrick to perform on cue like a trained animal. Mothershead pounds on the hospital reception desk so Merrick will do as he is told. While Treves is trying to examine him, Merrick is terrified by that same demanding pounding by another doctor outside the door. The pounding merges with the pounding of the Elephant Man's heart.

Even when the same noise is not heard in any extended pattern, the film has a dense texture of sound that is understood through the relationship of the noises. For example, water drips as Treves makes his way down a labyrinthine hallway to find Merrick. The ominous sound echoes in the similar soundtracking of the night porter's footsteps as he plunges into the hospital hallways to prey on the Elephant Man. The noises are exaggerated beyond normal hearing to sound as they would be felt: expressionistic sound design. Treves hears the slimy sounds of the dripping water while descending further and further down into the filth of Merrick's captivity. Sounds relentlessly stab the terrified Merrick waiting in this room to be still further degraded by yet another keeper.

The film appeals to the aural sense by supporting the story with auditory effects. Lynch orchestrates the sounds or their utter lack to enhance his film. Sound directly conveys feeling to the audience. The soundtrack is as inherent in *The Elephant Man* as are its uses in Lynch's style.

The film's visual design is also noteworthy. In a film created by a master of the film image, beautiful—and beautifully effective—images abound. For example, the film shows a hospital ward: quiet, sleeping institutional beds in orderly rows. A balanced pair of gaslight fixtures is dimmed. Order now reigns in Mothershead's world—a place for everything and everything in its place. Presiding over the ward is a portrait of Queen Victoria, regally and benevolently smiling over these, the humblest of her empire's citizens. As the camera pulls back, showing the expansive, ordered modern world, the hypocrisy of Victorian society is simultaneously exposed.

As in *Eraserhead* the images invite viewer input. The Victorian settings present images of the hypocrisy of Merrick's world and his own physical decay. "And as we are steeped in Lynch's somber reflection of London in 1884, in the seedy black alleys of poverty, the gaslit hospital corridors, the overstuffed elegance of a private house, the glitter of a Christmas panto performance, we too are disconcerted."[11] Hypocrisy is a significant theme in this film and in the other works of David Lynch. "Lynch achieves much of his purpose in *The Elephant Man* through the power of understatement" (Baker, 258). Lynch visualizes the theme with the camera. The audience understands the shot and sees the shot in the context of Lynch's film. This stylistic perspective, this painterly perspective, tells the story visually. Lynch envisions in film terms, translating his theme to pictures as a visual episode of his movie plot. The film images are striking photography; the audience is also affected by how they are made to see what appears on the screen.

Therefore, in *The Elephant Man* effective photographs of the subjects operate metaphorically as well. "From here," continues Henry Baker, "Lynch moves to another vision—that of industrial Victorian England. The superbly evocative black-and-white photography is beautiful and hellish at once—chimneys pour black smoke into the air, filth lines the streets of Whitechapel near London Hospital" (Baker, 258). Thus with audience interpretation, Lynch gives the photograph, in its composition and especially its context, a different meaning than that of the subject. This network of images moves Lynch into allegory.

Machinery is a spellbinding device in Lynch from as early a film as his *Six Men Getting Sick* with its looping projector. The man who pulls the lever on the ominous machine in the opening of *Eraserhead* triggers a film mechanism which is still running today. If any one image in Lynch's films could be considered emblematic of the artist, the industrial machine would have to be a candidate.

Researching the film, "Lynch expressed some disappointment in discovering that the Victorians didn't have 'more machinery around.' But after flying to England to shoot the film, he did what he could to keep the sound and imagery industrial; and *The Elephant Man* ultimately wound up with even more smoke, soot, and clanking machinery than *Eraserhead*" (Hoberman, 248).

Thus Lynch provides a network of images in sync with *The Elephant Man* on every level. First, the machine is an appropriate image of the Victorian age. This is, after all, the era which industrialized England. Here the overcrowded urban condition has its roots—factories—assembly lines—working machines. This is the height of the British Empire, when England ruled the world with military might and trade—war machines—weaponry—advanced technology. Experimentation and invention at this time gave us sweatshops and child labor, inside plumbing and locomotive power—mechanical devices—industrial machinery.

Here too, the price of scientific experimentation is the pain of human loss to mechanical progress. Images capture the sense of progress at any cost. The pictured machine then becomes screen image, expressing more than just a photographed subject. "Lynch was clearly interested most in the symbolic aspects of the story: he sees Merrick as a twisted, tragic metaphor of the wrenching dislocations of the industrial society that juggernauted with iron limbs into Victorian England. Lynch fills the screen with steel and smoke, images of relentlessly pumping machinery" (Kroll, 72). The audience sees the workers feeding the machines. Control of the machines gives men the modern world. The invention of technology has made man master of the universe. As the men toil, sweat, swaying back and forth, they become part of the process of the machines they operate.

And it seems suddenly that mastery is reversed and machines control men. Men are little more than fleshy cogs in the machinery of our modern society. The film shows the modern paradox: a surgery where the glistening, stripped body of a worker, like some human colossus mangled by the industrial predator, is being dissected—medical scientists using modern technology to repair the workings of the "human machine." Man is victim and beneficiary of the progress that ties him down, cuts him open, and restores him for the next industrial accident. Man and machine are shown as inseparably productive and destructive components of the modern world.

That conflict between nature and medical science in this age continues to be illustrated in mechanical imagery. The struggle between Treves's scientific curiosity and his human compassion pits images of medical tools and lab tests against images of pantomimes and teas. Treves realizes that treating Merrick as fodder for science, a subject on which to test the latest hospital equipment, is cruelly dehumanizing. But if progress is to be served, science must experiment, the sacrifice is inevitable.

Bytes and Treves have contradictory yet similar designs on Merrick; to destroy and to salvage through exhibition. Just as these relationships are paradoxical, machinery is imaged as savior and Satan of the times as it performs man's work. First a paddle wheel crosses the channel and then a steam engine rushes Merrick back, tearing through the British landscape. Images of modern transportation replace the pastoral image of the freaks' torchlights assisting Merrick's flight on foot across Belgian farms. So here too the mechanical has replaced the agricultural.

Thus the train speeds Merrick from hell to hell—and to his death. Its white smoke is reminiscent of the smoky explosion in the climax of the film's opening dream sequence. In that scene the image of the smoke was accompanied by the squealing cry of the newborn. Cry of the newborn age? Or screaming entry into an industrial chasm? Repetition of the image suggests the way in which man has been benefited and exploited by his modern world, simultaneously reaffirming how far society has advanced and how primitive society remains. Merrick's mechanical rebirth only rushes him to other brutalities. On arrival he will be beaten by a savage mob in the train-station urinal.

Machines are, of course, the quintessential modern image. They look like the age that produced them and that they produced—metal abstractions: complicated, systematic, and dynamic. They even look like pieces of modern art, functional and pragmatic, defining their times artistically and technically. "Their times" generate the brutal work code of London's sweatshops and introduce anesthesia in London hospitals. Victorian times then are recognized on the screen as the forerunner of the audience's dual environment. All of these levels of suggestion are invoked by the film's technical and industrial images. Therefore, as a film image in Lynch's work, machinery is what it is (replication), what it stands for (symbol), what it means (allegory), and how it looks (designed art abstraction). In the film the machinery depicts photographic subject, historical setting, art work, and a philosophy that is the despised, deified tenet of our age.

The Elephant Man is an interesting film for comparative study. Although differences between the film adaptation and its historical source are evident, their comparison and contrast provide a critical tool for identifying elements in Lynch's film style. Additionally, his film style, techniques, and aesthetics are found to be consistent with those of earlier and later film works. Ironically, the film is firmly in step with other Lynch films.

The Elephant Man is more suitable to Lynch's filmmaking than the subject at first suggests. Merrick's Victorian milieu is actually a rich source for Lynch's vision. Lynch has a vision of that society; Lynch sees that society as a visionary. Hypocrisy, social conventions, and class division identify the industrial years which closed the last century. Society in *The Elephant Man* is made up of people defined by how they view a set of elaborate, changing, arbitrary rules. Merrick galvanized the nexus of those realities. The collision of perspectives is eminently suitable to Lynch's aesthetics.

In the highest class, royalty, Merrick is a pathetic subject to be cared for with flair, if rarely seen. To convey this detachment, Lynch alters history. Princess Alexandra, it is noteworthy, did meet Joseph Merrick. But in Lynch's film this encounter is never seen. Lynch chooses to delete this fact. Rather Princess Alex shines her kindness on Merrick through a go-between, Carr Gomm, and the hospital board she deftly controls. Lynch gives us this scene of manipulation. The Princess of Wales saves the Elephant Man with a pithy letter from the Queen, but certainly not with a visit. Merrick is the worthiest of charities.

The smart set sees Merrick as an event. He is visited in his rooms at Bedstead Square by a lady shaken down to her teacup, evoking the reaction of a paying customer to Merrick's deformities in the film's opening freak show. Lynch creates the film's most lyrical sequence by telescoping Merrick's playgoing into a Christmas panto on the night Merrick will die, culminating in the audience's warm bursts of applause for Merrick, shaken by the magic of the moment.

The smart set—the theatrical world, of which Mrs. Kendal is a member—is after all the world of illusion, and Lynch determines—regardless of historical accuracy—to show Mrs. Kendal meeting Merrick. Lynch has them converse through a romantic reading of Shakespeare's dialogue for stage lovers: chaste, poetic, and theatrical. Thus Lynch shows everyone in Mrs. Kendal's genteel set, from prima donnas to the haute bourgeois, i.e., who see Merrick as this season's curiosity.

In the lowest class of cripples, pimps, tarts, victims, and drunks that people London's East End, Merrick is seen as a welcome diversion. Bytes, altered by Lynch, sees Merrick as the "freak of freaks." Even in Merrick's sanctuary in the hospital, these thrill seekers pursue and abduct him in a sequence invented for the film. Paying to get a glimpse of him raises the lowest class to the level of the social swells they mimic. Viewing him not only provides some good laughs and a good scare, but his deformity gives a little lift and a cheap thrill as well. He looks pathetic enough to make them feel a bit less disgusted with their own lot.

The hospital is a microcosm of the Victorian social order Merrick seeks and flees. All levels of Victorian society come to the hospital: from throne room to board room, from drama to tea party, from freak show to peep show. The hodgepodge of social perspectives within that world is reflected in the hospital environment. Lynch shows a world within another world, with its own added conventions. Doctors, nurses, and other members of the hospital community view Merrick here. Hospital society is "enlightened"; classes of a new order determined by the scientific tasks they perform put Merrick "in the proper light."

Treves exhibits Merrick to other doctors in a lecture hall under a spotlight's scrutiny. The display makes his fortune and career. But he exhibits the naked subject through a gauze screen with professional sensibility. Mothershead represents another echelon of the hospital staff. She plainly states that professional duty, her good Christian treatment of the Elephant Man, constitutes love. Not only is her love of Merrick beneficial, she declares, it is right. Hospital staff in its lowest reaches, as seen in the night porter's actions, has the ingenuity to turn some coins by making Merrick's exploitation a going small business, finding both a desperate subject and audience to exploit in the dockland rabble.

The hospital world is the perfect setting to convey the film's atmosphere. Modern and sterile. Also bloody and sweaty—rife with infection and disease. The hospital world stratifies into its own classes, from doctors to nurses to orderlies to the absolute bottom of society, whom they serve in the wards; it makes its own conventions. The medical community knows how to treat the freak; they know what is his proper place. It is a world based on assigned roles. It is a world of propriety. For example, Merrick entertains in his hospital room, starched white collar masking running sores and bony masses, teacup in hand. He strives to fit in properly. If incurable, he must be seen as trainable.

The Elephant Man is as he is seen. Merrick sees himself as a reflection of how each of the groups looks at him. Freak, monster, son, and patient, he is all of these things. Primping for a mirror, Merrick is a dandy—while caged with the monkeys, he is a battered animal—in the hospital auditorium, he is a physical specimen. The audience sees him as a sickening deformity.

Lynch adapts the facts of history to structure his artistic portrait. It's hard to imagine Merrick looking any worse. A great makeup job by Christopher Tucker explicitly details his pathetic abnormalities. The Elephant Man is certain ugliness.

Lynch chooses to display him before the camera. Merrick, shown in every light, is hideous enough to look inhuman. Yet by showing how he looks, Lynch shows who he is. Lynch forces the audience to admit that the medical assessment that Merrick is a freak is a painfully accurate diagnosis, but that the definition of what constitutes humanity is pitifully wrong.

When we see *The Elephant Man,* we see that any mirror can only provide a limited reflection. Lynch challenges the audience to abandon every looking glass—including the art of the motion picture—and to open instead their own eyes.

3

Future Perfect Lynch—*Dune*

The road of excess leads to the palace of wisdom.
—William Blake, *Proverbs of Hell*

Lynch next adapts Frank Herbert's novel to the screen, directing his own script. *Dune* is a future world. A messiah is born to lead the people of his time out of bondage under a despotic regime. The revolution centers on controlling the mining of a spice, melange, on Dune, a desert planet. The 1965 novel is a sci-fi classic. Frank Herbert writes an epic chapter of future history. The novel spawned four sequels and is estimated to have 30,000,000 readers worldwide.

As is typical of the critical reception to Lynch films, *Dune* on screen meets a range of reviews from raves to scathing condemnation. At the critical extreme, there are a few who see Lynch's adaptation as an audacious and important step forward in film. "*Dune* towers over most futuristic epics. It's richer and stranger than just about anything the commercial cinema has to offer."[1] The film's fans also include critics who recognize it as an interesting film, if an unsuccessful effort. "Lynch's failures—such as 'Dune'—are more fascinating than the successes of less gifted filmmakers."[2] However, this film is most often met by negative criticism, and the director faces an onslaught of critical abuse. "'You just do what you do, and the rest you can't control. In a way, I've already had one experience with being trashed and that's "Dune." Well, always with Roger Ebert and Rex Reed, but with "Dune" I had it pretty bad from a lot of people,' Lynch recalled" (Gary Thompson, 37).

Working on *Dune* gives support to Lynch's meteoric reputation. "Lynch's career thus far reads like a film student's fancy: an avant-garde feature made for $20,000; then a modestly budgeted ($5 million) no-star commercial movie, in black and white, that earned good reviews, a decent box-office take, and Oscar nominations for best picture and director; and now a $50 million epic that is dividing the critics and luring fantasy fans."[3] Lynch has again to postpone work on his small film "Ronnie Rocket" as Zoetrope Studios battles unsuccessfully for its financial life. *Dune,* his new project, is a mega-epic filmed in Mexico with 70 sets; he needs to clear $200,000,000 to show a profit. As a commercial film, whatever its ties to Lynch's career evolution, *Dune* is a critical failure.

Critics of the film as it was released include David Lynch. *Dune* has a checkered film-production history. Its production and distribution are affected by studio bankruptcy, changing screen credits, and convoluted rights. There is then, from the beginning, more than one version of *Dune.* The confusions with regard to *Dune* and its edited versions are far from over. The sci-fi epic is one of the few films that run longer after editing for television than at the movies. The telecast adds an additional 50 minutes to the film's running time. MCA-TV distributes the film with this additional, previously edited footage.

In the main, this footage attempts to explain still further the complicated story and make a clearer transition between unresolved scenes. The battle scenes are expanded and extended as one supposed clarification. Stills and diagrams are now included, adding more unmoving pictures to the already static story. Also several minutes of the film, particularly Harkonnen atrocities and perversions, are edited from the new version. "It is now credited as 'A Alan Smithee Film,' Smithee being a popular pseudonym employed by the Directors' Guild for members who want their real names deleted from a film's credits. What Mr. Lynch thinks of this 'complete and extensive adaptation' of his film can be detected in the pseudonym he chose for his writing credit: Judas Booth."[4] Nonetheless, if *Dune,* as it is theatrically released, carries some of its own abortive sequel within it, the expanded version made for TV does not resolve the confusion. Added expository footage further weighs the film down. *Dune* is still labeled a notoriously confusing film about inhabitants of the future. It stills lumbers like a titan until it suddenly—and without resolvution—fades to an anticlimactic ending.

The film's source, Frank Herbert's *Dune,* is a pop literary classic. It is a literary series that details a new world's language, decaying order, and moral salvation. The books revolve around the questions of morality and heroism. It is fascinating to observe Lynch trying his hand at adapting Herbert's novel to film. *Dune* asks a question—"Am I the one?" References are made throughout the film to test that question—"Is he the one?" More than a screenplay device, Lynch employs the question to give the enormous film some cohesion.

Paul Atreides (Kyle MacLachlan) fulfills his own destiny by acting out the text of religious prophecies. Thus *Dune* opens with the messiah's actions predetermined in prophecies. The messiah will avenge the assassination of his father and defeat the forces conspiring in the universe. When the Kwisatz Haderach leads his army of the just in a gigantic battle, he will show himself as the embodiment of right's quest and restore order to a warring universe. Paul has to be seen to act as the myths predicted the messiah would act. The plot fulfills preordained actions. *Dune*'s scenes are explained by their context in the myth. Events exist distinct from feelings and motives. The entire film is resolved in Alia's triumphant announcement in the final fade that Paul is the Kwisatz Haderach. The facts shown are interpreted in the voice-over narration of changing characters.

If the question works as a device to order the film—and that is in itself questionable—it certainly doesn't explain the story. Asked by Paul and other characters, as extrasensory communications, as dialogue, and as soliloquy, prompted by awe, resentment, or suspicion, the repeated question merely sounds cohesive. The audience of *Dune* still leaves the theater with too many other questions unanswered. Lynch essentially develops the surreal vision of the literary world on film. Because Lynch isn't merely making a space epic in *Dune,* elements of film as well as conventions from several different film genres surface in his story set in another world. The audience does not view the book's future; rather it enters the director's future world. Lynch's film must show Herbert's hallucinatory dreams, customs of a futuristic universe, and intellectual word riddles and prophecies.

Although Paul Atreides travels through space, the film is not really a space story. Lynch creates a future of gorgeously present evil and violence. A new moral order and a new language pervade his world of futurism—not just science-fiction film settings, but the creations of a cinematic visionary. The adaptation of Herbert's world isn't simply a depiction of Herbert's plot incidents for the camera. Futurism has an artistic genealogy in which *Metropolis* (1926) begat *The Exterminating Angel* (1962) begat *A Clockwork Orange* (1971) begat *Dune*. Lynch is a filmmaker and certainly film conscious, thus his medieval knights and dragons with the hyper-nuclear power to annihilate the universe are encoded as film myth.

Lynch crafts a cinematic mega-epic that leaves his audience sometimes awed by beauty, other times appalled and disgusted. *Dune* asks Herbert's questions, adds film questions, but doesn't answer—or, more conspiciously, doesn't really address—either set. Lynch just keeps expanding the exposition; he finds another premise. The film audience, whether Herbert readers or not, are therefore not intrigued; the audience is confused.

In *Dune,* as it stands in the screen or television versions, underlying elements cannot be meshed. Lynch's inherent sense of creating film images remains intact. The problem is not with the film as film. As film the final shots are very effective. The camera delves into the eye of Paul Atreides, now undisputed savior. The eye is a clear blue infinite; blue eyes solidify his status as a Fremen after years of fighting on the desert planet. Simultaneously, the blue waves fade into the frame and his eyes become the waves of Caladan. This ties Paul's roots visually back to the earliest shots of the film. He has fulfilled his promise. And visually so has the film.

Visual rhythm is intrinsic to a film created by images and their visual repetition. *Dune*'s close-ups of hands include Paul's signing or "weirding" power, Leto's hands beckoning just beyond his son's reach, and Paul's hands signifying that he survived drinking the "water of life," among many others. The pictured hands convey a message, and their depiction is frequent enough, varied enough, and representative enough to communicate on film through context. The frames are visually resolved.

The production design of the film is consistently excellent. In *Dune* Lynch's grafting of eras is intensified as the director images his lush tomorrow. "No science fiction film has ever been so inspired by the past, or so audaciously eclectic" (Ansen 1984, 93). The golden Byzantine of the throne room is invaded by a locomotive-like carriage bearing the gigantic amoeba who rules the universe. The distinctive look runs from the Reverend Mother's shaved head to Feyd-Rautha's spiked orange hair. The international cast includes Max von Sydow, Francesca Annis, Jose Ferrer, and Jurgen Prochnow, giving the film a global sound in its dialogue tinged by so many accents that the future world amalgamates a language unhindered by contemporary national boundaries. Rock star Sting appears, bringing a pop look to his villainous characterization. Stripped to gold lamé briefs, he is both om-

Scenes from *Dune*. Top: Virginia Madsen is the Princess Irulan. Bottom: Duke Leo Atreides, played by Jurgen Prochnow, with Francesca Annis as the Lady Francis and Kyle MacLachlan as the duke's son Paul. Courtesy of the Museum of Modern Art/ Film Stills Archives.

inous threat and adolescent pinup dream. His sexual presence and status as rock icon enhance Lynch's futuristic look. Lynch himself appears as a frantic radio operator on Arrakis. The actors wear costumes of quilted plastics which, according to the story, process the wearers' perspiration into drinking water while filtering out feces and urine. Military uniforms are covered with cossacklike fur-trimmed cloaks in a shot of Duke Leto, ensconced by his men, carrying a pet dog down a staircase. The eclectic costumes, hair styles, crafts, floating perverts, and metallic flowers are all part of Lynch's world.

The production's design evidences a longing for the past. Less than 50 years later, World War II is remembered as an age of honor, and the fifties already evoke nostalgia. The melancholy for the past is visually assimilated by Lynch into the production's costumes, sets, and makeup with enormous exaggeration into the increasingly foreign, technological future. Lynch's world has evolved, but not beyond recognition.

In fact, *Dune*'s future utopia is a telling illustration not only of Lynch's aesthetic vision, but of contemporary nostalgia. The audience seeks comfort in the familiarity of the known in the constantly changing future. But docu-media reduction of history, that syndrome exposing the clay feet on any real hero of the past, like "complete story" coverage of current situations, leads romantics to seek the ideal not in past or present but in a created, unreal future. The future holds on to the past for explanation. Arbitrarily. History, therefore, is evoked even if reprehensible because recognition is at least comfortable. In short, because current trends so demean past and present heroes by exposing their mistakes, weaknesses, and flaws, Lynch's contemporary audience, finding itself with all-too-human heroes, seeks its idols in fiction.

Lynch can only invent his superhero from the imagination of the future. Poetic references by T. S. Eliot illustrate the yearning for "future perfect" societies in a time of alienation. "Eliot's statement calls attention once again—as have many of the examples cited—to the fact that it is those artists, writers, and composers for whom creation is an act of impersonal discovery, a skillful ordering of objective materials rather than an expression of personal feeling, who have found the substance, forms, and procedures of the past most fruitful and who have used them most frequently and freely. They have also used them eclectically, some combining various pasts together with the present in a single work, others paraphrasing or simulating different pasts in different works, but always with a sense of the press of the present rather than a yearning for yesterday."[5]

As in Lynch's previous films, *Dune*'s world is one of sounds. This cohesive technique is present in the dialogue and music of *Dune*. Lynch features the Toto score, particularly the futuristic new sound of Brian Eno's "Prophecy Theme." The music is modern in sound, particularly in its use of a synthesizer. It is also romantic, dramatic, even inspirational, giving *Dune* a sound on the grand scale. The grandeur of the music is sometimes dirgelike, other times militaristic, always powerful. It enhances the epic look of the film.

Sound—and not sense—is best served in *Dune* by the dialogue. Lynch's screenplay adaptation is aurally masterful, but narratively bloated. The lines are written with simple statements describing the most outlandish things. Sentences are most often declarative, as if the world the audience has entered is somehow real. Lynch promotes the reality of his vision with first-person narration in voiceovers from alternating characters introducing scenes and events giving the film the sound of a legend passed down from generation to generation on scrolls read for the audience as part of a religious ceremony recalling the tenets of our new-world faith. It works.

Actors deliver their lines with the reverence of an ancient holy tract. The strange vocabulary further sounds the reality of a different world as its consistent inclusion without explanation furthers that world's credibility as a real society. Lines have a rhythm. For example, "Am I the one?" and "Is he the one?" are not only repeated enough to gain aural cadence in the film, but the levels of loudness between the whispers and proclamations and the pacing of statement and unspoken but heard musings make this auditory refrain musical, a refrain of sounds fluidly carrying the film forward.

The problem with *Dune* is that although Lynch provides a visual and auditory context, he labors under a heavy burden of unassimilated exposition. Narrative cohesion comes too late. Critics condemn the narrative's lack of focus and pacing: "The exposition doesn't seem to point the way to anything; the story isn't dramatized—it's merely acted out (and hurried through)."[6] The plot is so labyrinthine that it is excessive in fact and detail for most of the film and then undergoes (but does not survive) one of the most hurried and determined edits of actions in the movies. The plot first buries the audience under a mud slide of dates, names, predictions, atrocities, and events. Mind-reading soliloquies and voice-over transitions have blurred the sense of the film and the audience's senses. Then suddenly the story is wrapped up. Characters have come on just to die; the voice-overs substitute for scenes, as years, battles, and the film's resolution rush by the audience even in more of a hurry than they to get out of the theater in a conventional running time.

It is the convolutions of the story, Herbert's narrative on the screen (and Herbert has script approval), not Lynch's film, in which the audience has lost faith, perhaps even interest. The film is devoid of Lynch's lightning sense of humor. It lacks his usual sense of fun. It gives in to a temptation to preach. *Dune* is too careful with the source novel and too suspicious of audience limitations. It has a message. And the message is the text of Herbert's book. The film ends, but its story is never resolved. A viewer can only speculate on the unedited version, without the film's major concessions to editing determined by concerns other than Lynch's point of view. This is not going to happen to Lynch again. "I sold out on 'Dune'" Lynch says today. "I was making it for the producers, not for myself. That's why the right of final cut is crucial. One person has to be the filter for everything. I believe this is a lesson world; we're supposed to learn stuff. But 3½ years to learn that is too long" (Corliss 1990, 88).

Lynch's world is perverse and violent, peculiar and cruel; his future expands into an interplanetary arena. *Dune*'s images and incidents of violence and the grotesque also fall into different types that range from those occurring on tranquil, blue Caladan to the regal, burnished gold of Kaitain to the incendiary orange of fiery Giedi Prime to the colossal, tawny worms of Dune's desert landscape. The violence, cruelty, ugliness, and intrigue differ on each planet, ultimately converging, as do the film's different narrative lines, in Paul's confrontation with Feyd-Rautha on Dune. "The creatures of this film move toward a showdown like horror films, westerns, detective films, and all the other genres that point toward the good defeating the evil."[7]

Kaitain looks and is an idiosyncratic world of contradictions. The shaven-headed ladies of the court in their rich costumes and the almost Venetian luxury of the trappings of Padishah Emperor Shaddam IV's court belie the desperate, brutal intrigues that abound there. Customs are detailed, actions are veiled, and the plot events are convoluted and garbled. Most of the violence is labyrinthine and hypocritical.

Mind reading, lying, and eavesdropping are everywhere. The Space Guild navigator, a cracked soft-boiled egg of a bald-headed spokesman, makes his threatening messages over an anachronistic 1930s microphone system. The message is immediately transferred into a second language and voice. A parade of Tibetan-looking monks escorts an ominous, black locomotive encasing a tank; it intrudes into the regal setting and dominates it. Within one of life's apparently lowest forms, an amoeba, majestically conspires with a cowering emperor to hold the universe captive. Violence on this planet is unsettling, a surreal conglomeration of unexpected images juxtaposing the ornate surface and its hypocritically concealed dark, primeval underbelly.

The Duke Leto, Lady Jessica, and their son, Paul, rule Caladan. First shots of the world there are of blue ocean waves. Eno's musical accompaniment is lyrical. Both suggest infinity and abstraction in their cool flow of colors and sounds. Violence here is projected, suggestive, and intellectual. For example, most of the film's violence is predicted here in the waking or sleeping experiences of the characters. The murder of the duke and the conspiracy at his court, for example, is foretold here, as is the immense war and the epic fulfillment of the prophecy. But the violence does not happen in this place and time.

Historically *Dune*'s final conflict had begun on Caladan when Lady Jessica's love of Paul's father made her break her promise and bear the duke a son. But this is already the situation before the film begins. Paul's unlawful conception is of the past; the birth is not seen. Paul also sees the film's future, but the audience sees it misted by dreams. Paul sees the violent conflict in dreams, as he hears the violence in spoken and mental conversations.

Most illustrative of the suggestive and intellectual images here is the box of pain. Paul is given a mental workout, experiencing excruciating pain, in Reverend Mother Gaius Helen Mohiam's test. But the pain happens out of sight in a box, and when his hand is withdrawn, the grotesque deformity Paul Atreides and the audience expect is instead a shot of his hand perfectly restored. Paul takes on as many foes on Caladan as he will continue to battle throughout the film—mirrored automen, missiles, and computerized warriors. But these are the exercises of a student; Paul is in training against threatening devices of his teachers. Like Reverend Mother's box, these battles are learning experiences. They prepare him for the real enemy he will face on Arrakis.

Giedi Prime and the court of the Harkonnens is hideous, reeking with unexplained ugliness, violence, and perversion. The images here are often suggestive while their depiction is also vivid. For example, the baron's leering at Feyd-Rautha (Sting) is suggestive of homosexual incest. But the orange-haired, fat man (Kenneth McMillan) floating around near the ceiling has obvious other-world connotations. Baron Vladimir Harkonnen's attack on the serving boy sent into the room earlier in the scene has set the tone. Here a youngster with neon hair is forced into the room in obvious terror. While he haltingly arranges golden-stemmed blue flowers, the baron flies over him, mounts him, assaults and kills him. The baron pulls out the boy's heart plug, cooing with passion as blood splatters on him and on the ornate statuary in the otherwise minimalist decor of the room. Lynch's blend of sexual violence is colored here with a hint of futuristic vampirism. The graphic physical imagery continues.

The room is peopled by the Harkonnens, a flame-haired citizenry who rape and murder, animalistic in appearance and action. Lackeys are amused by the assaults, delighting in the sickening spectacle. The dim-witted nephew of the baron, the Beast Rabban, looks like a bloated jackal, but if anything more carnivorous and less intelligent. Baron Vladimir is having puss drawn from running facial sores with a long needle by an aid who desperately and ecstatically chants how beautiful the baron is. Giedi Prime is a world of violence and ugliness that is portrayed graphically enough to be repugnant. Whatever violence is the custom here, the Harkonnens carry with them to Dune in the war.

Arrakis is a barren, desolate place. It is a yellow wasteland interrupted by rocky patches, mining crafts, or worms. The Fremen, like the life-giving water, reside in stone caverns. These blue-eyed rebels fight to restore goodness to the universe and fertility to the arid desert planet that is their home. Held captive, they wait for a leader, a messiah to come to Dune to lead their revolt and fulfill religious prophecy. Their violence is for a cause, evil for good. Their monsters are both human and natural.

The Fremen are the good among Arrakis's evil. The evil is dual: the unnatural evil of the crafts which have been brought to the planet to mine the spice melange—technological monsters invading the desert landscape with relentless drilling and a mechanical back-up network to protect the mining industry—and the planetary monsters that live under the sand—the natural phenomenon of enormous worms seeking out the movement of the spice mining and devouring the miners.

It is on this planet that the final battle is waged. The worms and the spice are one, as good and evil are parts of Arrakis. Dreams and predictions, threats and conspiracies come to life here. The Reverend

Mother's fears take hold. The Fremen, both warriors and slaves, prepare to rebel and wait for Paul Atreides. The conception, gestation, and birth of the power of Alia are visualized. The emperor brings his unmitigated ambition, warring and turning on his allies with barbaric cruelty. Harkonnens plunder, murder, and deceive. Their vile and vicious manners image offenses like transfusing a cat in a bloody experiment, gleefully marking Lady Jessica's face with the baron's great wad of spit, and treacherously assassinating Leto as they attack the planet.

Here Lynch's dual world and Herbert's polar duality collide. Herbert, aware of the difficulty of creating a mythic hero, warns, "Messiahs can be hazardous to your health." Lynch, aware of the necessary exaggeration and separation of qualities of good and evil in a film, concedes, "Everybody's got many threads of both running through them. But I think in a film, white gets a little whiter, and black gets a little bit blacker, for the sake of the story. That's part of the beauty of it, that contrast, the power of it" (Breskin, 62).

Yet Lynch's cinematic vision and Herbert's literary world—now at a nexus in the film demanding resolution—hit a snag: the film abruptly and anticlimatically falls apart. The adaptation does not find balance in *Dune* as De Laurentis releases the film.

Dune is from the tradition of a developed film genre. According to Vincent Canby, there are four types of science-fiction film. These include contemporary comedies set in the future, adventure films, live-action cartoons, and "those that attempt to create their own universe from scratch, complete with their own histories, religions, languages, laws and bizarre rules of behavior." His division of these popular films appears to put *Dune* squarely in the category of new-world creations. In fact, Herbert's source novel is seen to present so complete an invented future world that some critics suggest that reading the Herbert text be a mandatory study assignment, as the film is as difficult to survive as a final exam; the videotape includes a printed glossary defining terms used in the film. And Canby concludes that *Dune* is a failure and continues by making the following "new-world creation" sci-fi movie hierarchy: "If the brightest films of this sort have been George Lucas's three *Star Wars* movies, *Dune* must be the absolute worst."[8] It is difficult to compare the *Star Wars* films, regardless of their commercial successes, to *Dune,* despite its artistic failures. The connection appears entirely superficial, although ironically, Lynch was asked "to direct *Return of the Jedi* (Lynch declined) and *Dune* (he accepted), a ten-ton flop."[9]

And because *Dune* changes from editing room through theater to TV release, it is impossible to attribute any version's flaws merely to Lynch's choice. Certainly Herbert's right of script approval seems noteworthy in his prose's confusing hold on the script. Many of *Dune*'s difficulties, especially the unbalance, may stem from the cuts the film sustained in order to gain release. But some of the problems must be seen as the result of Lynch's hedging in creating a film or transferring Herbert. If Lynch is seen as creating a film in the "new world order," other sci-fi books have more smoothly made that adaptation to film. In Radford's *1984* (1984) a future society has been dehumanized in a stark, colorless film. In Truffaut's *Fahrenheit 451* (1967) characters of the future are pursued by the police for reading books, dreaming, and thinking into metamorphosing into a living library. Here another literary future has avoided cartoon exaggeration. Clarke's novel is the source for Stanley Kubrick's enormous, lyric *2001* (1968). The film classic's shots of space are recalled in *Dune* in the warships' flights and travel between planets. The electronic dating and labeling of scenes in both films enhance a sense of scientific reality. The trip beyond Jupiter, floating the monolith through space, and the conception of a cosmic space fetus have resonance in *Dune*. Nonetheless, in Kubrick's film, HAL the computer, not the film's audience, shuts down with an overload of information. Although Kubrick's film is about infinity, and leaves his audience wondering, they question with the film not about the book—not about the end.

Comparison to another Kubrick new-world film based on a cult book isolates the distinction, thus an If-then relationship emerges concerning science-fiction films of the "new-world creation" type. It is far more accurate to posit: If the most fully realized of this sort has been Kubrick's *A Clockwork Orange,* then *Dune* must be the most frustrated—and frustrating."

A Clockwork Orange and *Dune* share essential similarities. Kubrick crafts a dense film, compelling the audience to enter his violent but enthralling world. *A Clockwork Orange* is aurally cohesive. A unique vocabulary is integral in portraying Kubrick's world. A song classic, "Singin' in the Rain," carries the film forward. The Gene Kelly ditty changes connotation from Alex's kicking, punching, and raping music while attacking victims. Sung by the reformed Alex in the tub, it later provides his own musical transport into the world of the victim.

A Clockwork Orange pictures a world in dishabille, weaving the best and worst of contemporary life with futurism: more expansive slum neighborhoods, Renaissance codpieces on futuristic jump suits, a red sports car on a darkened highway speeding a quartet of sadistic rapists with derbies and clown noses to their next crime scene. *A Clockwork Orange*'s violence is stylized: rapes look choreographed, crime spins in the hand-held camera's focus, crimes occur in shadowy, shimmering streets and the ruins of beautiful, gilded architecture.

As in the sci-fi film classification, both films are visions of a new world order. Lynch too leaves his audience sometimes awed by beauty, other times appalled at the violence. Both films are based on cult classics of pop literature. Visual and auditory innovations are employed by the filmmakers. Stylistically compatible as well as philosophically controversial, Lynch and Kubrick are both incendiary film innovators. Lynch's assessment legitimizes a connection: Lynch determines that "Kubrick is the coolest" (Woodward, 21). Yet *A Clockwork Orange* distinguishes an essential difference between the films.

Myth is an essential element of *Dune*. Whatever the future setting of the world, it is most importantly the creation of a mythical universe, not merely our world in a distant future. Concepts of redemption, sin and punishment, and revenge are present in both Western and Eastern mythologies. Historically, it is possible to tie many of the elements of *Dune* to religious myths: the redeemer, the mystic conception, and the life-giving water. A blood feud writhing with turns of barbarism and deceit, floodwaters, and a battle against giant foes also color many world legends. The *Mahabharata* and *Beowulf* are echoed by the screenplay; Venetian altarpieces and Thai temple robes are evoked by the shots.

If *Dune* is illuminated by studying any other science-fiction/fantasy films, a comparison of *Dune* to Bakshi's *Lord of the Rings* (1978), which adapts Tolkien's *Lord of the Rings* trilogy to the screen, seems most appropriate. Both literary sources lament a fall from grace which becomes Tolkien's and Herbert's rationale for their plots. Both worlds have a sense of the historical. Both share a feeling of loss and melancholy. Most important, these are not worlds of future realism; they are future worlds of surrealism. The bond establishes real kinship. Bakshi animates a cosmic cartoon and Lynch's enormous world exaggerates reality in bold colors and large, sweeping gestures. Akin to *Lord of the Rings, Dune* consecrates tomorrow's holy quest.

Actually, straddling the line between sci-fi and myth causes the confusion in viewing *Dune*. Lynch has a film intuition that propels his other films. Regardless of the narrative context—he creates virtual reality. The immensity of *Dune*'s world and the mythological tone of its quest in the fragmented film suggest that Herbert is, as was Tolkien, adapted to the cartoon. Lynch has in some aspects approached creating a live-action cartoon in *Dune*. But Lynch seems to equivocate between film and film tribute. When *Dune* begins to function as mythological cartoon—a cinematic allegory—with broad colors, bold, sweeping gestures, and captionlike language, it is quickly undercut by the laborious seriousness of transferring Herbert's message from his book into a serious new-world film. *Dune* as a film vision is buried in its own linear prose exposition.

Eastern religious myths are suggested, but the most overt mythological comparison in Western literature is to the Bible. The audience can make a much easier connection to Western theology and legends. The comparison is not a commentary on religious beliefs, but instead treats the narrative aspects of the Bible as the dominant story in Western society. Much of *Dune*'s mythology appears to be rooted in the New Testament.

Paul is sent by his father to save the universe. He has a mother of indomitable strength and a conception of mystical importance. After a secluded childhood preparing himself, his public actions are judged by friend and enemy in light of their conformity to actions predicted of the messiah. He teaches the secret of the water of life. He must conquer tremendous obstacles and he must expend his energy selflessly so that men will find the truth. Paul Atreides is a model of honor.

But Christian myth differs in some important ways. Most telling, Jesus Christ is a figure of great love. The New Testament teaches that the savior's price is his own death. Christ clearly refuses the rulership of any earthly kingdom. Thus the New Testament separates worldly and spiritual concerns and infuses its teachings with humanizing love. *Dune* does neither. Paul's triumph is glossed over as prophet (when he experiences the water of life) and as philosopher (when he moves from student to the teacher of the Fremen).

Paul Atreides triumphs as warrior. When he defeats Feyd-Rautha, the fight is hurried, and the fight is just too little and too late in the film. The fight is not as compelling as numerous special-effect battles which have preceded it, nor is Feyd-Rautha villain enough to elevate Paul's victory to a satisfying final test. There have been too many different battles with foes from worms to emperors. It is Dr. Yueh who was the Judas; it is Baron Vladimir Harkonnen who is Satan incarnate. The fight with Feyd-Rautha lacks the necessary concentration and impact to bring the film to a climax.

Therefore, *Dune*'s shortcomings rest in the narrative itself: as plot, as adaptation, and as film. Perhaps the simplified cartoon is easier to accept as moral fable on the screen. Herbert's complicated story on screen is flawed. "I needed more time . . . But at two hours and fifteen minutes [Dune] became like a garbage compactor. Things are supposed to be mysterious, not confusing."[10] Further Lynch's film is chopped and remade several times with increasingly fragmentary results.

Dune's plot is too disjointed as film myth. Heroism in thought and in the actions of the film is not balanced. The military conquest of the universe may convey the spiritual triumph of good over evil as a literary image, but it is just a war picture on screen. The film never convinces us that Paul believes in some higher philosophy; it never explains, much less deifies, his actions as the enactment of some abstract code. Giving lofty principles as motivation for action is possible for film heroes. For example, it works for Attenborough's biography of Gandhi, Roland Joffe's conflict between church and natives in Jesuit new America, and Hudson's Olympic athletes' pursuit of honor and gold medals. But it isn't there with Paul. Paul's actions don't demand the audience's respect.

On the other hand, Paul's conflicting tension of lofty, heroic principles with his humanity is also missing. Paul's actions never illustrate the human triumph of honor over selfishness, morality over weakness. There is never tension about his success. Paul's relationship with his mother is intellectual. His relationship with Chani, although the film shows him bare-chested in bed with her, is sketchy. His most emotionally involving relationship is with his father. But—in the main—the story of this relationship is not visualized but is rather telepathic. Paul Atreides's heroism is an abstraction. Paul's involvements don't invite the audience's support.

Paul achieves power in the film, but not stature. The character is kept so busy doing things that he is never shown accomplishing any. Too many things happen with no real dramatic development in the plot. Consequently, his final fight for the universe occurs in the film after so many lengthy declarations, fragmented confusions, and hurried inclusions that it is an unsatisfying climax to the plot. "On one level there's just too much in *Dune*; but on a deeper level, not enough."[11]

This circular deficiency is due in part to the film's myriad details. The continuous introduction of facts and characters comes at the expense of developing any of the material. No event is tangential to the story; each event is a tangent. Further, characters simply exist to be seen. They are on screen without actions to carry the plot. As quickly they are dismissed. Like all the supporting characters throughout Lynch's movie, Feyd-Rautha is fascinating. And like all the other *Dune* characters, Feyd-Rautha is not formidable. Oxymoronically, a character of hideous beauty, Feyd-Rautha provides the audience with a strange sensation to be sure, but he doesn't provide Paul Atreides with a worthy opponent. Without a nemesis to defeat at the climax, Paul merely fights again. Without any development in the film's context, their fight lacks importance. Paul's victory doesn't compel the audience's interest.

Paul's story on film isn't heroic, thus the literary myth does not transfer to film. Critics never admire the film's plot, but sometimes Lynch's adaptation is cited as successfully turning Herbert's convoluted narrative into a distinctive, moody film: "The strength of Lynch's movie is not in its storytelling. The easy stuff—making the audience cheer the hero—doesn't seem to interest him much. What Lynch does is to create a world, a haunted mesmerizing universe that envelopes an audience like a mist. A [sic] former painter obsessed with textures and inner organs, Lynch—who also directed *The Elephant Man*—thinks imagistically; he composes Dune more like a grand opera than a novel" (Ansen 1984, 93).

Other critics label the film too literal an adaptation of the novel. Regardless, the confusing plot in Lynch's film is generally criticized. In fact, the lack of Lynch's stamp on the material is the most frequent critical accusation in the reviews of *Dune*. "It doesn't take long to realize that basically this isn't a David Lynch movie—it's *Dune*. Lynch doesn't bring a fresh conception to the material; he doesn't make the story his own. Rather, he tried to apply his talents to Herbert's conception. He doesn't conquer the Goliath—he submits to it, as if he thought there was something to be learned from it" (Kael 1984, 74). Here Lynch is faulted for merely bringing Herbert's narrative confusions to film without turning the literary incidents into cinematic ones. The scenarist/director is faulted for not making *Dune* his own film vision.

Consequently, whatever position a critic argues about Lynch making *Dune*'s world his own, criticism clearly points to the major dilemma Lynch faced with *Dune*. He had to adapt a ponderous novel to the screen; he had to fashion a conventional feature release. There is too much plot in the film from the novel to dismiss it, not enough to care about it. The film keeps presenting the facts without clarification as a continuing narrative. The exposition is presented as the narrative. This narrative whirlwind sometimes merely confuses; other times the use of narrative for information already distilled into the film's images is redundant. In short, Lynch's film has a mixed attitude toward the Herbert source, and the audience receives the garbled message.

The adaptation poses an interesting question about turning novels into film: what is the responsibility to the source fiction? The novel on which it is based is labyrinthine. The film is complicated and filled with strange names and events. But Lynch's faithful adaptation—no matter how the responsibility to a literary source is perceived—is criticized as film. If readers of the fiction are not as confused by the film, that does not make *Dune* a better film. Critics conclude that if readers turn the filming of Herbert's book into a success, that doesn't turn *Dune* into a successful film. "It's going to be interesting to see if the fanatically loyal fans of the *Dune* novels will be able to turn this gigantic turkey of a movie into a financial success. I've not read a word of Mr. Herbert's prose and this movie is not the kind to make you rush off to buy some—does it sell by the pound?" (Canby 1984, 19).

It is fair to suggest that film has to operate as film. If the cinematic adaptation is to be criticized, it should be on its merits as film. The source novel, read or unread, carries little weight either as balm or as detractor to the film. *Dune*'s plot confusions as a movie are criticized by neophytes and fans of Herbert's book. *Dune* is a confusing movie.

The amount of details, facts, and information in *Dune* is immense. "Most sci-fi movies offer escape, a holiday from homework, but *Dune* is as difficult as a final exam. You have to cram for it."[12] Transferring that information becomes cumbersome. Initially the film is weighted down by the enormous exposition. Later the editing of the film hurries through deleting most of the book's material with the same vengeance which had painstakingly filled its earlier sequences with transferred fact upon fact. "Instead of streamlining either the language or plot of this lengthy book, David Lynch who directed the film and wrote the screenplay, tries to present it in unadulterated form."[13]

The ties to the prose overburden the film with facts. The need for exposition hurts the film. Ironically, the complicated retelling further confuses and also limits the film. Lynch paints his films with ambiguity, but his lush images and dense texture are seen as too conspicuous and labored when explained by lists of narrative facts and statistics. "It is a hopeless tangle of voice-over fills, dialogue used to explain missing legends, and a general emphasis on effect over substance. The book should be required reading before putting down five dollars to catch the imagery" (Hey, 97).

Dune's telepathy seems to be literary subject matter cumbersome to convey on film, providing technical and aesthetic illustration of the difficulty. But this mental process has been a film subject before. Films have given a character's thoughts separate from his shown actions. This is easy enough to do: the characters' thoughts are read over different actions depicted in the film in order to indicate that what is happening on screen and what is happening mentally are different. It works on film. It worked on film in Kubrick's *The Shining*. The reliance on telepathic communication, however, is identified by critics as a problem in *Dune*.

Cerebral as are *Dune*'s characters, many of them mind-read and mind-speak. Thereby, most of their activity is telepathic: checking information, culling prophetic innuendo, conspiring, communicating, and plain old musing and self-doubting are carried telepathically in the plot. Additionally, the plot actions are foreign, peculiar, numerous, and confusing. In the sweeping actions, characters often enter, fight, and die as other characters react to them in mental flashes. Telepathy is not a subject in Dune; telepathy is a system of communication within and without the film's world. Lynch confuses the film device of narration and the depiction of telepathy in the film. As a result, the film is again mired in a mode that muddies plot and structure.

Technically, the film is already using narration to provide exposition of the facts of the plot. The film uses voice-over to make the transition between scenes. The film uses voice-over as the narrative bridge between nonsequential edited scenes. Narration and telepathic soliloquy sound a lot alike. The film obscures divisions between what is happening, has happened, or will happen, as it blends what should happen, could happen, shouldn't happen, and could never happen (but often does, anyway). The vague and complicated effects on film trigger critical assaults. For example, Janet Maslin in a review titled "War of the Worms" asserts, "Several of the characters in *Dune* are psychic, which puts them in the unique position of being able to understand what goes on in this movie" (Maslin 1984, C18).

A second facet of the difficulty in using telepathy is illustrative of an aesthetic redundancy throughout the film. As the characters use voice inflections to convey the actual meaning of their literal statements, so too does the shot either support or make ironic comment on remarks to give them a context. The additional dialogue, the screenplay's events again discussed by characters, causes an overload.

It is not the distortion of these elements which hampers *Dune*. On the contrary, the interplay of aural and visual images to create message is a strong suit of Lynch's. It is a needless repetition of thoughts—spoken, heard, and pictured in actions on the screen—which not only further confuses *Dune* but also infuses the film with some uncharacteristic and tiresome over-explanations.

Watching the film conveys the impatience of seeing a silent classic. The one-reeler film often breaks to focus on a leaden placard writing out a line of dialogue to explain what the film has already shown. The audience understands the film's message. The placard is like an insurance policy to be sure the audience is able to follow the film. But such insurance policies, the wording of dialogue or voice-over exposition are so intrusive that not only is the new information not understood, but the whole effort of trying to understand our understanding becomes an ordeal. *Dune* interrupts its fluidity to provide Herbert's narrative context. The lines don't further the film experience, they interrupt it.

Watching the film conveys the frustration of not speaking the language of the film. Subtitles intrude to convey realism with too much frequency; they are distracting. Bad dubbing is remembered: one of those scenes in an Italian movie where the character's hands gesture furiously, eyes inflamed with emotion, words sounding for line after line at a rapid clip, and a weak, small "I don't agree" appears on the bottom of the screen.

The language of Lynch's film is expression through film. And when *Dune* works, his film works there. All of the devotion to Herbert's prose—or more to Herbert's prose audience—is detrimental to the film. "But if you can't remember all the names of the planets and the warring feudal factions, simply submit to the images and the story will soon fall into place. In a Lynch film, the images are all" (Ansen 1984, 93). Albeit inconsistent as released, viewing Lynch's film, not looking for Herbert's book, still yields a treasury of film images and—if in part—intriguing film work.

In conclusion, watching *Dune* is most like watching *The Magnificent Ambersons* (1942). True, the film doesn't work. True, it's too reverential to the source book. True, it is often heavy-handed. True, blame must fall to the screenwriter/director of the film. Lynch, like Welles before him, may fall victim to his own reputation. But blame must also fall to studio butchering of the film. "A messy, sluggish film, it is nonetheless visually enthralling" (Woodward, 43). It is impossible, even with additional footage or later explanation, to distinguish the director's vision from the film as released.

Dune's business involvements with Lynch and Dino De Laurentis's studio are obvious. The film's budget immediately involves it with industry concerns. The filming is covered by *Forbes* magazine as a financial event.[14] And Lynch expresses concerns during the prolonged production of the film. The film's difficulties prompt Lynch to take steps to protect his future films. "He vows never to make a movie without the right of final cut" (Ansen, April 1990, 71).

Lynch is working in several areas at this time. He begins to run his cartoon "The Angriest Dog in the World," a picture remaining constant while the captions change. He is also painting. Lynch remains a painter throughout his filmmaking career. There is also little time between Lynch's production of *Dune* and his next film. In fact, he is working on the new screenplay while *Dune* is in production. Lynch's artistic endeavors are so varied that he seems to be juggling several at one time. His interests include an increasing involvement through distribution of the film. Lynch is not a man to flinch from business aspects of motion-picture production or, for that matter, of twentieth-century art.

Several of his techniques and themes overlap. This is true within and without his movie productions. It's fun to offer Lynch's next film hero, Jeffrey Beaumont, also played by *Dune*'s Kyle MacLachlan, as a dark messiah in a twentieth-century world of violence and sadomasochism. But in truth, much more credible connections can be made, not in the plot of this and his next film, but rather in the role of *Dune* in the evolution of Lynch as an artist and filmmaker. This is particularly significant in the self-assured tone of his next film, which is distinctly the creation of David Lynch.

When asked how his next film is affected by *Dune,* Lynch answers, "It is what I've learned. I've just finished that script." Further pressed to delineate the ways in which *Dune* influences his work, Lynch mentions the changes to script as an indication of the emergence of his philosophy as a filmmaker. "It was way different before, not nearly as good. I've learned a lot, and I want to try to do films that are commercial and artistic. I want to have a strong story, but I want to have a story that has room for mood, where the whole is greater than the sum of the parts. As long as I can do that, I'll be real, real, real happy" (Griswold, 56).

Lynch's next film is a very different project than *Dune*. The film is met with critical accolades and commercial success. Usually considered one of the most important films of its decade, *Blue Velvet* is the film Lynch learned from *Dune*.

4

Lynch at His Best—*Blue Velvet*

> "Listen!" it said. "We'll tell you the last, the most beautiful and secret story—shut your eyes—it is a very small story—a story that gets smaller and smaller—it comes inward instead of opening like a flower—it is a flower becoming a seed—a little cold seed—do you hear? we are leaning closer to you—"
>
> —Conrad Aiken, *Silent Snow, Secret Snow*

Blue Velvet is plainly Lynch's masterpiece—thus far. "Brilliant and unsettling . . . this is the work of an all-American visionary—and a master film stylist."[1] In his 1986 film, Lynch is in complete control of the images that are to become part of his world. He projects them with a clarity not evident in his earlier films and an economy and restraint not typical of the other Lynch films through *Wild at Heart* that follow. The film generates excitement and exudes mood from its first shots. In fact, *Blue Velvet* sets up its cinematic premise from the opening credits.

The lettering of the opening credits is fluid and romantic. The title and the fabric background are dense and sensual; the Badalamenti music is lush. Immediately senses of sight and sound are mingled hypnotically. The opening takes us back to the magic of yesterday's films: luxuriant scores, mysterious plots, and fabulous color cinematography.

Drawing on our collective experience of the movies—memories of childhood movie houses and the aroma of fresh popcorn at the Saturday matinee—the opening summons us to a world of illusion. The score triggers both the remembered sanctuary of the theater and the apprehension of rushing down streets suddenly dark and unfamiliar to find our way back home from this fantasy world. Responding to Lynch's evocation, we nudge the person next to us and pronounce our regrets: "They don't make movies like this anymore."

Unlike preceding Lynch work, color is necessary to the film. Color is an artistic element. It is as blue as depression. It is as hopeful as the budding yellow tulips, as youthfully intense as the blood red flowers of the first shots. It is as cavernous and black in shots of the insect-infested earth as Jeffrey's deep, dark secret. *Blue Velvet*'s hues range vividly from the serene violet stained glass of Lumberton church windows to the lurid neon pink glow of the cadaverstrewn Lincoln Avenue murder scene. Bold, unabashed color paints the film.

Lynch creates a world of his own. The film presents each scene as vividly and crafts each shot as graphically as possible. But Lynch never comments—he presents. He uses incidents of a story and elements of film to fashion his movie world. He tells us that the world is an amalgamation of contradictions. Life is both good and bad, as is everyone who lives it.

Blue Velvet first appears to have adopted the conventions of film noir. But there is also a 1950s B-movie feeling to the film. Even a budget in excess of $7,000,000 doesn't destroy the artificiality of the sets or the staid delivery of some stiff dialogue.

But *Blue Velvet* is not a clone of old Hollywood films. With changes, reinterpretations, and other additions, Lynch uses and reinvents genre conventions. MacLachlan's performance is somehow rooted in the leaden teen stars of another era, but it is more. Something of the 1950s screen teen dream flutters about Dern. There is a sense of other popular young stars: Troy Donahue, Sandra Dee, Connie Stevens, Tab Hunter, John Saxon. *Blue Velvet* has the ultra-technicolor look of a Negulesco film, with colors brighter than life. "The more expansive *Blue Velvet,* alternating the 1950s and the 1980s, bland sunlight and rich obscurity, teenage innocence and ripe adult corruption, is practically a new genre: the demented matinee."[2]

Lynch's reality is subjective. What the audience sees is both ominous and promising, depending on its changing perspectives. Lynch creates his characters between extremes—light and dark, pleasure and pain, reality and illusion. Lynch uses the camera to take the audience into what a character sees. Lynch uses sounds so the audience can hear what a character hears. The audience is left between the same extremes.

Lynch insinuates fear into the most pedestrian shot and tinges the most brutal shot with a hint of sly humor. The audience remembers childhood fears of the commonplace: fear of a toy's coming to life in the darkened bedroom. It remembers fighting back a snicker when a nasty in-law provoked the neighbor's Doberman. Lynch plays on knowing that the audience remembers.

Blue Velvet centers on the myriad inconsistencies that make up reality. The film recreates the pattern of dream and nightmare. Lynch gives the audience tickets to Lumberton, but demands that they bring their own maps.

Gliding through dreamlike shots in slow motion, the film opens to image Lynch's pastoral America. The montage of small-town people, streets and celebrations, topples onto the screen; the Bobby Vinton oldie warbles all so familiar and easy; it is both aurally and visually nostalgic. The setting is a hodgepodge of the decades that make up the audience's recollections. Thus the opening evokes memories of the audience's childhood—unsophisticated, sentimental, even a bit tacky. The opening is a collective romantic rendering of innocence lost by America's move from its small-town, agricultural childhood to industrial, sterile, urban maturity. The pictures are set to music by the title song, which if outdated is as reassuring as the favorite song of everyone's older brother. Deftly, Lynch fills the screen with certain images and sets the images to a cadence. The opening has the rhythm of illusion—dreamlike and bittersweet.

These opening moments of *Blue Velvet* visually anchor us in a specific time and place. Shot in Wilmington and Lumberton, North Carolina, the film has the look of rural U.S.A. "Blue Velvet is a very American movie. The look of it was inspired by my childhood in Spokane, Washington," director David Lynch says. "Lumberton is a real name; there are many Lumbertons in America. I picked it because we could get police insignias and stuff, because it was an actual town. But then it took off in my mind" (Chute, 32).

Because it "took off" in the scenarist/director's mind, Lumberton's geography is Lynch's mental terrain. Although we enter a town of a specific time and place, Lumberton is larger. Lynch borrows from times and places, experience, and the world of motion pictures. Cars may be of one era, telephones of a different era, costumes of a third. The divergent sources are arranged into a single movie setting. Lumberton gains a life of its own as a cinematic image.

The image is enhanced by the selection of music, breadth of the production design, casting, and the use of other motion-picture conventions, prompts the audience to assimilate its own memories into

Blue Velvet's local color. "That is to say, it's a real movie, the first one in a long time that turns the viewer's passivity into furious cognitive activity" (Rafferty, 1986, 383). Because the image of the town demands audience input to complete Lynch's cinematic vision, Lumberton is whenever and wherever the audience lost its innocence.

Valuing the message is never Lynch's prerogative. The coexistence of reality and illusion is Lynch's province. Scenes portray his world as both image and story. Because a frame's composition may convey a different message than does its subject, shots in *Blue Velvet* are both visual and narrative. As the film progresses we recognize that Lynch's images are double: narrative reality is often different than visual context.

For example, in the opening shots of the film, we watch a man watering his lawn. The spurting hose, loosened from the water spigot, tangles and knots itself around a branch as the man gyrates and falls to the ground. Pressure thrusts the hose forward around old Mr. Beaumont, who looks like a glorified geriatric *Manneken-Pis*. A dog rushes into the frame wagging his tail, playing in the shower. Ironically, Beaumont is having a heart attack (narrative reality). Ironically again, it is another hose that will be attached to him as the hospital lifeline (visual context). But we will learn to recognize these as ironies only in a later context; we will learn to see them as symbols only in a later reality. The camera, like the innocent child, sees only what is before it: a playful dog and a funny old man rolling around on his lawn. Lynch shows what each of us as a child also saw.

Blue Velvet is also—equally—a film of and about sound. The film centers on the finding of an ear and presents its story from within that ear as we follow the camera into a universe of sound. It is also a film of sounds owing to its richly orchestrated score, its highly charged dialogue, a plethora of noises, and its use of eerie quiet. Lynch claims its genesis was music. "It was hearing Bobby Vinton's version of the song that got things rolling" (Robertson, 11). Strains of music, industrial and mechanical sounds (celebrated Lynch touches), comic and graphic expletives are so integral to *Blue Velvet* that mute moments become just as loud, just as heard. From the very beginning of the movie, it is impossible not to enter the world of music, dialogue, noises, and silence.

Use of sound is a technique that often gains its meanings in context and adds to the narrative reality of the film. The title song, for example, as originally sung by Bobby Vinton, is nostalgic when it is heard over the opening credits. The old pop song with its musical connotations in the film's opening has a place in the audio-fabric of the film but provides no narrative link.

The song is again without context in the film's narrative when it is sung by Dorothy Vallens (Isabella Rossellini) as part of her floor show. Her version lacks Vinton's nostalgia. Costuming and lighting suggest a cohesive inclusion of the song into the visual texture of the film; it resembles the opening credits. But the song continues to have no narrative implications.

When Dorothy next sings the song, it exudes sexual innuendo. It is during her second rendition, when Jeffrey (Kyle MacLachlan) realizes that Frank (Dennis Hopper) is in the audience holding the loathsome scrap of blue velvet, that the song gains a narrative connotation. The song gains new meaning from within the film's narrative—and gives new meaning to the scene.

In the final scene, accompanying a shot of Dorothy and her son on a park bench, the song last creates a dual message. Its narrative connotation gnaws at the visual of her tearstained face. The film's conclusion suggests that the close is not entirely painful; at least, that pain is not without its attraction for Dorothy. Lynch loads the scene with the aural/visual context and narrative reality.

Throughout the film, aural devices often enhance the visual of shots. The visual occurs in tandem or in tension with the auditory, independent of the narrative reality. The film's soundtrack operates in a network similar to, but distinct from, the network of visual images. Since shots consist of both sight and sound, auditory and visual aspects of the film intermingle and interact. The sensory images within the shots are, therefore, paired, compared, contrasted, or juxtaposed.

Consequently, what we see and hear often is only a part of what we get. Shots are two-sided; they contain a visual/auditory charge and a narrative charge. *Blue Velvet* presents shots that are subjective. Shots show the audience how a scene is seen or heard. Some *Blue Velvet* shots express what's seen, heard, and meant. Still other shots generate a third meaning by comparing the sight and soundtrack of the shot to its different narrative context.

Bazin in *What is Cinema?* suggests that the object in reality and its reproduced image on the screen share a bond: no matter the treatment of the object in the film, the image of the object must always be seen to represent that object in reality.[3]

Consequently, Bazin's view would recognize the blue velvet robe in the film only as a photograph of a blue velvet robe. We understand and recognize it to be that. But Lynch alters and distorts this image on film—aurally and visually—to endow it artistically with new meanings. Lynch's uses of the robe, its place in the composition of the shots, its relationship or juxtaposition with other visual and auditory elements in a shot and sequence of shots convey new meanings.

The ear is an example of how Lynch endows an object with expanded metaphoric meaning. The prop ear, realistically made by Dean Jones of Alamance County, North Carolina[4] first looks to Jeffrey and the audience like a hairy human ear. But the severed ear will become a symbol for what is beyond understanding and for the pursued secret. It is also symbolic for the heard, the auditory, as an abstraction; it is a concrete object for the camera.

It implies Vincent Van Gogh, the painter who severed his ear. It compares Jeffrey's dark pursuit of the meaning of the ear and the reality of his day-to-day life. Lynch adds metaphoric meanings to the ear; it implies Jeffrey's invention and artistic creation within the film, which is an invention and artistic creation of Lynch and the audience. The ear becomes the film's metaphor for new illusions within the film's visual context.

Thus the ear metaphorically distinguishes the creative reality of art from the virtual reality of the film. The audience goes through the severed ear into Jeffrey's world; but the ear that they later pass through to return to Lumberton is Jeffrey's. The ear is the gate to the creative brain. The ear becomes the film's central metaphor as the audience goes easily beyond questioning, "What does it mean?" to, "Is it real or unreal as a film device?" Lynch's use of the ear, both as a metaphor and as an unsettling image, demands input from the audience to give meanings to the ear. The ear becomes a metaphor for ingress into the world of the imagined.

True to Bazin's theory, Lynch understands that the audience's unqualified recognition and acceptance of the ear is a limitation of the symbolic and metaphoric possibilities of cinema. But Lynch moves beyond. When the nuances of the ear confuse, Lynch strives to separate the photographed image from film's narrative reality.

Lynch's operation beyond this limitation is significant. Pushing beyond the limitation becomes Lynch's rationale for sight and sound choices in the film. For instance, the sound of industrial or mechanical equipment is heard louder and more frequently than the narratively real makers of the sounds are pictured. At times the sounds are heard completely outside the narrative reality—the slice-of-life level—of the film. Their inclusion takes the audience to a level beyond that of the photographed image's replication of reality.

Moreover, new possibilities in meaning are generated by the changing combinations of auditory and visual elements. For example, Lynch terminates the visual tone of the opening shots with an auditory jolt. Nostalgic scenes and music are shattered by the film's first words. Suddenly the tranquil waterfront of Lumberton cuts to an intruding billboard, a jarring chorus of "Lumberton," and an ominous invitation to "get out your chain saws." Without a narrative context, this invitation is as frightening as the auditory jolt that started it.

In the first moments the film plays one of its most provocative tricks through a mixing of sight and soundtrack messages. There is tension in the shot of Jeffrey trekking in the Lumberton forest. He walks toward his peculiar adventure of finding the ear. Dressed in a dark suit, looking like neither college student nor camper in the shot, Jeffrey is solemn and determined. Visually, the elements are incongruous, but the composition is not.

There is a strange visual truth in this scene shaped by Lynch's cinematic aesthetic. "There is an autobiographical level to the movie. Kyle is dressed like me. My father was a research scientist for the Department of Agriculture in Washington. We were in the woods all the time" (Chute, 32). The visual message lies in the juxtaposition of visual elements of the shot, not in any narrative reality of plot and characterization.

The scene also is paradoxical as an auditory scene. The audience hears not sounds of the woods but rather sounds of woods on a radio, playing somewhere within or without the hearing of Jeffrey. As he continues his walk, the recorded sounds of falling/felling trees on the radio continue. The sounds gain a charge not as background to the narrative but as sounds on film. The sounds are larger than the life of the narrative.

Lynch demands that we enter this scene to provide its meaning. Tension is increased as the film invites the audience to graft the visual and auditory messages. Jeffrey is seen on his solitary walk in the woods. He is dressed for a mission. A radio plays the sound of a falling tree. The audience is seeing a well-dressed hiker and hearing the soundtrack or it has entered Jeffrey's interior—heard—world. As with the visuals of the opening scene—Lynch's credits interrupted by an intruding billboard, which cannot be read simply as narrative reality—the audience finds that they are involved with soundtrack too as film narrative and as film device.

So, one muses, if a tree is not seen to fall in the woods but somebody hears it, did it really fall? And if an ear is found in the woods . . . Thus the film is made to operate on both literal and metaphoric levels. Quickly Lynch invites us into a world of fact, nuance, and innuendo. "There's no mistaking the exhilarating fact," writes Janet Maslin in her *New York Times* review of *Blue Velvet,* "that it's one of a kind."[5]

Dual realities permeate the film. There are shifts and evolutions from light into dark and from silence to sound. Polarity is illustrated in day and night shots, romantic and brooding shots, even in shots of blondes and brunettes. Sounds shift and evolve from the silence of the woods to Badalamenti's romantic score to the roar of Frank's engine. Jeffrey goes into the unknown (darkness of the Deep River) from the known (light of his convertible ride with Sandy). Jeffrey dares not listen to the conventional (police and parental warnings) but dares to hear within himself the taboo and the forbidden (ominous gusts of silence).

This is Lynch's world. This is the world we are given. Themes are carried by and become the mode of their presentation. Realities are as they are perceived to be. There is real and virtual. Fact couples illusions. Good and bad commingle and coexist. Boundaries are dangerous and enticing to cross. Perception is never objective. The refrain of sights and sounds in the film is a leitmotif of pleasurable and painful expressions.

But Lynch's film presents a world that is not good *or* bad but rather is good *and* bad. Sights and sounds contain both elements; the audience supplies its hierarchy. So the pink neon of the sleazy Slow Club is as bright as the lurid pink of the apartment where Jeffrey's darkest wishes/fears and then experiences/dreams come to light. Watching from the closet while Dorothy is beaten, Jeffrey breathes heavily because he is scared to death and because he is sexually aroused. This is a dual world—and it is Jeffrey's dual world.

Blue Velvet drags the audience into Jeffrey's reality by juxtaposing the somber underground colors seen by Jeffrey in his visit as an exterminator to #710 with the Day Glo pink of the same aptly named Deep River apartment when Jeffrey returns to see it as the murder scene (visual). The film juxtaposes intrusions from radio jingles shattering the quiet of the woods the violent sounds of a sadomasochistic rape which fascinates Jeffrey into his lurid silence (auditory). It is a film about seeing and being seen, voyeurism and exploitation. It is a film about hearing and listening, appetites and conventions.

Lynch presents a world in which waking and sleeping, dream and nightmare, wishes and fear, reality and illusions are strands of a fabric. *Blue Velvet*'s world is both real and represented. Multiple facets and perspectives are interwoven: what the actor sees, what the character sees, what the audience sees; what the actor hears, what the character hears, what the audience hears. Piling layer upon layers, Lynch weaves tactile, dense textures of sight and sound.

These sensory charges blend. We enter Lynch's world through a vision of the auditory, a shot of an ear. *Blue Velvet* looks, sounds, and feels coherent if one enters the world of Lynch's movie. *Blue Velvet* is not to "read" as a story. The film's visual/auditory images are woven into a fabric that is not "sensible" but is "sense cohesive."

Blue Velvet's earliest shots start to build the film's visual impact: brightly colored flowers in front of a white picket fence under blue skies and the ominous black world under the green grass. These wide images are shot in CinemaScope ratio, 2.35 to 1, making them larger than life. The sky is hyperbolically blue (velvet?) in this lovely scene of the technicolor garden. The flowers are garishly colored as they sway top-heavy with ripeness.

This glorious image of a garden and picket fence under a bright summer sun is followed by an equally grotesque image of darkness filled with savage bugs in a predatory war beneath the backyard's thin surface. The warring bugs are gargantuan. The ferocity of their slaughter is epic. Eisenstein determined cinema's pattern as an artistic compilation of individual parts in *Film Form*.[6] Lynch records photographic fragments of nature that he combines in montage.

This visual contrast restates what the previous shots have already created; the images repeat a tension. The visual context of the garden and the bugs suggests symbols; the cannibalistic reality shows us garden and bugs. This chilling juxtaposition of images assaults us with a sick but recognizable message, a feeling of foreboding; we know that what looks good is too good to be true. And because it is too good to be true, our worst suspicions are aroused.

In the first moments of the film, we recognize and fear the combination of bloom, death, and decay. From the first frame of the credits on crushed velvet through the first shots of the small town with its lost American calm, the audience is aware of a lethal combination. Lynch has alerted us to a central truth of his world; his truth gnaws at us through the rest of the film. He reinforces this truth with abrupt cuts from scenes of beauty to scenes of terrifying hideousness. He creates in his audience an expectation—an expectation of duality.

Lynch understands the appeal of the film's nightmare logic. In the *Blue Velvet* world, we find pictured what we have learned to dread—the inevitability of decay, the inevitability of death. We are not shocked by the small-town decay under a bucolic facade; we are compelled to look at the corruption of values that we know to be true. We learn not to be disillusioned but to expect disillusionment—to expect other façades. This is the melancholy that *Blue Velvet* makes us remember. Melancholy is the film's pervasive tone.

The audience may be startled by individual pictures that flood the screen, but they are entranced by the fluid evolution of a visual world. They are lifted out of a learned point of view, out of a literary, narrative sense; they recognize that, just like images in dreams, each vivid shot flows visually into the next. A slow-motion shot of a waving fireman atop his truck cuts to a group of school kids, lunch boxes in hand, dejectedly putting aside summer fun and being "policed" into returning to school. The nostalgia for childhood adventures and for all our lost summers is thereby evoked, although the narrative thread is never continued.

It is significant to note that the opening visual images take us into an auditory world of sounds and silence. Scenes are scored with quiet. Without music, noise, or words, Jeffrey boyishly skips stones in a vacant lot before visiting his father in the hospital. The hospital scene is static, sterile, and institutional. In the hospital bed, the hoses into the old man's nose look like a high-tech nightmare. Although Jeffrey makes an attempt to speak, the scene's painful silence screams of thwarted messages between fallen father and maturing son. As father and son grasp each other's hands, Mr. Beaumont garbles incomprehensibly; neither of them can communicate. At the sickbed, Jeffrey never manages to say what he wants. Equally important, Jeffrey does not hear what he wants to hear.

Blue Velvet's world is also chronologically structured to move the characters and the audience from night into day. The feeling of awakening from the night is reinforced by characters coming from the dark, where so many of the film's gruesome events transpire, to the realization of Sandy's dream of peaceful, bright days of the future. Nevertheless, this awaited better day is underscored with a feeling of melancholy: students return to the Lumberton school, leaving parades and summer behind, and walking into the apprehension of facing the new year. The varsity football team prepares for the new season. Images renew in the audience the nostalgia for the glories of their youth. The film begins as summer turns to autumn, as full bloom turns to death and decay. Ironically, in playing the story in the context of the school year calendar, Lynch invites the audience to think not of death and decay but of fall's clean slate with all new things possible.

The film ends in the season of promise, a comforting sense that with the passing of the cold, hard season of the year, order has been restored. It ends in spring, the season for new life and resurrection. Ironically, Lynch invites the audience to remember high school's end, signing yearbooks and unkept vows of lasting friendships.

The passing of the school year must distance the characters, as it did the audience, from childhood's security. Therefore, as the changing seasons bring the film into the sun at the school year's end, Lynch also coerces the audience into a hard look at reality in the glaring light. The film's conclusion is dual: Jeffrey is safer, he is also wiser and sadder in the daylight of Lumberton spring.

Thus Lynch invites the audience into his world but insists on its input. The audience follows the camera into that ear and is assaulted by brutal images until the robins arrive as the insect-devouring harbingers of spring renewal. The camera will take the audience out of the blood-splattered ear, but even after the film's final frames, it is unlikely that the audience can so easily escape from this powerful, disturbing world.

A great deal of pain, violence, and sex fills the screen. The film is aware of both the duality and subjectivity of each of its scenes. Through the film's metaphoric rendering of images of sight and sound, *Blue Velvet* snares the viewer into responding to the film. The setting and the time, the mood and the pacing support Lynch's *Blue Velvet* world.

But *Blue Velvet* does tell a narrative. Jeffrey has come home from college to join his mother and live-in aunt Barbara at his father's bedside. As he heads again into the vacant lot on his route to the hospital, Jeffrey finds an ear. Here, "just beyond Vista," just the other side of a local street, and just out of our range of sight, Jeffrey has dared to go beyond the secure parameters of his youth.

In trying to discover the story of the severed ear, Jeffrey becomes involved with club singer Dorothy Vallens as well as with a police detective's daughter, Sandy (Laura Dern). Jeffrey enters Dorothy's story: she is under the control of drug dealing/using Frank Booth, who holds her son and husband—who is missing an ear—captive. Jeffrey's obsession with Dorothy and her life of corruption and sadomasochism propels his pursuit of the case. Jeffrey and Sandy's romance is fueled by her being the only person who will listen to his theories about Lumberton's criminal underbelly. Jeffrey's world is no longer ordered by his work at a hardware store and visits to an antiseptic hospital room.

Jeffrey enters a dark world through the ear, but Jeffrey's initiation occurs on Lincoln Avenue. The severed ear leads by all clues to Dorothy. Despite being advised not to seek out Dorothy Vallens, Jeffrey concocts a plan with his friend Sandy to disguise himself as an exterminator to search Dorothy's apartment.

The first step of Jeffrey's plan gets him into her apartment by a simple knock on the door. Dorothy lets Jeffrey—now the exterminator—go from room to room. His next steps fall in place by serendipity. In her kitchen, Jeffrey finds a spare key to let himself back in later. Dorothy is distracted by a stranger to Jeffrey who appears at the door. Thus Jeffrey's plans are augmented by fate. Almost dreamlike, events lead where he wants to go, even if things don't go the way he planned. Jeffrey is fascinated not by his being there, by reality, but rather by the possibilities in the muted sounds of a conversation near the front door. It is a conversation that he can see—but cannot hear.

Jeffrey has played exterminator to enter the forbidden world of the mysterious, dangerous Dorothy Vallens. In this scene Dorothy is as Jeffrey sees her—the complete object to be studied under the microscope.

The film has already shown enormous insects throbbing under the calm surface. The close-up slaughter of the insects in the film's opening resonates. The shot of a robin devouring a gigantic black bug in the film's conclusion is foreshadowed.

The next step in Jeffrey's plan is to search Dorothy Vallens's apartment. He watches her perform at the sleazy roadhouse on a decoy date with Sandy. On stage in a blue fog, she first sings the title song behind a 1930s Art Deco microphone, almost an iron sculpture, and under an incongruous mixture of pink neon and antlers advertising Club Slow. While she is on stage, he sneaks back into her Deep River apartment

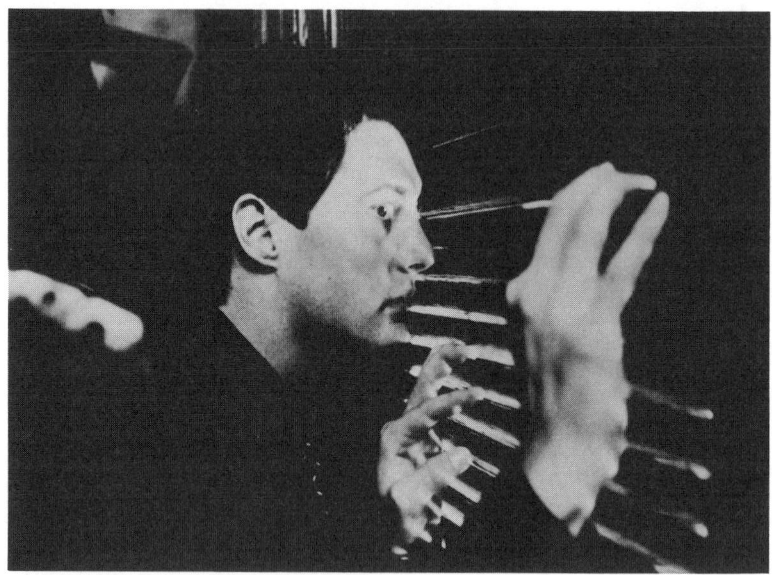

Jeffrey watches Dorothy through the slats of the closet doors in *Blue Velvet*. Courtesy of the Museum of Modern Art/Film Stills Archives.

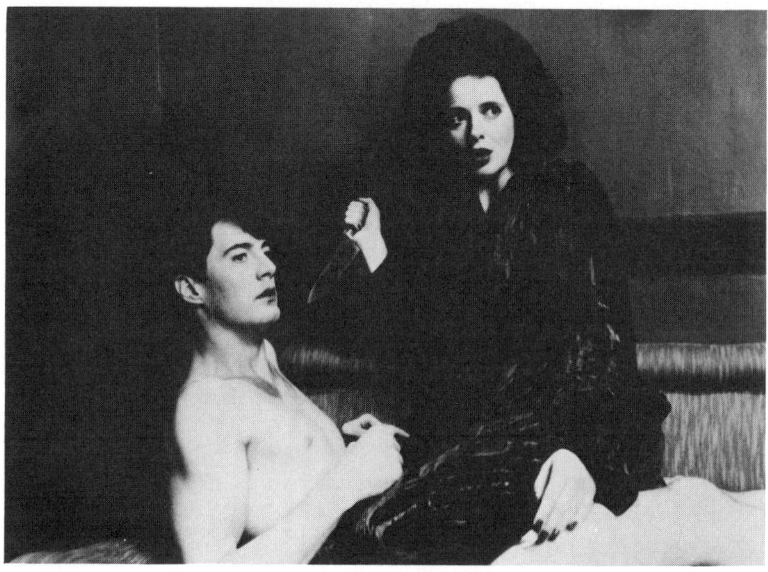

Dorothy turns the tables on Jeffrey in *Blue Velvet*. Courtesy of the Museum of Modern Art/Film Stills Archives.

with the key he's stolen from her kitchen cabinet. Inside the stillness of her vacant apartment, Jeffrey searches for evidence of Dorothy's life. It is appropriate that his collegiate interest in beer—Heineken—interrupts his search, causing him to have to urinate. In flushing the toilet, he drowns out the coded sounds of Sandy's warning horn blast. Dorothy is heard entering the apartment and Jeffrey has to choose between hiding or being seen.

Jeffrey watches Dorothy through the slats of the closet doors. Voyeuristically he savors her detailed, silent ritual until the mood is shattered by the ringing phone. Jeffrey listens to her cryptic phone conversation, a strange scenario of power and brutality. Jeffrey is fascinated by the power of his sexual espionage. He watches enthralled through the shards of light.

The crosscutting between Dorothy in the room and the tight close-ups of Jeffrey in the closet build a tension and erotic voyeurism in the scene. Although Jeffrey is shot in close-up, Dorothy is shot as if at a great distance, surrounded by the almost melted decor of her apartment. Jeffrey fears both looking and being caught looking and yet is held in sexual bondage, compelled to watch. The intimacy of the scene is too intense, too awful. With just heartbeats and quiet between his assaults on Dorothy's privacy, Jeffrey's power over her solitude ends when she hears noises from the closet. She is suddenly the master of her—and his—fate.

Dorothy makes Jeffrey come out of his hiding place in the closet. She turns the scene's exploitation around by intimidating Jeffrey and forcing him to disrobe. Held at knife-point Jeffrey is ordered to stand. Now the camera places the audience in the role of the voyeur, looking from the closet as Jeffrey, who had so enjoyed watching Dorothy, now himself becomes the prey. "Don't touch me or I'll kill you. . . . Do you like talk like that?" Dorothy asks, fondling him. The scene regains sexual energy and suggests the contradictions of pain and pleasure, power and humiliation.

"Kneeling in front of him, the knife poised threateningly at his crotch, Dorothy arouses her victim while ordering him not to touch her or look at her. She turns the tables on him by denying him his look, forcing him to appear naked and vulnerable, and appropriating a male gaze and sexuality, here clearly associated with violence."[7] This is quite emphatically role reversal in an almost mirror image of the "male gaze" as labeled in scopophilic theory. This current trend in film criticism analyzes the camera as an exponent of the male point of view. Dorothy is in power here and Jeffrey is under her control. She has already cut his face with the blade. Finally, both sexually used and physically threatened by the danger of continued maiming, he becomes an object to be studied.

Violent and graphic exploitation continues in the scene, evidences of an uncensored, contemporary liberality. After crouching while disrobing on command, Jeffrey must next stand motionless. Denied even the right to continue undressing himself, he is stripped. Naked, he looks slight and young, demeaned and trapped by his fascination with the eroticism of the moment.

The sadomasochistic reversal and the duality of excitement and humiliation continue to spin in the scene. As it is in rape and other acts of violence, Jeffrey's fear and horror at being the victim, stripped and defenseless, is part of the aggressor's thrill.

Jeffrey is sexually threatened again later by a man. Frank attacks him and fondles him with his gun, crushing Jeffrey's lips with kisses in a parking lot after a frenzied joyride in view of the audience and oncamera viewers. Punctuating his sexual assault with a salvo of punches, Frank makes Jeffrey again the object of sexual violence. Allowed this time to keep his pants on, Jeffrey is nevertheless stripped again as an object.

In the first assault at Deep River, Jeffrey looks clinically rather than sexually nude. His body is first exposed, then overexposed by the camera, like a butchered side of beef. Few characters have been stripped as pitilessly for the camera as Jeffrey: his bare flank and buttocks pale, almost on the lens, in the scene's next turn, he runs as the photography continues, his frontal nudity included briefly.

Frank knocks loudly at the door. His sudden intrusion taunts Jeffrey and makes his degradation laughable. He rushes about the room clad only in a pair of socks, coltlike, cringing clumsily, awkwardly clutching for his clothes. Unable to hide his nakedness, Jeffrey finally hides himself again in the closet.

When first ordered to undress, Jeffrey is kneeling. Consequently, his undressing is not seen but is heard. The abrupt, loud tearing sound of his fly being unzipped shatters the still air; the audience hears it as Jeffrey does. We hear it as the denial of any shred of modesty, the certainty of his submission, and to a knife.

Told to stand, Jeffrey is free from his subservient kneeling, but ironically he is exposed to even greater danger and to even more humiliation. The camera concentrates on his bare midsection but intercuts shots of his face showing his degradation, resignation, and arousal.

He is seen as utterly defenseless in his capture—forcibly exposed, aroused, and terrified by that arousal.

But as passion bests fear, they move entangled to the sofa. Jeffrey, naked except for his black socks, begins to look like a character in a cheap pornographic film, somehow shifting Jeffrey's battered-object status. He is still under command and naked, but the sequence looks more sexual than violent. The scene again loses sexual overtones with the arrival of Frank.

When Frank is heard pounding at the door, Jeffrey looks surprised and confused, frustrated and ridiculous. Now his nudity is comic as in some frothy French farce. Clad only in a pair of socks, Jeffrey looks like a schoolboy in the team room, towelless after his shower, surprised by pranksters.

In this sequence we hear and see not what happens but what Jeffrey sees and hears happening. The role of Lynch's camera is to show us Jeffrey's world. The camera does not editorialize; it gives us Jeffrey's reality. His reality is everything—and the only thing—to Jeffrey. Jeffrey sees and hears as he does, and therefore, he sees and hears what he does. Jeffrey Beaumont establishes his own reality. The camera shows it to us.

Frank's appearance and the sadomasochistic ordeal that follows is the film's most disturbing scene. Frank immediately demands his bourbon as if he had waited for hours. He orders Dorothy, Jeffrey's erstwhile master, now victim, to engage in acts of perversity and shame. The scene gains a distasteful aura in the frequency of Oedipal references—first Frank with his profane Freudian maternal references, then Jeffrey, who is encountering this tirade of sex and violence of "mommy" and "daddy" from his closet. The scene is shot for its cruelty, eroticism embedded in repulsive violence. Hopper pulls out all the stops in his performance as Frank, so the audience is quite believing of his later threat/boast/lament that he'll "fuck anything that moves."

The emotional, physical, and sexual abuse is heightened when Frank, distorted under a mask, inhales gas. His drug use and the medical apparatus for it heap hallucinatory and frightening medico-sexual innuendo into the scene. In this graphic sexual encounter Frank debases Dorothy as whore and mother while she wears a blue velvet robe, a symbol of their relationship. The image will color forever the old Vinton classic. He shoves a fragment of the robe into his mouth for heightened sexual gratification. Jeffrey hears the language and the ambiguous choked sounds of power and pain accompanying these acts. Furthermore, the camera forces us to experience again the same feelings of fascination, revulsion, fearful shame, and bondage as Jeffrey. "The style might be described as hallucinatory clinical realism."[8]

The voyeurism of this sequence expands in concentric circles. First we watch Jeffrey watch Dorothy. Next we watch Dorothy watch Jeffrey. Now we watch Jeffrey watching Frank watching Dorothy. There are two noteworthy modifications: first, unlike the other two characters, Frank never appears without the protection of his clothing—he even wears a second skin of leather and a face mask; second, only Frank thinks he is committing his vile acts in private. By this stage Dorothy knows Jeffrey is behind her closet doors watching, Jeffrey is doing the watching—and everybody in the audience sees them and can see Frank. This spins an unending circle of aggressor and victim, watcher-and-watched relationships.

More important, the audience knows of these intrusions, feels these intrusions—because of the soundtrack and camera work. It is quiet enough to hear the heightened breathing of Jeffrey as he becomes aroused. The audience too is brutalized by the punches assailing Dorothy. The audience moves closer and withdraws farther with the spectator in the closet or drops to its knees as the camera changes perspectives.

Here the film reveals streaks of expressionism from Lynch's training as a painter. It furthers the evolution of cinematic expressionism going back to Wiene's *Cabinet of Dr. Caligari*. The cruelty is too barbarous. The scene first so dark framing Frank and Dorothy like grotesques of a ballet, then in overlighted welts on Jeffrey's face, unreal and distracting, yet sometimes horribly rich as in a Renaissance oil painting.

Images of sex and violence are painfully interwoven, as are the sounds of pain and ecstasy. An inherent duality of the pleasure and/or pain of the seen and heard expressions of sexual frenzy is illuminated by the constantly changing perspectives of Jeffrey, Frank, and Dorothy. The camera spins and the audience sees how each sees and is seen; the audience hears while craning forward, ashamed of its heinous curiosity.

The scene melds content with presentation inextricably in our disquietude as we watch first for Dorothy and then for Jeffrey. It further goads and humiliates the viewer, first for watching Dorothy, then for watching Jeffrey, then for noting—perhaps understanding—the erotic pleasure in watching, using, being used. Yet it compels through its cinematic texture of color and sound that viewers cannot turn away.

Finally, viewers are assaulted by their own confusion about their voyeurism. Neither the audience's uneasiness nor its fears of exposure is the final turn that concludes the scene.

After Frank leaves, Jeffrey comes from the closet to comfort Dorothy. This impulsive kindness sparks the final role reversal of victim and aggressor.

Jeffrey has put on the romantic guise of the knight-protector along with his undershorts and tries to take control. He responds emotionally to Dorothy. A rapid exchange of violent dialogue is heard. Instantly, the auditory and visual connotation of the scene reverts from tender lovemaking to brutal sex. Quickly violence forced upon violence is seen as a sadomasochistic choice.

Jeffrey, alarmed by Dorothy's request to hit her, dresses to leave. Alone in the room he checks under the sofa for the photograph and papers she had clung to in what she had assumed was her solitude. He is shocked to find that the papers prove she's married. His shock at such a minor detail may be a sliver of his remaining innocence; the sex and violence were frightening enough, but with a married woman . . .

Jeffrey again loses himself in pursuing the mystery of the ear. He seeks the trappings of the mysterious tale, the photographs, the papers, and the clues. He leaps beyond the recent dominance and sadomasochism and returns to the mystery of the ear.

No wonder the film garners such mixed reactions. Lynch is not without his detractors, and *Blue Velvet* is a controversial film. Early reviews and newspaper accounts are peppered with anecdotes about the intertwined fascination and repulsion in audience responses. "'Unbelievable,' the guy with the tattoo was saying as he and his date stumbled out of the theater in Cambridge, Mass. 'I don't know which was weirder—the movie or the people watching it.' 'Yeah,' his girlfriend mumbled, looking slightly dazed. 'Wow . . . I think I might have hated it.'"[9]

Even some of the critical raves recognize the difficulty, perhaps the impossibility, of all filmgoers accepting Lynch's vision. *Blue Velvet* is a rough movie, and the closet scene with Jeffrey, Dorothy, and Frank is among the hardest hitting in the film. The artistic contributions of Lynch are not for everyone. "Lynch will never be everyone's cup of tea, but he's the real McCoy, a wondrously American combination of morbid obsession and true blue sincerity."[10]

Works of art are not necessarily pretty. Artists have chosen throughout history to take an unsettling approach, to shock, or to portray ugliness to make a statement. Michelangelo's slaves are contorted and in agony. There are very few good-humored laughs in Swift's pithy satires. Hieronymus Bosch's world is frighteningly ugly, vividly illustrating the gamut of sexual perversity in his paintings; Bruegel's cripples are deformed yet brilliantly colored as they hobble or drag themselves out to beg. The literature of Poe includes necrophilia, murder, and animal abuse.

In fact, in the twentieth century even more artists find their universe cruel and deformed. Accidents, cannibalism, gender, racial, drug, and class abuses, military slaughters, and nuclear holocaust permeate contemporary art. Jarred, Shapiro, Picasso, Millay, Tennessee Williams, Orton, Shirley Jackson, King, Genet, O'Neill, Ensor, and a seemingly endless list of artists have portrayed ugliness in its many forms. The same tradition exists in cinema, from the silent films of Luis Buñuel to Philip Ridley's *The Reflecting Skin*.

This is not an assumption of Lynch's inclusion in this list. Rather it recognizes his position in the world of innovators. His attraction to the grotesque is part of our artistic tradition. What separates him from predecessors in his film style is his sense of humor and his sense of the movies. What apparently makes Lynch difficult to accept is his frequent abandonment of narrative exposition, his dual point of view, and a tendency to be coy.

In the vanguard of Lynch critics, John Simon and Roger Ebert are consistently unimpressed, and Ebert's reviews seem particularly enraged. After watching *Blue Velvet*'s bouts of sex, violence, and sadomasochism, Ebert finishes his review with a question: "What's worse? Slapping somebody around, or standing back and finding the whole thing funny?"[11]

This question is well addressed to the scene of Jeffrey in Dorothy's closet, but Lynch does not offer an answer to the question. After the final role in the Deep River apartment, the camera follows Jeffrey descending the building's staircase into darkness, where the scene recedes in its own fade to black. The absolute blackness is held for some length. Lynch forgoes editorializing. He passes the opportunity to preach. The blunt perversity of the sequence remains intact.

In an earlier dark sequence too we see Jeffrey descend a staircase into absolute blackness. He leaves the brightly lighted room at the top of the stairs in his own home. He is beginning his night and seeking an adventure. He is admonished by his aunt rather than by his mother, who sits silently beside her. Before reaching the front door, Jeffrey is cautioned against wandering toward Lincoln Avenue. Lincoln Avenue is the part of town that a good boy avoids. Jeffrey placates Aunt Barbara by giving his word that he'll stay close to home.

The women watch a television program. Like the black-and-white TV scene of a pistol that Mrs. Beaumont watches in the film's opening sequence, this TV scene is also ominous. Here the focus is on a man's shoes as he creeps on a staircase slowly and with determination. The TV scene fills the film's frames. The television story again usurps the film action.

The parallel of the filmed and televised trips on the stairs is significant. Their placement here in the film increases the tension between the film scene (now the audience's reality) and the scene within the scene (the audience's and characters' illusion), a TV program viewed by characters in the film's reality. Lynch includes another level of illusion within his virtual world: the audience watches actors watching actors. The audience watches the descent of a staircase in the film and the actors watch the descent of a staircase in the television scene in the film. Where is reality? Where is illusion?

The parallel images suggest Jeffrey's duplicity in claiming to be home from college simply to assist in a family emergency and at the same time surrendering to his urge to break from convention and explore the ear's mystery. His pursuit causes him to lie about staying close to home and avoiding Lincoln Avenue.

The juxtaposed images also suggest the duality of Jeffrey's actions. Jeffrey's descent into the darkness literally foreshadows his descent into the secrets of his Lumberton life. The TV character's ascending the stairs into an unknown is echoed in the plot several times by Jeffrey's long, hard climbs up the stairs into the secrets of the Deep River Apartments.

Hours after he has brought the ear to Williams's office, and minutes after his promise to his aunt, Jeffrey walks to the police detective's home to check on the investigation. Hunting the secret in the dark streets of his own neighborhood, Jeffrey passes a man walking a dog. The audience sees that the man wears glasses too black to see through on this dark night. Jeffrey is not particularly interested in the blind character so close to home. Ironically, in the next sequence, set in daylight, Jeffrey is delighted by a fellow hardware-store clerk's ability to see quite clearly although blind. At night, on the other hand, seeking new, uncharted streets, Jeffrey is not interested in eyes and vision, but in the ear and truth.

On this walk among dark trees and shadows, the image of Jeffrey fades into a shot deep into the ear. This fade is accompanied by the soundtrack of a roaring implosion. Jeffrey is submerged into the ear. As the sound subsides, Jeffrey knocks on the Williamses' door. In complete contrast to this surreal imagery, Jeffrey enters the Williams home, a comfortable, pleasant two-story.

Both the exterior and interior and some of the furnishings of the Williams home are those of an actual home. The real people and properties in this scene in the film enhance the dual visual perspective. The two-story Tudor home at 128 Northern Boulevard in Sunset Park, North Carolina, used in the film belongs to the Spencer family, who spent 46 consecutive days away from the home during the filming. All of the phases of preproduction and production were completed there in July, August, and November, 1985.

During the filming the owners were most impressed with MacLachlan and Dern, who were kitchen cookie eaters, and met Lynch and the crew, who used the backyard for football. Dorothy's nude scene on their front lawn and other filming experiences disrupted the household and the neighborhood—except for the family cat, who wouldn't cooperate even for a role in the film. "I wouldn't discourage anyone from letting anyone make a movie in their house," the owner, Mrs. Spencer, suggests in her recollections about the filming in her home, but she wouldn't do it again "unless the filmmaker were Disney."[12]

Lynch used other local Wilmington sites like the Carolina Apartments on Fifth and Market streets (for the Deep River Apartments), the New Hanover Public High School, Memorial Hospital, and the Wilmington Police Department. Local people, including the ambulance squad, also appear in the film.

It is an effective juxtaposition that while entering the maelstrom of the ear, Jeffrey is actually seen entering the front door of this lovely house. As do the other visual compositions of real-location elements and cinematic ones in *Blue Velvet,* the shot combines elements of the surreal with elements of the real. After making small talk with Mrs. Williams, Jeffrey heads for the den to pose his questions about the ear to her detective husband.

A shot of a glossy photograph introduces the next scene. Sandy's photograph, an idealized, retouched likeness of a lovely girl next door, not the character herself, is the first image of Sandy Williams in *Blue Velvet*. The photograph, like the earlier television scenes, draws attention to the difference between what is seen and how it is seen.

The mise-en-scène places a colorful duck decoy in front of Sandy's picture as her father and Jeffrey talk. The decoy might surprise Billy Baldwin with its rustic if unlikely position in the set—but it foreshadows Sandy's use to Jeffrey in much of the film. As with the sound of the falling tree heard earlier on the radio, virtual and real elements blend interchangeably in *Blue Velvet*'s world. Again a visual context develops.

The scene between Sandy's father and Jeffrey begins after a discussion of the investigation of the ear. The audience never hears Jeffrey's questions. The audience can only infer from hearing Williams's answers that it has been the earlier topic of their discussion.

We do hear Detective Williams's admonition to Jeffrey to keep out of the case followed by Jeffrey's reassuring answer—echoes of his answer to his aunt. Williams also warns that the curious nature that he and Jeffrey share has already led him to some painful insights. He melodramatically warns that this two-sided awareness will be as disquieting for Jeffrey.

The character of Detective Williams is one of the film's loose ends. According to critics, many of the film's drawbacks are found in the screenplay's loose ends. With Lynch's detective the problem seems to be not a conscious artistic ambiguity but rather an unresolved characterization. Although the film treats the good and evil in each of us as a simultaneous duality, this neither rationalizes nor excuses the vagueness in the character of Williams.

Although Lynch's major characters from Sandy to Frank Booth do not suffer from this shortcoming, it seems to hamper other figures of the police department, who also remain unfinished. The script seems better able to reveal the bad side of the good characters or the reverse than it is able to portray average characters. This leads Lynch to rely on flamboyant characterization. It also leads to problems of simplification and repetition in characters and lack of resolve in his plots.

But this criticism of the screenplay, although understandable, is significant neither to the film nor to Lynch's style. In fact, concern with development of the characterizations or plot resolution is painfully shortsighted. As Pauline Kael wrote in the *New Yorker,* "Lynch skimps on these commercial-movie basics and fouls up on them, too, but it's as if he were reinventing movies. His work goes back to the avant-garde filmmakers of the twenties and thirties, who were often painters—and he himself trained to be one. He takes off from the experimental traditions that Hollywood has usually ignored" (Kael 1985, 102).

By the time Jeffrey again reaches the street outside the Williams home, the film snaps back into focus. Lynch accomplishes this again by emphasizing a message through visual and sound images, not narrative devices. Jeffrey's resolve to stay a good boy, if it were ever genuine, has disappeared into the darkness. And then—out of the complete darkness—he hears a woman's voice ask if he is the one "who found the ear." From the shadows Sandy emerges dressed in a billowy pink dress.

Sandy, unlike every other character seen with Jeffrey, is immediately interested in Jeffrey and in the severed ear. In a stylistic inversion of Jeffrey's moves from the light into the dark in the film, Sandy comes out of complete darkness and into the light.

The nighttime scene continues an air of mystery and promise. Earlier, Jeffrey saw the ear pictured and heard its roar as he walked into the night. Now he hears Sandy's voice questioning him about the ear and she appears out of the darkness. Lynch's genius as a technician bonds the film here with his evolving visual energy: sound and vision create meaning outside the film's reality.

It is noteworthy that before Jeffrey sees Dorothy Vallens, or her apartment, he keeps hearing about her. Sandy insists that, based on what she has heard, his pursuit of Dorothy will only expose him to dangerous possibilities. She says this as a warning but Jeffrey hears it as an invitation. Jeffrey has heard tonight from his aunt Barbara that Lincoln Avenue (where Dorothy lives) is a place to avoid. He has heard Detective Williams tell him to avoid seeking information about the ear (Dorothy's blackmail bondage). When Sandy warns him that Dorothy herself is notorious and should be avoided, the pattern of seeing or hearing about characters before their actual appearances in the film is extended. Meeting Dorothy becomes more enticing to Jeffrey and the audience.

Jeffrey listens to Sandy's information about Dorothy: "I hear things," she tells him. And, as with the severed ear, she qualifies her eavesdropping "in bits and pieces." Sandy soothes Jeffrey by understanding his now-insatiable urge to see the Vallens woman's apartment. She volunteers her support before Jeffrey has to solicit it. She is immediately a balm for Jeffrey, and Sandy accepts his quest into the mystery of the ear from the start.

In Lumberton, even the unsavory streets are just around the corner. As Sandy and Jeffrey cross into a treeless, more urban, seedier part of Lumberton, a group of toughs breaks the romantic spell of their walk by shouting suggestive taunts from a passing car. The ominous potential of this expedition is further underscored by a shot of the Lincoln Avenue street sign and Badalamenti's musical flourish as Jeffrey and Sandy conspire across the street from Dorothy's apartment. Typical of Lynch, this shot evokes simultaneously both the real dangers of Jeffrey's next actions and the melodrama of such actions in the world of the film noir. It is a shot which is conscious of itself as a convention of B-movie mysteries.

The youngsters head back home "and Mr. Lynch paints the small town of Lumberton as ludicrously idyllic."[13] The mood is entirely different as they stroll homewards in the warm and balmy evening. The streets look inviting and safe. Trees arch over them with familiar warmth. Here is the wholesome, naive first date of small-town Americans, or more accurately the Hollywood interpretation of one.

The scene is a provocative one in analyzing the film. It suggests a streak of romanticism that belies the film's darkness. The old maxim "Under the pessimist's sorrow lies the idealist's heart" may underlie the scene. True, the audience sees and will never escape from seeing the bad in everything in the film. But because the film refuses to make a judgmental presentation, the audience also sees the reverse. Because good and bad both exist, scenes show the spark of promise in the darkness of the Lumberton night.

Jeffrey and Sandy's nocturnal walk recalls Capra's *It's a Wonderful Life*. The young lovers walk discussing their dreams. They amble side by side, both shyly keeping their hands in their pockets. Trying to impress her, he performs his animated "chicken walk." Part tribal courtship dance, part animal mating display, the male struggles to attract the female's attention. The incidents emphasize the innocent qualities of Jeffrey and Sandy. They find themselves capable of speaking the same things at the same time; they finish each other's sentences. She appears more rational than he, with wisdom beyond her years. He looks impulsive, pseudosophisticated, anxious to gain her approval.

George Bailey and Mary took this same movie walk as first steps in their romance. They also shared and exchanged dreams. In an obvious parallel to the scene of the earlier film, Jeffrey and Sandy pass a boarded-up and empty house on the street, just as George and Mary passed the deserted house in the Capra classic. The dream house was to be salvaged. Brimming with promise, nurtured by love, it was going to blossom into George and Mary's home.

But Jeffrey and Sandy do not find themselves entranced by her hopes of starting a life together in the restored dream cottage. In *Blue Velvet* Jeffrey Beaumont blurts out a recollection about a childhood classmate with the world's largest tongue who lived in the now-deserted house. The image of the boarded-up house goes awry from Capra. In order not to succumb to a surgical division of good and evil, screenwriter Lynch gives Jeffrey this anecdote inappropriate to the narrative but within the context of the film's images. This possibly romantic image is tied to the grotesque.

The anecdote is met with neither scrutiny nor suspicion by Sandy. She hears what she wants to hear Jeffrey say. But what does the audience hear? The tongue flicks of passion during sexual intercourse, of Eden's serpent, of oral sex; the red-lipsticked, tongue-on-teeth mouth of Dorothy begging for abuse in her sadomasochistic sexual frenzy is foreshadowed—as are Frank's wet-tongued kisses on Jeffrey's lips. "It must be that Lynch's use of irrational material works the way it's supposed to: at some not fully conscious level we read his images" (Kael 1985, 101).

These darker cinematic connotations easily distinguish Jeffrey from George Bailey in the movie of 50 years ago. Yet the texture of the *Blue Velvet* scene is enhanced in Lynch by recalling the Capra sequence. Comparatively, both characters are seen in a different light, yet the two characters have more in common than was originally seen.

As it was with George, this is a most affecting scene in the characterization of Jeffrey. It wins audience sympathy for him in the twists and turns ahead. In *Blue Velvet* apparently little will suggest anyone gaining angel wings. Lynch's movie isn't the stuff that holiday classics are made of.

Yet as the century nears an end, Jeffrey's dreams—even his nightmares—might actually be understandable to celluloid grandpa George Bailey. The age of terrorism, cloning, and computers slithers in Lumberton, but still somewhere outside of Jeffrey's neighborhood. And in this scene Jeffrey is safely at home where he can imagine. "The global village might be called Bedford Falls, or even Lumberton, but we're stuck together in it—the world that dreams are made of, Our Town."[14]

And what are our heroes' small-town dreams? They both dream that there is something more, something that will imbue life with value. They both want to achieve. They both want to know the great big world outside of their tiny communities. And nightmares? They both fear that they must accomplish great things or be nothing. They are both haunted by the realization that there might be something they will never know. They both dread the something they will miss. And they are both caught between their realities and fantasies.

Kinky sex, terror, and violent ordeals aside, Jeffrey shares with George common elements in character. The brutality of the explicit *Blue Velvet* world is a different landscape than Bedford Falls. George Bailey's being involved in almost any action of Lynch's plot is sacrilegious. But each man wants to know what it's all for—why he has a hungry need.

Lynch's universe belongs to tomorrow's cold headlines. But Lynch as screenwriter creates a much more "American" set of values than the obvious nudity, violence, and sex. David Lynch has gone back to Lumberton—and Jeffrey Beaumont decides to stay there—because something of small-town values looks right.

Life in Lumberton is potentially just as wonderful for Beaumont as life looks to Bailey. Out of the darkness, there is the warm light of a spring day. In all of the evil, there is also good. Sure George saved the bank, a crotchety old lady only needed to borrow $17.50, but the depression did hit Bedford Falls. George Bailey did contemplate suicide. Capra doesn't say Bedford Falls has no Lincoln Avenue, he just doesn't detour down there with his camera.

Sandy is *Blue Velvet*'s sweet angel in training; her character adds Harold's mysticism to Mary's ideal American woman. Sandy dreams the American Dream of peace, prosperity, and goodness. She brings her vision to Jeffrey. Sandy's belief in him provides Jeffrey with a confidante. She sees herself as his lifeline. Infinitely supportive, Sandy listens with rapt attention to all his stories. She even listens, is the only one who listens, to Jeffrey's version of his exploits with Dorothy.

Reporting his involvement with Dorothy to Sandy mingles the two plots. Without an ally from the neighborhood for Jeffrey to talk to, there would be no conduit between the film's stories. Without Sandy, Jeffrey would also have no bridge from dark to light, evil to good, or illusion to reality.

But more important, sharing Jeffrey's obsession makes Sandy Jeffrey's ear. Jeffrey is able to express himself to Sandy, revealing the seemingly conflicting elements of his psyche, albeit with varying degrees of acceptance. In the film's conclusion Sandy will know and accept both parts of Jeffrey's world. Jeffrey looks out of his darkness to see Sandy as a creature of the light.

At the end of the scene, Sandy and Jeffrey have not yet finished their stroll. The camera pans back and we see them in a context of streets they know, shared school experiences, and each other's company. Music begins. We hear them laughing not derisively but contentedly. This seems a Hollywood ending.

But the roaring, dense sound of the ear—that auditory fall into the abyss, that soundtrack of falling, falling—again is heard. And the fade to black that ends this scene seems long and black indeed.

Jeffrey's involvement with Dorothy occurs in that bleak darkness. Until she is seen at the film's conclusion on a bench in the park, Dorothy is a creature of the night. Her occupation as a club singer supports this body clock. Undoubtedly, her relationship with Jeffrey is better staged in muted tones, darkness, and unnatural electric or stark neon fading into blackest black. A black wig covering her equally dark hair, Dorothy conforms to other dark ladies of film conventions. Her sexual and moral feeding on Jeffrey heightens the illustrative possibilities of these cinematic conventions as she becomes almost vampiric.

Sandy had also come out of one of Jeffrey's nights. She assists him in his pursuit of the ear on the first night—and it is at night that she realizes both that she loves Jeffrey and that he is involved in sadomasochistic sexual activities with Dorothy.

But unlike his meetings with Dorothy, which are always in the secrecy of the night, incidents in the evolving relationship of Jeffrey and Sandy take place in broad daylight. Thus Sandy is seen to function in both night and day; the film presents her in several important scenes of daylight. Visually, setting the pain of her discovery of Jeffrey's nocturnal activities in the darkness and the joy of her dream come true in daylight at the film's closure illustrates the flow of brooding dark and bright happiness in Lynch's context.

On a sunny day outside of the high school, Jeffrey picks Sandy up to explain his plans for pursuing Dorothy. Seen with a group of her school friends, Sandy is concerned that Mike, her football-playing beau, remains in the dark about her involvement with Jeffrey. The film shoots Jeffrey and Sandy from the back seat of his car as they drive off from Sandy's girlfriends.

Driving a convertible that harkens back to the Beach Boys and senior proms, Jeffrey and Sandy are quite the teen dream couple. Their conversation is breezy. Their lively dialogue is tempered by a bit of good-natured teasing. On their way to Arlene's diner—a local spot to which Sandy informs Jeffrey she has also certainly been—Jeffrey and she look as bright and act as young as can be.

Before the diner comes into view, the scene is brutally interrupted by a massive log-carrying truck rolling down the street. This open truck reminds us of the Lumberton radio jingle about felling trees, evoking again Jeffrey's walk in the woods. But do we stop to wonder how this industrial dinosaur got on the rural street corner of this small town?

At a booth in the diner, the colors are again so vibrant and the photography is so close that *Blue Velvet* sends another of its telegraphic film messages. The repetition of the stylistic techniques that define the opening shots is effective. Like the technicolored flowers and their dark undercurrent of bugs in the Beaumont yard, this light and refreshing scene has its own very dark undercurrent: the daytime discussion is a tactical one to formulate strategies for the night's assault on Lincoln Avenue.

In this scene Jeffrey reveals his urge to explore the unknowns that fascinate him. He wants to go out and experience everything new. His role as guide to Sandy is one he adopts with a bit too much relish; he is didactic to the point of being patronizing as he pontificates about his desire to experience everything. Lynch characteristically companions his theme with his style. Maintaining cinematic objectivity, Lynch shows the discussion as both serious and comic.

The audience fully appreciates Jeffrey's courage in breaking away from the smothering constraints of middle-class morality and the security of mediocrity. He flies here with Shelley, Gandhi, and Einstein. The audience may be tempted to rally to his support. Of course, it may be just as tempted to lean over to his booth, squash his showing off, and break his spell of ever-so-intense philosophizing with a bit of advice: "See how you'll feel about this when you grow up."

Later in *Blue Velvet* they will again find themselves witness to dual realities. They are torn between absolute revulsion at witnessing Jeffrey's humiliating ordeal in Dorothy's apartment and sarcasm. Jeffrey's trauma is a relentless assault. Yet observing him jump, watching that continuing horror show through the slats, it's tempting to tap him on his shoulder with a question: "Learn anything new today?"

Lynch operates as screenwriter and director with an awareness of this dual potential. Lynch's world of reality and illusion is a dual world. *Blue Velvet* structurally and technically confirms that "cinema is like dream in the mode of its presentation: it creates a virtual present, an order of direct apparition. That is the mode of dream."[15] The creative possibilities extended to the evolution of metaphor in film by Lynch's perspective are best illustrated in *Blue Velvet* appropriately in the introduction by Jeffrey and Sandy into the world of their dreams.

"A wise man said, 'Normal people are the strangest people,' and Jeffrey is about the very strangest. Nice boy right out of a Fifties boy scout troop. But there are anomalies: that hoop earring he wears; his goofy rendition of 'the chicken walk' (David Byrne, take note); his allusion to an old school friend, the one with "the biggest tongue in the world" (Corliss 1986, 12). Jeffrey's reality is sometimes as difficult to distinguish from his dreams as are his nightmares.

After Jeffrey leaves Dorothy Vallens's apartment his first night on Lincoln Avenue, he is seen in a black outfit descending the stairs into the dark night. As he walks the murky streets, the film slips into Jeffrey's dark dream. First there comes the by-now-recognizable howling whisper of the ear. Pauline Kael suggests that listening to this ear is, in fact, like listening into a conch shell and hearing the enormous power of the sea.

Appropriately, it is his own pulse he hears in the conch's mysterious call. It is the sounds of the interior world, expansive and deep as the ocean, that beckon. Jeffrey drowns in the black void of hissing sounds. Sinking deeper into darkness, even deeper than into the deep river suggested by Dorothy's address, Jeffrey now becomes enveloped listening to the sounds of the ear. He flounders—drowning—in the unnavigable deepness.

Sounds at an excruciatingly slow speed roar from faces Jeffrey sees melting into each other as the dream continues. One of the faces is Frank's as Frank obliges Dorothy by punching her loudly in the face. Another is Dorothy's as she begs to be hit, begs for physical abuse. And there are those red lips. Enormous. Passionate. Liquid redness relentlessly taunting, inviting, disgusting. The overpowering soundtrack and the extreme close-up flame being extinguished thunders.

Jeffrey's dream wakes him. Boyish, hair askew, clad in his striped pajamas, Jeffrey sits on the edge of his bed. He looks for the comfort of consciousness in the surroundings of his own bedroom. He takes note of the familiar wall beside his bed. Here in broad daylight his childhood room appears to be, after his dream, some grotesque juxtaposition. "Man oh man," he hears himself moan.

Jeffrey has found a severed ear in a vacant lot. He has watched Dorothy beaten in a sadomasochistic act of sexual bondage. He has watched Dorothy beg to be abused. He has been stripped naked and slashed with a knife. He has demeaned. He has been demeaned. He has deplored the degradation. He has thrilled at the degradation. He has seen Frank's perverse cruelty, heard the vile venom spat from his lips. He will taste Frank's blood red lips. When this dream ends. If this dream ends. But when did the dream start?

And what does the dream mean? Can the audience decipher it? The dream isn't intended to replicate reality on the screen. It operates as film images. In the safety of a dream Jeffrey need not face the scrutiny—nor need Lynch—of putting images into a linear narrative. The images gain context from—and as—film.

The audience may think they enter Jeffrey's dream because they understand Jeffrey. But the camera has only visualized the dream, not given it meaning. So it isn't possible for the audience to understand the "real" meaning, as one is simply not shown. What Lynch has done in *Blue Velvet* is to make the audience enter Jeffrey's dream because they know they don't understand it any better than they understand their own dreams.

That night Jeffrey meets Sandy to fill her in. Calling her to make the date was his first action when he woke from his dreams that morning. Jeffrey and Sandy's nighttime conversation begins in her car. Close-ups of them are bordered by the darkness. In the background is a white shape and the hint of color—rather like the camera under the dark ground looking upward at flowers near the white picket fence of a summer garden.

Jeffrey's mood is certainly down. He is suffering as mothers warn children they will. Discomfort increases as the sun goes down and the fever returns; a bruise hurts more on the following day than when the injury happens. And Jeffrey has been injured.

He tells Sandy in a halting, broken delivery of the events of the past night. Jeffrey edits everything that really happened to him, everything that he did or dreamed, merely outlining the facts he has learned about Dorothy. He states the ugly facts without feeling or details. Sandy watches his pain with intense empathy. Finally, he asks—and it appears he needs her answer to what must be the granddaddy of rhetorical questions—why must life be so unhappy?

The religious strains of organ music and the singing of innocent, unafraid crickets become more noticeable as Sandy answers Jeffrey. Although he has not told her about his dream, which the audience has already watched, Sandy shares the secret of her dream with him and with the camera. Like Jeffrey, the audience hears Sandy tell what she saw in her dream. It is her description and not the dream which the camera shows.

This was her dream on the night she met Jeffrey. The night he passed a man whose glasses were so dark that his wearing them infinitely increased his blindness in the dark night. The night Sandy and Jeffrey laughed and had fun. The night they talked about his investigation of the ear. The night she led him to—and back from—Lincoln Avenue.

It was a dark world and had been dark for a long time because there were no robins. The robins, as she explains her dream imagery, represent love. Suddenly—and here the organ music swells as in some 1950s black-and-white lunch-time soap opera—the robins appear. Her dream is bright, filled with the "blinding Light of Love." The world awakens out of its somber sleep, and the day of peace, happiness, and love arrives.

Jeffrey is spellbound and finally sees something other than what is paraded before his eyes. He buys, not Sandy's dream, but its message. He tells her she's a "neat girl" and she counters that he's a "neat girl" too. This affectionate slip is less cataclysmic to him than was Dorothy's clinical exploration of his "neatness" as a boy.

Conspicuous by its absence, there are no physical assertions between Jeffrey and Sandy. Jeffrey and Sandy are comfortable together. What they see in each other is good for them. Jeffrey's nightmares and sadomasochistic actions are not reflected in Sandy's eyes; her needs and doubts are not reflected in his. To each other, Sandy and Jeffrey look "neat" and, therefore, they are "neat."

As they pull away in the car, mutually comforted, the white church behind them comes clearly into focus. The bright light of its beautiful stained-glass windows stands as testament to the human spirit. The organ music rises in the night sky. This shot concludes the scene uncustomarily. The characters do not fade into the darkness. Jeffrey and Sandy take action and find together the strength to move on. No darkness fading to black here. The shot is clear, stressing promise in color and light.

It is without promise but with a sense of apprehension that Jeffrey faces the bold #710 of Dorothy's Deep River Apartments, which opens the next scene. In a peculiar conversation the quirky "I looked for you in my closet tonight" to the understated "I like you" and his answer, "I like you too," Dorothy and Jeffrey talk themselves back into sex. Their sexual involvement will continue in the film beyond

Jeffrey's ability to awaken from this bad dream. "*Blue Velvet* is a mystery . . . a masterpiece . . . a visionary story of sexual awakening, of good and evil, a trip to the underworld."[16] The film is in the genre of maturation stories. In Lynch's world Jeffrey becomes a man, not because of his initiation into varied sexual experiences, but rather because he realizes the dark seed in himself and the ugliness and beauty in the world it reflects.

Since first watching Dorothy through her closet doors, Jeffrey has also been observing Frank. Introduced by a shot of his Heineken bottle at the bar, Jeffrey is seen on another night watching Frank listening to Dorothy's "Blue Velvet" in the Slow Club. Frank is mesmerized by her rendition, clutching the sordid shred of blue velvet from her bathrobe. Later that night Jeffrey continues his investigation of the ear and follows Frank and his criminal friends, recording with his camera the suspicious exploits in Lumberton.

Another Heineken and a crumpled bag of chips on his dashboard making a visual connection, Jeffrey's surveillance of the widening spiral of unsavory activities is retold to Sandy in a flashback of the events. Sandy has chosen once again to ride away with Jeffrey after being spied on by Mike from behind the fence at after-school football practice. They drive via the old route, complete with log hauler, back to Arlene's diner so she can hear his story. High-school romances, football heroes, small-town diners fill the screen. "Part, but not all, of what makes *Blue Velvet* so unsettling is that Lynch's nightmare has a sort of irregular, homemade quality, as if it had been cooked up with familiar but not entirely wholesome ingredients—a fresh apple pie with a couple of worms poking through the crust" (Rafferty 1986, 384).

Seeing the danger Jeffrey courts in his continued involvement with Dorothy, Sandy asks him why he won't stop. "I'm seeing something that was always hidden," explains Jeffrey. "I'm involved in a mystery. I'm in the middle of a mystery. And it's all secret." Jeffrey speaks with determined relish. His remarks have evolved from explanation to excuse to credo. The fervor of his quest makes the meeting of Jeffrey and Frank inevitable. And one night outside Deep River #710, it happens.

Vinton's "Blue Velvet" is heard in the background, Dorothy is dressed in red, Jeffrey arrives and is silently led into her bedroom. "The movie is *Blue Velvet,* and it is one of the bravest, strangest and most intensely personal works ever to come out of Hollywood . . .

one of the few great films of the 80s, could be the most sensational work of cinema since 'Last Tango in Paris.'"[17] She'll let him do "anything," but of course she begs, "I want you to hurt me." The cacophonous, elongated sounds of their sexual groaning penetrate the cavernous whispering of the ear. Close-up shots cut from bodies and faces to the burning heat of a flame being extinguished by hot breath. "Hit me." Louder: "*Hit me*!" The moist red mouth—the tongue, the sharp teeth. The scene is, of course, Jeffrey's dream. Again. And he hits Dorothy. It is Jeffrey's nightmare. So he hits her again. And again.

Dressed and in Dorothy's living room after this encounter, Jeffrey is aware of the scope of the cruel streak he and Dorothy share. How is the abuse different from the violent sadomasochism Jeffrey observed with shock between Frank and Dorothy his first night in her closet? It gnaws at Jeffrey's need to question. Sexual pain and degradation are enticing to Jeffrey. The association mirrors Jeffrey's nightmares. And in his abusive return to Deep River, Jeffrey himself opens the Deep River door to let Frank in.

Frank is instinctively jealous and compensates by intimidating Jeffrey. Building on Dorothy's introduction of him as a good kid "from the neighborhood," Frank and his goon squad taunt Jeffrey, threaten, ridicule, and finally assault him. This is another night that goes haywire down on Lincoln Avenue. But the dark antics of this night spill into other secret places, leaving Jeffrey bruised in the daylight.

The changing connotations of Jeffrey's status as a "neighbor" are interesting in the context of the uses of the term in the film. First, there is a level of truth to the term. Lumberton is small-town America, where everyone is a neighbor. Both Aunt Barbara and Sandy have made it clear that Lincoln Avenue is geographically in Jeffrey's neighborhood; thus Jeffrey is rightly considered a neighbor. Frank also makes synonymous Jeffrey's sexual relationship with Dorothy and the sarcastic label of acting "like a good neighbor," making the term accurate on an analogous level. Finally, after Frank has roughed Jeffrey up, had a sexual taste of him, and accused him face-to-face of being just like him, it becomes a description of the sexually aberrant bent that Jeffrey and Frank share as "neighbors."

The joyride of that night begins with the peeling of tires and the screaming of the motor. The headlights are exposed and locked into place, making the car look like a military vehicle preparing itself for battle. Shots of the wheels spinning wildly cut to Frank driving fiendishly next to Dorothy in her blue velvet robe, or Jeffrey wedged in back with the seedy looking Raymond (Brad Dourif) and the slow-speaking, straw-hatted Paul (Jack Nance of *Eraserhead*). The dialogue, loaded with cursing and four-letter words, is abrasive and cruel. Close-ups and cutting among the faces and the mechanical parts of the car, tracking shots in a near blur of the road's yellow lines, and the eerie changes in lighting from the headlights of the oncoming traffic make the fluid scene as frightening as the ride to Ben's.

There is a discussion about buying beer in which Jeffrey's acknowledged preference for Heineken further disgusts Frank Booth. Beer slogans recur to characterize the stereotypes of beer by brands. Consequently, Frank's diehard devotion to Pabst Blue Ribbon separates him from Jeffrey socially and culturally. Beer drinkers are not only different types, chanting advertising slogans like pop-culture mutants—each is seen as a member of a different class, initiated into a club by the beer he drinks.

The party at Ben's reaches a low-life nadir, no matter the beer choice, and satirizes the barbarism of Frank and his cronies in the refined ritual of toasting, "Here's to your fuck, Frank," with mismatched glasses of beer. Frank's gang is the antithesis of Jeffrey's imported-beer-drinking circle at college. There is little chance of confusing the gang at Ben's with a party of Yalies passing the traditional silver cup at Morey's.

Ben's party includes several bloated, overly made-up prostitutes, a fat man, another whore, and presumably little Donny, Dorothy's son, secreted in another room. Ben himself is heavy on the makeup and effeminate. His softness of delivery—calling everybody "darling" like some drag queen dragon lady from 1930s Art Deco Hollywood—causes Frank twice to remark with awe that Ben is "one suave fucker."

This is a brutal scene physically as well. Jeffrey is again threatened with a knife in this sequence, recalling Dorothy's violent attack on Jeffrey. Now, during a toast he is forced to make to Ben, Jeffrey takes first a punch from Frank and then—in a surprising show of brute force—a punch to the stomach from Ben himself.

Assimilating the violence, Jeffrey eavesdrops on Frank and Ben discussing "Gordon, the man" while they do drugs in an alcove and listens to Dorothy in a pitiful discussion wailing, "Donny, Mommy loves you," from behind the closed door. Instead of continuing with ambiguous voices heard outside the room, the film as ambiguously now features confusing voices within the room—at least in clear sight, if not clear sound.

Blue Velvet again employs remembered connotations of songs of the past top forty. Frank convinces Ben to sing "In Dreams." The lyrics about reality and illusion in love take on new meanings in the context of the film. However, the lip-syncing and grotesque staged lighting of Ben's version immediately color its use. In fact Lynch succeeds in molding the music into an anthem in the film for secrets within each of us. Typical of Lynch's auditory style, the song has different uses in quick succession. First, Roy Orbison's song appears to be sung to Frank by Ben, then it is used by Frank to thwart the biting effects of the first version in a mimicking delivery of the song to Jeffrey.

Also important is that each time "In Dreams" appears to be sung, the voice heard is actually a prerecorded voice, not the voice of either "singer" seen in the shot. It is also impossible not to note that the visual contexts of the song both times are utterly harrowing. *Blue Velvet* reveals the thematic message of the ear's secret now in auditory form.

In its first rendition Ben lip-syncs Roy Orbison's song as if, like Dorothy earlier, he is a singer on stage. In the brothel he grotesquely lights his performance with a workman's industrial flashlight that he holds up too closely to his face as a pretend microphone. He sings with melodramatic gesture and grimace to Frank. One hesitates to psychoanalyze Frank without a road map, but it appears the homosexual contortions of Ben while intoning "in dreams you walk with me" agitate Frank. Suave as Frank claims Ben is, Ben's suggestion that he and Frank are two of a kind offends Frank, who abruptly halts the first version.

Frank and his cohorts, Jeffrey, Dorothy, and a stray tart continue their screeching auto ride. Wearing his mask to gain his sadomasochistic sexual charge, Frank gleefully points out that Jeffrey is just like him. Then, moving to the next phase of degrading Dorothy, Frank finally torments the heretofore-petrified Jeffrey into hitting him.

Jeffrey is dragged from the car. Frank smears on red lipstick and continually forces kisses on Jeffrey's mouth during a sadistic sexual tirade. Ordering the song played again, Frank now lip-syncs the lines to the captive Jeffrey while beating him severely. Now the context of the song's lyrics stresses how alike Frank and Jeffrey are in their dreams.

The song is used as soundtrack and as a metronome by which Frank both humiliates and assaults Jeffrey sexually and violently. The suggestion of the lyrics is still that singer and listener are two of a kind in their dreams. Although singer and listener are now different characters, Ben's version to Frank echoes. But are they really different men? Ben's song had found a secret fear in Frank. Is there in the lyrics' message of violent sexual attraction between singer and listener another level of painful understanding now hideously awakened in Frank and Jeffrey?

During the beating and the musical interlude, the tart in her tight miniskirt dances on the car roof. Dorothy screams for Frank to stop. The car tape blares. The scene is narratively ambiguous. The scene is a rush of dual aural and visual images, each given context by the film. In the muted shadows of the deformed and discarded metal of the junkyard, Frank continues to punch Jeffrey into unconsciousness. Is the slattern on the car moving trancelike to the throbbing of the music or to the rhythm of the beating? Regardless, her movement to the violence is cohesive with the sounds and visually balanced in the shot's gritty composition. "This is the real nightmare stuff, inexplicable and thus inescapable: we don't know where it's coming from, so we don't know which way to run" (Rafferty 1986, 383).

Jeffrey's swollen face rises the next morning reflected in a muddy puddle. The lot is now quiet. He attempts with pain to get himself out of the dirt. The camera focuses his bleary gaze on a street sign reading "Meadow Lane." He is still in the green fields of small-town U.S.A. He is still in Lumberton. But is he still in the middle of a "mystery . . . where everything is secret"?

Later that morning, after crying himself out, Jeffrey sits in his striped pajamas on his bed back in his old room. He goes down to breakfast in his sunny kitchen. In answer to Aunt Barbara's prodding about his visible cuts and bruises, he quips, "Aunt Barbara, I love you, but you're going to get it." The suggestion of violence has seeped into his home, his family, his daylight life.

The duality of this remark as both a serious threat and a good-natured retort illustrates again the techniques employed throughout *Blue Velvet.* In fact, from its first shots, the film is one of tension resulting from the alternating and dual composition of the scenes. The visual and aural messages, objective and subjective presentation, gruesome and comic scenes, editing style, and even the casting alternate between real and cinematic depiction—*Blue Velvet* is two-toned. The film thus cannot only be received in two ways—it can, in fact it must, often be interpreted a third way, metaphorically, resulting from the combination and juxtaposition of the apparently conflicting and certainly separate elements.

This is masterfully, subtly, and consistently done by Lynch. For example, a 1930s microphone adorns a 1980s stage. TV programming takes its place in the plot events of the story. We hear sounds but find they are recorded: saws, songs, trees, even radio promotions. A scene of a violent beating is choreographed with a woman suddenly dancing on the roof of a car. When the narrative gets creepy and perhaps too "real," a cold scientific discussion develops to identify the forensic who, how, when, and why of the severed ear for the plot. The film scene cuts to the yellow "crime scene" tape being cut by a shiny pair of scissors—a play on the ear and its amputation, and a play on the distancing cut of the movie camera. Simultaneously repellent and fascinating, sickening and erotic, frightening and amusing, *Blue Velvet*'s world is a film universe of images sewn together for and by the viewer.

This duality is also important to Lynch in casting. The film's powerful performers are characters of the story as well as screen actors, further enhancing Lynch's vision. Jack Nance is a member of the Lynch repertory; Kyle MacLachlan is *Dune*'s hero. A repetition in casting the same actors in many of his films makes in Lynch, as in other contemporary writer/directors, a movie more identifiable as a part of a filmmaker's artistic creations. Their casting makes the film more immediately recognized as a movie—a David Lynch movie.

And Lynch has the uncanny knack of going a step further in blurring lines of character and actor. Laura Dern is daughter of an actor recognized for playing some notoriously unconventional roles. Isabella Rossellini brings an accent and brooding beauty to her role that is inseparable from the voice and face of her mother, Ingrid Bergman, a legendary film actress. Thus these casting choices integrate movie history and its conventions into *Blue Velvet*'s shots.

In an essay, James M. Wall extends the possibilities of these implied connections to biographical scandals and to roles in previous cult films. Casting a child star like Dean Stockwell as Ben adds something to the audience's feeling that Ben is somehow tarnished and soured. Frank Booth also resonates as a character of seedy, dated disillusionment. "While it is not essential to appreciating the movie, the film gains a certain additional resonance from the viewer's sense that

Hopper's character is the middle-aged descendent of the free spirit he portrayed in *Easy Rider,* the quintessential 1960s road movie about drugs in an oppressive society."[18]

In the film's concluding sequence, Sandy and Jeffrey declare their love after Jeffrey has relinquished his investigation to the Lumberton police. They dance at a teen party in a basement rec room, lost in each other's arms. On the way home they are chased by another car and battered by the threatening maniac driver. Surprisingly, this collision derby has nothing to do with Jeffrey's treasured ear—it is unrequited love on a rampage, Sandy's cuckolded boyfriend, Mike.

Mike's adolescent, joking innuendo about Jeffrey's mother falls abysmally flat when the Beaumont house becomes the setting for the naked Dorothy wandering arms akimbo on the front lawn. Dorothy is a beaten victim of almost continual violence in the film. She is utterly vulnerable and pathetic. Her nudity suggests not eroticism but a medical victim, as did the naked Jeffrey stripped earlier for the camera. The human body in these scenes is just a live cadaver prepared for dissection.

In this scene Dorothy again makes reference to having Jeffrey inside of her. But she announces their intercourse as a metaphor of the contagious spreading of disease. Jeffrey's sperm is the seed of disease. Certainly this graphic accusation is sexual. The remark is distasteful to Sandy, who, being exposed to Jeffrey's sordid activities, slaps Jeffrey in the face as her mother covers the naked Dorothy with a coat.

But the allusion—in this sex-filled movie—is not only sexual. Jeffrey's secret is not about his male organ and ejaculation. Jeffrey's secret is not about having orgasms, but is about being human: he carries the potential of corruption. Within him is the power to create and to kill. He's not reckoning with sexual climax; Jeffrey is struggling with human conscience. Now that he knows what cruelty he can and will engender, he can never be the young Beaumont boy again. Jeffrey has lost his innocence. Jeffrey has heard what it is he sought from the ear.

Dorothy lies masked in the rescue-squad ambulance, aimlessly yelling Frank Booth–like as she is carried away. Sandy forgives Jeffrey's unfaithfulness. The film's plot has come to its resolution. Jeffrey is left alone to bring the action of the film's story and its sensory universe to climax back on Lincoln Ave.

Walking up the familiar Deep River Apartment steps, Jeffrey faces the foe with whom he has danced since his first experience in #710's closet. In the ghastly pink glare of Jeffrey's mind, the murder scene stands suspended. Murderers and victims, gunshot holes in their heads, coagulated bloody wounds, one-eared Don and Detective Gordon propped on display. The sounds of "Love Letters Straight from Your Heart" singing/signing Frank's signature on the slaughter to Jeffrey.

In his frantic attempt to escape, Jeffrey—fully dressed but captured somehow naked, this time in the Deep River—hears the jumbled radio messages while calling the police for help. He realizes that Frank has the calls bugged and that this makes his confrontation with Frank inevitable. He uses the radio message as a decoy, setting Frank up for the kill. Jeffrey hides himself to wait—and watch—again in Dorothy's closet.

Frank enters and searches for Jeffrey. When he forces himself on Jeffrey in the closet, the game is up. Jeffrey looks straight into the face of Frank, the monster who has always seen that he and Jeffrey are alike, sees that part of himself—and annihilates the mirror by firing bullets into Frank's face. Now Jeffrey can leave the darkness of Lincoln Avenue, and robin-filled spring can come to Lumberton. It is Sandy's dream—but it is Jeffrey's epiphany.

A long shot from Jeffrey's ear pans out of his head and into the yard where the film began. Mr. Beaumont, no longer heart-attack victim but backyard chef, engages in "manly" conversation with Detective Williams in the green outdoors. Their wives complete this extended family, chatting about "ladies' things" with apparent familiarity and ease in the more refined but cozy interior of the house. This is what small-town America is.

The conclusion is also an almost-Shakespearean restoration of order. The color and pacing of the film as well as the musical score are once again bright and easy, nostalgic and romantic. If more fuel is needed for this message, the camera gives the audience a shot of one of the world's most contented robins. And they are even directed by Sandy to this shot as she underscores that we have all entered her dream.

A shot of the notorious bug dangling from the carnivorous bird's beak visually underscores the parallel existence of the beautiful and the ugly. An absolutely splendid image—twice. In itself the dual image is brilliantly attractive and, of course, repulsive as a film shot. Adding the connotations of Sandy's dream, the film's theme, and the audience's expectations, the shot is also an image that takes on meaning with the input of the viewer, beyond the replication of reality.

Watching the spring feeding from the kitchen are Sandy, Jeffrey, and Aunt Barbara. The lovers see the dream come true of a brighter, more enlightened future. They have devoured their bugs and enabled themselves to fly high above the ground. The film has beautifully realized its story. Here is the happy ending.

And Aunt Barbara? The funny old lady who warned Jeffrey first about straying down to Lincoln Avenue? The intruding busybody who questioned Jeffrey about his exploits where impaired father and TV-watching mother feared to tread? She's busy looking for the potato salad, so she tries not to be bothered by the sight of still another bird eating just another bug. They are, after all, ugly and only birds and insects, seen everywhere in the spring. And this fat puffy robin looks a little like a mechanical movie prop anyway. Thus David Lynch abandons message and spins us back into the movie.

Dorothy and her little boy are reunited on a park bench. The sounds of Dorothy's version of "Blue Velvet" echo in the background. As Dorothy looks to the blue sky, mommy cradling her little boy, tears fill her eyes. Is she crying tears of joy at having her son, grateful her ordeal is behind her? Or tears of pain drawn from the well of memory that, even under the blue skies, Dorothy is incapable of escaping?

Dorothy will ever see blue velvet, joy and pain intertwined. She is both melancholy and happy in that pain. The shot suggests all of these. But what Lynch shows us before the final fade is a film shot: Dorothy sitting on a park bench. And so he concludes his film.

Lynch is accused of several offenses in *Blue Velvet*. Recognizing the range of critical reaction to his work, two are still of particular interest to address, as they underlie a misunderstanding of the film. First, the film is called a defamation of the women of the world. In an interview Lynch denies falling victim to a current trend in movie politicizing. Jeffrey is not every man stripped by his mother as an object of maternity bashing, any more than Shakespeare's Hamlet is a societal indictment that portrays all men as incapable of taking action. Thus the brutalizing of Dorothy in the film is not defended by Lynch, but is instead explained as the visualizing of one woman's trauma, the victimizing of one character/female.

"Now, let me bring up a touchy subject, the position of women in your films. For *Blue Velvet* you took some abuse about—"begins

Breskin in a *Rolling Stone* interview with Lynch. The director of *Blue Velvet* responds, "Because people have an idea that Dorothy was Everywoman, instead of just being Dorothy. That's where the problem starts. If it's just Dorothy, and it's her story—which it is to me—then everything is fine . . . When you start talking about 'women' versus 'a woman,' then you're getting into this area of generalizations, and you can't win. There is no generalization. There's a billion different stories and possibilities." "In the naked city," Breskin finishes, and Lynch answers emphatically, "You betcha!" (Breskin, 63).

Lynch has been the target of some criticism for demeaning a symbol of womanhood. Dorothy would certainly be a sorry emblem. Yet to limit art by making a character in film suddenly carry the burden of being all people of that sex is ridiculous. Dorothy is not all of the women in history; she is a woman character in a film. One shudders to think of Ben as the image of men in film, but no more than at labeling Raymond as the universal male. All men are not Frank Booth. Sandy or Aunt Barbara too are only individual characters in the world of *Blue Velvet,* different from Dorothy and no more universal.

In fact in *Blue Velvet* finding a role model for anyone's sons and daughters is a difficult enough task, let alone finding the universal mother, father, or American. Thus viewing the film as a medieval morality play—with whatever selected extension—is inaccurate as well as arbitrary. And in *Blue Velvet* particularly shortsighted.

It is the distinctively individual universes of each character that Lynch presents. It is the absolute reality of one character on a collision course with another because of the diametrically opposed way each sees the same incident. This is what gives *Blue Velvet* its rich texture—and its multiplicity of meanings.

The abuse is disquieting. Abuse is at its most disquieting because Dorothy's ordeals are tinged with laughter. The assaults border on burlesques of obsessions. Laughter may well be, as evidenced during screenings, the audience's only outlet in a scene of such sick, violent intensity. And Lynch is perceptive and unrelenting enough to underscore his scene's grotesquely comic possibility. "During *Blue Velvet,* when you were filming the scenes of Frank abusing and raping Dorothy, apparently you were beside yourself with laughter. You thought this was funny on some level?" the interviewer accosts Lynch. Lynch responds by making an aesthetic not a moral call: "I'm sure pretty near every psychiatrist could tell me right now why I was laughing, but I don't know. It was hysterically funny to me. Frank was completely obsessed. He was like a dog in a chocolate store. He could not help himself. He was completely into it. But because I was laughing and I am a human being, there must be some logical reason why. It has something to do with the fact that it was so horrible and so frightening and so intense and violent, that there was also this layer of humor. It has to do with the degree of obsession where people cannot help themselves" (Breskin, 62).

Fundamental to the film, assault is pictured with consistent brutality. A rock song in the background, Jeffrey certainly gets the dark experiences he has sought in Frank's passion. Lynch presents Frank's assault on Jeffrey with the same barbaric bent of ridicule as he does the assault on Dorothy. Jeffrey is sexually and physically abused in the dark night while a fleshy hooker dances on the car roof. The violence against Jeffrey is also dehumanizing. Violence is always dehumanizing. Violence has no possible excuse. In fact, sex in *Blue Velvet* has little to do with sex at all. The film is obviously a foray into the dark world of violence and abuse, a world not of sex, but of sexual violence.

In fact, in all of the reversals, exploitation, and graphic sex apparently rampant in *Blue Velvet,* brutality is the subject. Lynch's world looks most explicit in the sordid fantasy and violent foreplay. Scenes focus longest on the exposure of depravity and force. Sex in either a romantic or trenchant context is never visualized. Perpetrating violence—viewing violence—being amused or assaulted by violence—is neither soft-pedaled, separated nor singled out for censure or pity by Lynch. In *Blue Velvet*—they all only are. And each is all. It is sexual aggression-rape-power that spellbinds and tantalizes in the dark on Lincoln Avenue, no matter the roles—voyeur, master, or victim. Lynch refuses to give the audience the solace of distancing these roles as items in a hierarchy.

One can easily imagine *Blue Velvet*'s difficulties in gaining commercial audiences and distribution. The film won both critical praise and ridicule. "Members of the National Society of Film Critics yesterday voted David Lynch's 'Blue Velvet' best film of 1986. Mr. Lynch, who wrote and directed 'Blue Velvet' and described it as 'a film about things that are hidden—within a small city and within people,' was named best director."[19] Dennis Hopper won Best Supporting actor, and Frederick Elmes was voted the best achievement in cinematography.

Blue Velvet was also the object of critical disdain at its release. "It's a stylistic tour de force, but I think it finally unravels. By the end of Thursday's preview, the other reviewers and I were laughing at the 'serious' parts."[20]

At its release it was nominated for the Academy Award for best film and best director. *Blue Velvet* provided the Oscar telecast a challenge as well. *US News and World Report* suggested how inappropriate many *Blue Velvet* scenes were for inclusion in the world-viewed Oscar telecast. David Denby of *New York* magazine further questioned the ramifications of this out-of-the-mainstream choice. "David Lynch's nomination is a guilty notice that there is a world out there that Hollywood is not touching on—and other people are."[21]

Its undeniable mastery makes Lynch's film a ground breaker. *Blue Velvet* is a film which would previously have been an "art film" with a limited audience, not an Oscar contender. "But by nominating Lynch for his direction of the film, the movie establishment has legitimized such controversial work—albeit reluctantly. It is clear that Hollywood is headed into some unfamiliar terrain." (Horn, 75)

Most of the published lists of the best films of the 1980s acknowledge Lynch's *Blue Velvet* as "one of a kind." This is a David Lynch film—probably his best, and perhaps one of *the* best. His techniques enhance the film, identify it as a part of Lynch's vision, and immeasurably elevate its stature in American film history.

But it is *Blue Velvet*'s ingress into its "unfamiliar terrain" that makes it a masterpiece. Quite simply, the cinematic vision of Lynch is the landscape of twenty-first-century film.

5

Lynch on TV—*Twin Peaks*

It was hard by the dim lake of Auber,
In the misty mid region of Weir—
It was down by the dank tarn of Auber,
In the ghoul-haunted woodland of Weir.
—Edgar Allan Poe, "Ulalume"

"Twin Peaks" is poetic suspense, film noir, television series, and classic pop phenomenon. With Mark Frost, Lynch is credited as originator of the idea, and he produces, writes, directs, and acts in some to all of the one-hour episodes and special movies running two seasons on U.S. and European television. A European feature version is released on videotape. A series of commercials based on the works of great authors, using actors from "Twin Peaks" and directed by Lynch, runs during the series. The show spawns a small industry of books and audiotapes. Lynch also writes and directs a further feature film based on the series after its second-season television cancellation.

The four years between *Blue Velvet* and "Twin Peaks" is a busy time for Lynch. He continues to paint, exhibiting in Philadelphia, New York City, Hawaii, and Paris. From 1982 he continues to run his weekly cartoon, "The Angriest Dog in the World." Lynch designs and wins the Rossellini Award for Film Direction. He writes song lyrics and, with composer Angelo Badalamenti, coproduces *Floating into the Night,* an album for singer Julie Cruise; a concert performance at the Brooklyn Academy of Music; and a videotape, *Industrial Symphony No. 1.* He also continues to work on some favorite film projects. "Lynch spent a good deal of time trying to launch projects such as 'Ronnie Rocket,' in which a detective travels inside the consciousness of a young idiot savant dwarf rock 'n' roller, and 'One Saliva Bubble,' the title of which (never mind the content) couldn't be counterbalanced even by the proposed casting of box office names Steve Martin and Martin Short" (Campbell, 34). The bankruptcy of DGI, Dino De Laurentis's studio, and the unrealized film projects have kept Lynch's name off the big screen as writer and director.

This does not mean Lynch does not appear on the screen. In 1988, David Lynch appears in Tina Rathborne's *Zelly and Me*. Lynch has consistently performed in capacities beyond writer/director in his own films. In his early films he conceived and performed technical, photographic, and sound tasks while supplying paintings for Jack Fisk's production design of *Heart Beat* (1980). Lynch acts in *Dune*; he will also appear as a character in "Twin Peaks."

In *Zelly and Me,* Lynch, working for another director, gives an appealing, credible performance as Willy, a manservant impersonating his employer. It cannot easily escape notice that the gentle, romantic character Lynch plays and the feature film in which he chooses to appear seem a far distance from the characters and films he writes and directs. "Whether he intended to be or not, Mr. Lynch, the director of *Elephant Man, Dune* and *Blue Velvet,* is a creepy sort of screen presence."[1] But more noteworthy, Lynch's understanding of films and realization of how they work continue to expand with his wide-ranging film credits. Lynch creates film from his own experience as painter, writer, technician, director, and actor. So Lynch's move to the small screen of television and his work as producer further enhance his perspective as filmmaker.

His interests include television. He and Mark Frost have collaborated before. They have envisioned "The Lamurians," a cops-and-aliens program. They have worked on an unproduced scenario, "Goddess," based on the life of Marilyn Monroe, and on "American Chronicles," a short-lived half-hour series documenting cities or events of American importance. Together they create "Twin Peaks."

"Twin Peaks" is an appropriate arena for Lynch. It is an American television product about an American small town with American values. Lynch is an American artist—product himself of the idealistic explosion of the sixties, turned chronicler of the national decay into mediocrity and secularism of the nineties. He records without comment the trend to trivialize everything from rural mass murders to urban poverty in disposable, programmable video episodes. He somehow placates concurrent and polar American cliques defined by racial,

The director as actor. David Lynch plays opposite Isabella Rossellini in *Zelly and Me*. Courtesy of the Museum of Modern Art/Film Stills Archives.

gender, and political differences. His vision is of a dual world encompassing both American Dream and American Disillusionment.

The suspense series itself is an American genre rooted in the grisly tales of the American tradition. Many of these tales have—as violence unfortunately continues to have—a place in American history. And certainly both U.S. legends and letters include a somber look at death, betraying a fascination with evil and crime. Nowhere in American literature is this better illustrated than in the classic verses and tales of Edgar Allan Poe. And Lynch's place in the tradition of Poe determines the scope of his TV suspense series.

In his "Theory of Composition" and his "Poetic Principle," Poe devised an aesthetic for literature. He demanded that its province be universal. As the only universal, death is the most appropriate subject. Poe writes to evoke a universal response, and sorrow is an emotion felt by everyone. Thus Poe determines that the death of a beautiful, young girl, the most intense and painful beauty, is the most perfected subject.

Poe creates a nether world—somewhere between history and legend, somewhere between dream and nightmare. His stories and poems detail the bizarre; his characters ominously move toward unraveled secrets. They involve themselves in dark acts. His grand houses and mausoleums chill the audience, while his medieval kingdoms and the mythical El Dorado warm their imaginations. Poe is also, of course, credited with the invention of stories of ratiocination, the detection of crimes by use of reason.

Poe's world gains cohesion from point of view. A narrator makes necrophilia, live burial, and murderous gorillas seem like a part of reality. First-person perspective also turns the same objective focus on the cold dispatch of a cat. Straightforward narration channels Poe's vision. Because of its point of view, Poe's world becomes visible to the audience, if never understandable to them.

Moreover, Poe is a stylist who seeks sound over sense. His poetry creates vivid images and builds rhythms in the audience's mind with refrains, assonance, and alliteration. Poe's influence extends to the school of French symbolism with his hypnotic patterns and startling hues of a melancholy world. The poet sparks too the vision of Lynch's television world. Lynch is a filmmaker who often creates expressionist works with the dynamics of poetic composition. Poe masters tone and mood; Poe spins a fabric of colors and textures. Lynch on the screen—particularly in "Twin Peaks"—is on Poe's wavelength.

The film begins with a corpse, a corpse in lyric decomposition. The lovely young blonde, ice blue from her watery grave and wrapped in plastic, pops up on the shores of a serene lake in an idyllic wood. She is a beauty, prom queen, best friend, sweetheart, daughter, small-town girl who tends a local retarded boy. Her loss is tragic and her murder is insidious. Laura Palmer is a beautiful corpse.

The series is overloaded with images: mournful—a traffic light's solitary beacon drowns in the black Washington sky; lyric—night blankets a pristine Pacific Northwest forest; erotic—a beautiful young woman slips into red high heels at her school locker. The shots are consistently "beautiful and moody and everything that American television isn't."[2] Lynch has pictured a promised land where the American Dream is ever possible, and hopelessly infected by disease. The small-town cleanliness, the freshness of youth, the wide open spaces of the northwestern frontier belie the corruption and crime that seem possible everywhere and at every moment. "Although terrible things happen, or seem about to, in *Twin Peaks,* it has the air of an enchanted place, a fairy-tale woodland"[3]

"Twin Peaks" spins a lyric woodland peopled by lumberjacks, a gentle town doctor, and honest police. The audience buys into this world because it exists in American folklore. As in Poe, Lynch vividly sets his atmosphere. His credits of rural sawmills, small-town population signs, the open road, and contented birds in the woods on the shores of a bucolic lake are accompanied by the music of sweet bird songs and the meter of the saw's lulling mechanism. A dirge of foghorns wails as a prom queen's blue-blonde corpse is found cocooned in plastic. It is a world of the senses, operating with an immediacy and an intensity not of narrative development, but of the poetic concentration of its images and sounds.

Like Poe's verse, "Twin Peaks" is poetic—inherently rhythmic. It has a first-person speaker: the straightest, fairest, most literal hero, Dale Cooper. In the televised serial, Agent Cooper even reads impressions into a tape recorder, thus not only making the audience party to his telling, but involving it through his language, his rhythm, and the sounds of his voice. As in Poe's world, no matter the peculiarities of the incidents, the audience is assured by the speaker's voice. Ironically, neither offers a universal world; rather comfort is found in idiosyncracies: Cooper is as distinctive a first-person speaker as any found in Poe's poetry.

Following the patterning of images that seek emotional response rather than narrative sense, Lynch also operates in his sound network. It is consistently the power of sound in Lynch that supports his visual images and completes the sensory experience of entering his world. Lynch uses a particular kind of music as an important part of sound communication. This was evident as early as his use of Tractor's music in his early Philadelphia films; but the score of "Twin Peaks" is heard by critics as collaboration on a heightened level. "One reason Mr. Badalamenti's music works so well—and why people who scorned, say, Rick Wakeman like the score for "Twin Peaks"—is that music of this sort combines so readily with images."[4]

Therefore, in a very real sense, Lynch evokes the emotional involvement one feels with poetry. "Now as a poem is literally a poem, it belongs, in its literal context, to the class of things called poems, which in their turn form part of the larger class known as works of art. The poem from this point of view presents a flow of sounds approximating music on one side, and an integrated pattern of imagery approximating the pictorial on the other. "Literally, then, a poem's narrative is its rhythm or its movement of words."[5] Because Lynch brings this concise flow of images to the television screen, "Twin Peaks" breaks the traditional conventions of a series and instead generates new film conventions for TV.

Here, as in the poetry of artist and mystic William Blake, Lynch has created a dense, rich world expanding beyond Poe's vision of the macabre. Images paint a physical and spiritual world: an entire cosmos of characters both innocent and experienced, nature both beautiful and cruel, spirits, demons, and mythic characters of good and evil. The audience is immersed in the world and caught in the flow of its images. And—as with Blake's "Sick Rose," in which dark properties of nature are shown in the beautiful garden flower—perversion lurks in Lynch's Pacific Northwestern Garden of Eden. In fact, this "weirdness of Northwest Noir,"[6] as the *New York Times* will later call it, will be explored in various ways by Lynch, director Gus Van Sant, cartoonist Gary Larson, and painter Mark Tobey, revealing an awareness of sickness festering under the healthy great American outdoors.

Thus, as suspense tale, "Twin Peaks," film and series, visualizes and sounds the language-composition theories of Poe. The TV episodes, like Blake's dense verses, bring to life through motion pictures a diseased world. Lynch creates a mood. Mood pervades his town, seen through the eyes of his observer. It is a poetic world with a definite point of view, if without any moral indictment. There is a crime to investigate, but it is the feel of this entire world, not merely a crime, which compels the audience. Lynch, like Blake, creates a lush universe of colors, textures, and sounds. "Twin Peaks" is, therefore, immediately recognized as a TV first. "It may be the most hauntingly original work ever done for American TV . . . . Its distinctiveness is almost purely a matter of style. The pace is slow and hypnotic, the atmosphere suffused with creepy foreboding, the emotions eerily heightened."[7] The television breakthrough, however, has roots in literary tradition—and in a celebrated film genre.

Once again Lynch creates in the American tradition of film noir. "Twin Peaks" uses the conventions of the genre in its production. References to film noir movies are recognizable throughout Lynch's TV work. This is true especially in the dark characterization, setting, and tone. It is also true in Lynch's asides and in jokes; Lynch borrows from movie history, even from movie trivia. For example, he uses the title of a 1944 Gene Tierney film.

But it is the scope of "Twin Peaks" that most conveys the feel of classic film noir. Lynch refuses to underestimate the audience's intelligence or to overemphasize the limitations of the small screen of television. "Twin Peaks" operates on television, the small screen, with the aesthetics, techniques, and conventions of the motion picture. This not only expands writing, producing, and filming techniques; it liberates artistic philosophy.

Thus critics recognize the potential world Lynch opens to television programming by bringing motion-picture conventions to the small screen. Critics praise the innovations of the television production. "Basically, it's this: 'Twin Peaks' goes beyond usual and customary television procedure—it's unafraid of utterly absurd characters, chilling screams and weird camera angles—to pack more into one episode than a whole night of normal television contains."[8] More important, critics appreciate the aesthetic potential for television in Lynch's film aesthetic. "It's as if Lynch didn't recognize any difference between the highest movie art and the lowest television craft" (Rafferty, April 1990, 86).

Therefore, Lynch selects conventions of film noir to achieve the feeling of film noir. His use of the smoldering dark lady in the series, for example, evokes film noir conventions and even film noir history. The characters recall both film noir women and classic film noir actors, specifically Mary Astor, Lauren Bacall, and Jane Greer. Audrey Horne smolders with sensuous possibilities. Donna Hayward hides a secret passion. Norma Jennings too has a past forbidden affair. Josie Packard hides a crime that her icy sister-in-law schemes to uncover. These women know things they'll lie to protect.

The male characters in "Twin Peaks" also come from film noir history. Andrew is the suspiciously missing older man with the young wife. Hank Jennings is the soon-to-be-released hard-luck loser doing his time in prison. Big Ed is the husband in love with another man's wife. Leo Johnson is the woman-beating punk. Ben Horne is the two-timing millionaire with ties to the mob. These men have dark passions they'll violently pursue.

The settings of the story have film noir models. Scenes in the police station, morgue, and roadhouse abound. As the story progresses, motor cycles and tractor trailers, FBI men and murderers are lost in the dark nights on bleak, unmarked roads. Characters are held captive in deserted mountain cabins and in abandoned train cars. A guarded brothel fronting a drug-running border operation looms across the Canadian frontier. The locations are dark and seedy film noir settings. And they, like the characters, evoke a tone, the mood of film noir.

David Lynch sees the idea of setting "Twin Peaks" out there in the ominous Washington woods as essential to the film. "What is it about the ambience of that town and the dark firs looming in the deep wood carvings that lends itself to this time, this mystery and this sense of doubleness about all the characters? Just picture this kind of darkness and this wind going through these needles of the Douglas firs and you start getting a little bit of a mood coming along. And if you hear footsteps and you see a little in the window and you start moving toward it, little by little you're sucked in. And a mood, this fantastic mood and a sense of place comes along, and hopefully you like to go back and feel this each week."[9]

An example of using characterization and setting to conjure up film noir and film noir movies is the diner in "Twin Peaks," the Double R. Here waitresses and truck drivers converse in hard-boiled jargon. Food and decor are plain and neon-lighted in a world operating on its own hours and with its own language. The style becomes the reality. Gumshoes order "cups of Joe" from sultry waitresses. It's the B-movie hash house: Bob Mitchum flirts with Ida Lupino—the audience sees Bogey smile and hears Lizbeth Scott's sultry double entendre. Lynch invites the audience into the film noir, the movie of its mind.

"Twin Peaks" is both part of TV's tradition and a new direction in TV. Its significance to TV is its vision. Lynch's vision. But the series operates successfully as television. Television production schedules suit Lynch. Often a fast worker, Lynch conceives the show with Mark Frost in TV terms and with TV production demands in mind. He is aware of how television works. "The plot was written in only nine days and shot in 23, Lynch was apprehensive about the restrictions of TV . . ." (Zoglin, 97). Operating within these commercial considerations, Lynch's style, story, and filming methods come to TV, and the network gives Lynch's venture its support.

The first two-hour movie, written and directed by Lynch, captures a Sunday-night audience. From the opening shots of the beautiful Josie staring languidly, humming in her mirror, to the final fade of the mysterious Hank Jennings suggestively licking a domino during a cryptic telephone call, Lynch brings television to an unprecedented and unequaled high. Advance word and advertising are strong. The first show is an event, scheduled to attract a large audience. "ABC last week said it will air the two-hour premiere of the new series 'Twin Peaks' on Sunday, April 8, with 20 percent fewer commercials."[10] This reduction in advertising time makes the series more watchable and makes the story more approachable.

From the beginning the show is intended to reach a specific audience. "Twin Peaks" is geared to reach Lynch's movie audience on TV. "ABC executives never expected *Twin Peaks* to score with a mass audience. But they did hope its high artistry might recover a demographic group largely lost to network TV: Upscale young urbanites with large amounts of disposable income" (Horn 1990, 56).

However, not a man to put stock in send-up, Lynch fashions "Twin Peaks" in a specific television genre. It operates within the conventions of soap opera. The series is also a unique high watermark for television, sustaining its individuality and uncompromising standards throughout its first season. Lynch spins his tale so masterfully that any division in time, sense, or senselessness between the first episode and the following season seems academic. And, as confusing episode runs into confusing episode, real or remembered evil twins, amnesia victims, resuscitated bodies, and unresolved cliff-hangers are assimilated into this classic TV series. "Twin Peaks" does not include the ploys of soap opera; "Twin Peaks" understands TV and plays as soap opera.

The soap opera is an episodic structure which creates and continues a story of ever-expanding events. Complications intervene, leaving resolution until a next episode. Like an emotional rendering of yesteryear's movie adventure serials, this television genre has always been a daytime staple, including a Gothic daytime drama, "Dark Shadows." For over a decade before "Twin Peaks," soap operas like "Dallas," "Knot's Landing," and "Dynasty" have been regular prime-time programming as well.

Certain techniques and devices have determined the conventions of the form. Lynch, who spent time during his years in Philadelphia "keeping up with *Another World,*"[11] is familiar with these conventions. For example: "Backed by strains of emotional organ music from a TV soap, Big Ed cradles Nadine, who has been crushed by rejection. 'There are plenty of patent attorneys,' he tells his eye-patched wife. We just need to find one that understands drape-runners" (Storm, May 1990, 10). The scene attracts the viewer's attention, invites emotional involvement, and piques viewer curiosity. The subject matter, mysterious actions, unresolved incidents, acting technique, and music are from conventional television soap opera.

Meeting the demands of the television genre is seen by some critics as beneficial to Lynch. "*Twin Peaks,* subject to TV's constraints of decency and decorum, shows that Lynch can give his intuition subtler expression when he doesn't make use of shocking extremes."[12] Therefore, TV evidences some new techniques and alterations of others in Lynch's style. The experience working with these constraints expands Lynch's experience in directing, writing, acting, and producing.

Ratings are a reality of television, and the show is fashioned to maintain audience ratings. As with any other soap opera, this means stringing along the loyal viewers, holding the intermittent but frequent viewer, and attracting a new audience. Lynch and Frost intended to have an audience. "The series definitely doesn't insult anyone's intelligence," says Frost. "We have embedded clues for the careful viewer throughout—but it is also rewarding for the casual viewer."[13]

In fact, far from denying its television format, the TV show, like Lynch movies, revels in its genre. Conventions of television genres and TV history become a part of the series's fabric. Some of the characters evoke small-screen forerunners. Critics note that tying the program to TV is part of the experience. "Where is that one-armed man who's mentioned in the final credits? Didn't he die when Lt. Gerard shot him in *The Fugitive*?"[14] In fact, it is the use of the familiar that gives Lynch a point of reference for the show's unique departure from conventions. Thus, although the show operates within commercial concerns and conventions, its status as a classic is determined by its revolutionary difference. "Where so many—almost all—shows ignore the vision part of television, Lynch wallows in it" (Storm, April 1990, IL).

Lynch knows where television has been; Lynch understands where it is. But Lynch sees where it could be. Conscious of television's conventions, Lynch refuses to consider them as limitations. Whatever the ratings, "Twin Peaks" has an enormous audience. "Twin Peaks" is classic, one-of-a-kind television. Lynch gives his viewers a show unprecedented in potential. "He has proved that an eccentric artist can toil in American TV without compromising his vision, and in doing so he helped loose the bonds of the prime-time straitjacket" (Corliss 1990, 84).

Lynch's series amalgamates. Consequently, suspense, film noir, and television are molded; evil and good coexist; comedy and horror overlap; parody and reverence intermingle. Solving the murder of Laura Palmer is not really the issue of "Twin Peaks." A TV soap opera, "Invitation to Love," is intermittently televised in the show—the only programming shown other than news reports. Its inclusion further comments on the soap-opera reality viewed by an audience watching the show's characters-as-audience. Therefore, the plot, characters, setting, and tone are all classic Lynch. The story line includes characters in a plot and a mysterious subtext. A stalwart detective investigates the murder of a small-town beauty with the assistance of a local sheriff. But Laura Palmer is also promiscuous, cruel, and drug-addicted. The sheriff is having an affair with the mill owner's widow. The FBI agent hides a secret about his past. Clues are outnumbered by MacGuffins; in-jokes and film references toss the series between earnest horror and guessing game. The rustic town is good with an evil underbelly.

Laura's classmates include TV's most sultry trollop and Laura's cyclist boyfriend, who is really in love with her best friend. At the diner one waitress waiting for her husband's release from prison loves a gas-station owner married to a woman with an eye patch who works to invent new drape runners; another waitress has an affair with Laura's best friend's boyfriend, a sullen high-school son of an army savant, while her sadistic, drug-running husband is on the road. Citizens include a schizophrenic, a reclusive hothouse gardener, a rowdy group of Norwegians, and a woman who talks to a log she carries; dreams include dwarfs talking backward, owls, and giants. This is before the food critic, space aliens, or the caustic forensic expert arrive on the scene.

The peculiarity of the characters is continued in the suggestive casting, which includes Russ Tamblyn and Richard Beymer, who were both gang members in Hollywood's record Oscar-winning musical, *West Side Story*; Kyle MacLachlan, star of *Dune* and *Blue Velvet*; Eric De Ra, son of fifties star Aldo Ray; Jack Nance of *Eraserhead,* a Lynch-cast regular; Peggy Lipton of TV's "Mod Squad"; Jane Greer, star of the quintessential film noir *Out of the Past* (1947); and David Lynch as Gordon Cole, a character name from Billy Wilder's *Sunset Boulevard* (1950).

The series is distinctive in the images and sounds that give the settings mood and give the series tone. A prison cell cages howling youths, sawmill machinery choreographs the workdays, a whirling sock hides a bar of soap as a lethal weapon. Foghorns, winds, and cycle motors sound. A distinctive vocabulary is scored by a lush, sometimes ominous soundtrack. Visual and auditory are combined and juxtaposed. A school official makes the announcement of Laura Palmer's murder to a stunned student body as a screaming student is heard and seen through the windows fleeing hysterically.

Lynch's creation is, as is the case in his films, a world with visual and aural context. The inclusion of more comic and direct references to TV history and conventions is a stylistic addition. "Twin Peaks" operates as a network of sights and sounds playing with and against each other. Essentially Lynch has created for television his visual and auditory world. Because he does not water down his vision for television, he elevates TV conventions. A critic recognizes the grand scale of Lynch's vision for the small screen—less soap than opera. "Opera is a far more malleable term than ordinarily understood. It doesn't just mean stentorian onslaughts at the Met. It can mean any dramatic work in which music plays a vital role. This applies to 'Twin Peaks' as much as to 'Gotterdammerung,' and it helps explain the allures not only of Mr. Badalamenti's music but of David Lynch's brooding filmic visions of America as well." (Rockwell, 20).

"Twin Peaks" is American art. It deals with the American Dream. Poe's theories of death and melancholy intact, Lynch's suspense-tale power is enhanced by a swipe at American values, the security of the small town, and by an increasing exposure in the U.S. to violent crime. Violence is graphic and sometimes darkly comic. The story itself begins with the murder of an American icon, the prom queen. And, of course, because this is Lynch, oddities and hypocrisy are omnipresent. Some events are exactly as expected—others are surprising. Thus fear of both the known and the unknown pervades the town and the series. Lynch says, "There are certain things about it that deal with human nature that are going to strike human beings, and there are certain things about it that deal with human nature that are going to strike human beings, and there are certain things about it that are very American."[15]

The show works because it is so earnest and just as earnestly unimpressed with itself. Nothing that happens is a certainty. There is nothing that is not grisly, romantic, and self-aware. The suspense story is itself one of tangents, false starts, and mystery, keeping the audience consistently suspicious. Lynch uses conventions of the MacGuffin of Hitchcock and trades on explicit conventions of gothic literature, from Poe-like dead birds to messages hidden under a cadaver's fingernails, to keep the audience constantly emotionally involved. He anchors them with scenes of routine: high school, diners, and family dinners. He peppers everyday small-town life with everyday perversion: drug running, prostitution, domestic violence, and murder. Lynch's point of view and especially his constant sense of humor keep the series spinning and fresh. This distinctive originality obviously separates "Twin Peaks" from other programming as surely as it growingly disorients an audience that is accustomed to seeing television with few surprises and almost no demand for thinking. Lynch operates—as in his films—expecting the audience to contribute to the series.

Lynch further undermines the viewer's security with the myriad complications of the murky world of film noir. Lynch's series operates like film. An awareness of illusion spawned by the "dream factory" is assimilated into his filmmaking aesthetics and transferred to television expectations. Characters break down the "fourth wall" convention. This is a film world. Lynch is again film conscious. Episodes employ cliff-hangers but delete their resolution. Pets are named for movie models, so are characters, so is the show. Sets are made to look like sets and backdrops; the show consciously recalls filmed predecessors.

Most significant, soap opera is a genre of disbelief: ratings resurrect characters when no medical or mystical rationale is otherwise possible; casting determines forgotten grown children suddenly found; years pass unequally for different family members aging on their own clocks. The audience recognizes the incidents as non sequiturs of the genre. "The thing that particularly attracts them about 'Twin Peaks' is its unfathomability. Are the spooky doings here a put-on of soap opera or a put-down of small-town America? Are the inhabitants caricatures, or are they—pardon me, Diane—embodiments of the darker impulses of the America psyche? Wasn't it Dr. Johnson who said a person could write such stuff forever if he would give his mind to it? Please check that out. I say it's huckleberry pie, and I say the hell with it."[16]

Film is conscious of conventions and history. Current cinema revels in film's two-dimensional artificiality and glorious theatricality. Peter Greenaway's *The Cook, the Thief, His Wife and Her Lover* (1989) not only uses gigantic sliding doors and moves from scene to scene along the horizontal, but begins and ends with the filmed parting of theater curtains. Greenaway's costume designer is the same man who has made lingerie a fashion statement of the time.

Recognizing the inherent artificiality of the everyday as well as recognizing the pragmatic need for theatricality has become part of [illegible]
Thus contemporary film, on the big screen, has an aura—a postr

ernist "look." It has the look of our contemporary reality. And why not? Film operates in spaces, blocks not unlike today's decor. It employs every up-to-the-minute camera technique in its post-cinema-studies Kodak school of brilliant colors. Consequently, the realization of the duality of dress and costume and content and presentation in the movies has resulted in its inclusion in our culture. And this contemporary perspective is further reinforced through prompting its self-generating inclusion again in our movies, continuing the cycle.

Film in theatrical release is also devoted to game playing. Part Nintendo fetish, part twenty-first century cinematic aesthetic, films invite active audience participation. The contemporary audience works computers and has survived the Cold War. It stands in line costumed to call back lines to *Rocky Horror Picture Show* committed to memory from frequent viewings. This is the audience for Lynch films; this is the audience Lynch films have helped create. Thus, by recalling collective motion-picture heritage, Lynch generates an emerging twenty-first-century point of view. This is also Lynch's television audience. And so around the water coolers the next day people buzz with discussion, imitation, and laughter as the audience pieces together the hints, in jokes, and nuances of last night's "Twin Peaks."

Consequently, Lynch's sense of humor invades the American mainstream: television creates and finds the audience. Lynch's sense of humor feels the pulse of his times. It is a reverence with a knowing touch of ridicule. Along with numerous theories speculating on Laura's murderer, critics include frequent lists of series jokes in the papers: "The Horne brothers plot fraud while one eats ice cream. 'Needs more pecans,' he tells his sibling. The Hornes' first names are Ben and Jerry . . . 'These are fresh,' says a law-enforcement officer at the scene of a crime. Has he just discovered a set of freshly minted fingerprints? Nah. A new batch of doughnuts has just arrived. He's talking crullers, not crooks" (Storm, May 1990, 10D).

Adding television conventions to the experience is a masterstroke. Television is the communication medium par excellence. This hypnotic member of the family resides in most homes, sometimes several sets per household. The audience knows what it expects and doesn't expect from television. And Lynch plays and doesn't play the expectations for all they're worth. He adapts his film aesthetic to television.

His humor is particularly appropriate to television and to the audience that grew up in TV's inescapable web. Television provides a cultural common denominator as literary and art canons fall victim to cultural illiteracy. Old television is also a safe, recognizable basis for humor. Television programming prompts almost endless trivia questions. Bittersweet twenty-year reunions televise aging TV casts. Sitcoms in continuous syndication reach enormous audiences. Poor television programming becomes the object of nostalgia, treasured as childhood memory, and thus plays comfortably on the screen. In Chicago, lines of people wait to see staged scripts of "The Brady Bunch" to relive the episodes. TV conventions and Lynch's knowing evocation of them, sometimes humorous, other times nostalgic, make television his terrain and put "Twin Peaks" on the map.

"Twin Peaks" is concerned with reality, absurdity, and surrealism. The circular convolutions of these three perspectives, the ultimate merging of the three, are Lynch's vision. The connection is recognized in the massive amount of critical and popular response to the series. "Perhaps the show's appeal lies in its unprecedented similarity to real life. Think about it: what else but life is as absurd as "Twin Peaks"? And where else but in real life can you get such good cherry pie?" (Leershen, 59).

Reality and absurdity? Lynch's sources, facts of history and geography, suggest the ridiculous possibilities in reality. For example, the waterfall shown in the opening credits is Snoqualmie Falls. Surprisingly, Snoqualmie Falls reaches 268 feet, 100 feet higher than its more famous rival, Niagara Falls. The location, with the lodge and the Puget Power generating plant built in 1898, is a real place. "Indian tradition has it, that years ago the Yakimas came over the mountains with the intention of annihilating the coastal Indian nation. Chief Seattle set up a powwow and was to meet the eastern Indians somewhere above the falls and convey them to a potlatch by canoe. They came down the river singing their war chants totally unaware of the existence of the Snoqualmie Falls. When they reached this rock, Chief Seattle in the lead jumped out on it, saved himself, but his enemies were swept over the falls and plunged to their deaths."[17]

Other tragedies occurred near the falls before Laura Palmer's murder. For example, "In 1890 Charlie Anderson made a parachute jump into the canyon of Snoqualmie Falls . . . He used a fictitious name so that his parents would not hear about it . . . When he jumped, the chute opened and an air current drove him straight towards the falls." The local historical record continues with finding Charlie at the bottom. "He was still alive and his mouth contained his shattered teeth. They held the train up in order to get him to a doctor in Seattle.

Charlie died that night and his mother and father found out later in the evening that it was their son that all the fuss had been made over." (Evans, 4).

The details of geography and history contain the absurdity of a publicity release for the show, plot incidents, or one of Dale Cooper's dreams. Lynch sees more than simple facts. North Bend and Snoqualmie are real towns, but his town is the best and worst of all towns in reality. Lynch sees the nuances, the interpretations, and the contradictions. His world, like twentieth-century plastic art, shows reality simultaneously from front, back, both profiles.

Television as a medium contains this same real and absurd potential. TV enjoys familiarity as part of daily life. Most of the fact (news shows and documentaries make viewers immediate members of the global community) and most of the fiction (consider the average TV viewing time of Americans) of U.S. life come through the television screen. Television has ingress to American homes that the cinema does not. Once the silver screen's biggest competition, ironically, videotape now makes television of major significance even to the film experience. Still, this most powerful communication tool is frequently found to be inane, "the boob tube." Television is live coverage of a political coup on the other side of the world and a bargain bonanza on home shopping.

The television programming of "Twin Peaks" strengthens the real/absurd/really absurd continuum. Intruding commercials force another brand of film fiction/reality into the reality of "Twin Peaks." And, of course, there is the pacing of the TV soap opera. Only life provides the audience more time to see unresolved incidents unravel. The series ambles along absurdly week after week, evoking the real absurdity—life. "David Lynch is fond of pointing out that people don't expect life to make sense, yet they demand that TV shows do" (Gary Thompson, 33).

Depicting the absurdity of life in art—a moose head on a table, a sheriff named Harry S. Truman, a fish in a percolator—must still have structure. The images have been selected and ordered. Thus, an audience seeks narrative explanation for the absurd: a family's pathetically saccharine sing-along, interrupted by a visiting father's hearty rendition of a ditty, must really mask Leland's anguished mourning for his daughter. In the tale of detection, musings get more complicated: the audience keeps looking for a reason that Donna's mother is in a wheelchair, it waits for the oft-mentioned Diane to appear, it

Snoqualmie Falls. Photo courtesy of the author.

The setting for "Twin Peaks" is small-town America. North Bend and Snoqualmie are real towns. Photo courtesy of the author.

listens for the roar of Leo's truck's engine on a deserted mountain road. Still more complications are sought in a series that owes its origin to David Lynch. Lynch uses his visual and aural context and his notorious movie mania to embellish the events with still other meanings: the plastic that wraps Laura's dead body is recalled in the plastic-lined walls of Leo's cabin, a scene suggests Mount Rushmore, then *North by Northwest*. "A beautiful bird soars gracefully in the distance. As the camera closes in, we see it's really a frightening, scruffy raven. The camera focuses closer on the bird's eye. Taught in the first episode that clues can be reflected in the light of an eye, we strain to see what's there. The bird just blinks, and we can imagine Lynch and Frost saying, 'Gottcha' . . . Drape-runners, drug-runners. One-eyed Jacks. One-eyed Nadine . . . There's got to be a connection" (Storm, May 1990, 10D). Here is an arena in which Lynch is undisputed master.

"Twin Peaks" is in the world of surrealism. Working with Frost to conceive and produce the series throughout the episodes, Lynch is master here of a tremendously sophisticated surreal dream/reality vision. "His work often brings to mind the European surrealists Buñuel and Cocteau, but in person he is wholesomely American" (Woodward, 20). It is the grafting of this intellectual European art movement on television, that most American of institutions, that makes "Twin Peaks" powerful and unique. Thus it is Lynch's vision and his role as visionary that transports "Twin Peaks" into a realm of classic TV. The series is about and of television. If not historically the first television program to build on this self-awareness, it is easily the most far reaching. Its influences then on television and television audiences are irrevocable.

The early surrealists found that life was continually nonsensical. They drew from life and from pieces of art in a hat. They were attracted to the serial, which maintained reality in spurts. They appreciated its exaltation of parts dominating the whole.

The world Lynch sees is well served by television. Rather than inhibiting him, television as a medium suits Lynch's vision of "Twin Peaks." The small screen is a striking reminder of his painterly perspective. A canvas is a small, static area on which to work—yet the painter has made it and its tension with reality his world. And David Lynch is a filmmaker who is a painter.

Critics recognize the surreal aspects of Lynch's television soap opera. Once again he is paired with early great surrealist Buñuel. The comparison here, moreover, suggests how appropriate the American TV genre of "Twin Peaks" is to surrealist expression. "Works like Buñuel's and Lynch's derive their force—even their narrative force—from the swift movement of the artist's mind, a strong current of ideas and imaginative energy. Lynch sets us drifting through a vivid dream of American life, and wakes us, two hours later, with the message that all dreams (and all soap operas) imply: To Be Continued" (Rafferty, April 1990, 87).

Finally, the series is definitive Lynch because it deals with abstraction. In fact, where Lynch has been using sight or sound to abstract through sensory images, "Twin Peaks" goes one step further. Critic J. Knipfel sees it this way: "Since his debut with *Eraserhead* in 1978, each of Lynch's successive films has dealt, in more and more complex terms, with some basic physical sensation. *Eraserhead* was about noise (the severed ear which opens *Blue Velvet* would've been a much more appropriate icon for Henry. The ear, having been severed from its connection to the brain, no longer had the ability to discern specific noises, capable only of letting the whole whitewash pass through it). *Dune* was about thought (and maybe that's why people didn't get it). *Blue Velvet* was about depth perception. And now *Twin Peaks* is about light—specifically, color and reflection."[18]

Whether the ear is a better device for one film or another or whether each of the categories is well made or exclusive is not the point. The point is that the sense image takes the audience into the world of process. Lynch, as discussed in the previous chapters, deals with the process of perception throughout his films. In Lynch movies it is not what Jeffrey hears, Henry sees, Paul Atreides believes, but rather how they watch, listen, and think—that they watch, listen, and think—that is Lynch's world. He is a consumate technician: he employs visual composition, sound effects, music, camera angles, dialogue, casting, set design, props, costuming, and more to create his film in an artistic context. His vision is the subjective—the infinitely changing worlds, not of what is to be experienced, not even of how it is experienced, but rather *that* it is experienced.

The severed head in *Eraserhead* takes the audience into Henry Spencer's thinking process and into his mind. The head is obviously more than just a symbol of thought. However, a head must be a symbol of thinking. It must be recognized on that level; it is where the audience thinks. Lynch continues technical reinforcement with the camera to focus and compose his scenes as the vision of his subjective world. He uses form (techniques) as his content (subjectivity of his world as film).

In "Twin Peaks" the log is farther removed from any sensory connotation. It becomes a far less recognizable symbol and nearer the abstraction. TV episodes will give Lynch a new freedom to further fragment a narrative line. Therefore, creating visual and aural rather than merely a narrative context continues. And the complications of a subjective world will expand in the series.

His artistry explains the critical accolades lavished on the first TV installment. Lynch uncovers an unexplored potential of television. Because of his style the first episode succeeds in itself. "Even with the narrative unfinished, these first two hours are thoroughly satisfying," says the *New Yorker* in an uncustomary review of television programming (Rafferty, April 1990, 87). Because of Lynch's style, "Twin Peaks" becomes a cultural phenomenon.

The show is a sensation. Ratings are enormous. "Twin Peaks" hits a popular nerve. Lynch knows how to get an audience, and "in addition to its confounding plot line, the series plays like a pop-culture Hall of Fame, resonating against everything from *The Fugitive*'s one-armed man to Tibetan asceticism to the namesake 1944 thriller that starred Gene Tierney."[19] The jargon catches on, the lingo, the casting, the hints. Books, tapes, and quizzes follow. Itineraries are printed for touring Twin Peaks. There is rumor of coffee labels and promotional mugs. The killer of Laura Palmer becomes a topic for TV talk shows, magazines, newspapers, and everyone's office. Cartoons appear, parodies on other shows, and inevitably all sorts of imitations.

The series is renewed after its first season in the States. It begins in Europe with the same gusto. "The opening 90-minute pilot attracted 8.15 million viewers in the first week, one of BBC-2's largest audiences ever. How the second episode did isn't known yet, but some London households have begun to keep Tuesday evenings free, if that's any indication. Broadcast time is 9 P.M., with a repeat late Saturday night."[20] At the end of its first season, "Twin Peaks" is, against all television odds, riding high.

Lynch creates a critical and popular bonanza. "The critics loved it. So did TV viewers. But would the TV industry buy 'Twin Peaks'? By awarding it 14 Emmy nominations—more than any other show this year—those who work in television answered with a resounding 'yes' Thursday. But it's too early to say whether this murder mystery–

"Funky Winkerbean" watches "Twin Peaks." Reprinted with special permission of North America Syndicate. © King Features (North America Syndicate).

soap opera–black comedy from director David Lynch will win on Emmy night Sept. 16 . . . Will 'Twin Peaks' win? That could be the biggest TV question since, well, 'Who killed Laura Palmer?' "[21]

"Twin Peaks" is canceled during its second season. Thus both TV questions are quickly resolved. First, in a narrative stroke that disappoints some of the audience, Laura Palmer's murderer is revealed. The hype that focused on solving the murder, the necessity for immediate television gratification, and the minute attention span of the audience are simultaneously the murderers of the series. Second, the televised Emmy Award night comes and goes. "It wasn't just that we lost." says Lynch, "but that we lost so spectacularly. As the evening wore on, I began thinking of the event as a sort of Theater of the Absurd. I couldn't get upset about not winning, because the concept of absurdity is something I'm attracted to."[22] These answers are a palimpsest revealing a third, more important, question: what does "Twin Peaks" mean to filmmaking and to David Lynch, the filmmaker?

"I have a soft spot for secret passageways, bookshelves that open onto silence, staircases that go down into a void, and hidden safes. I even have one myself, but I won't tell you where . . . At the other end of the spectrum are statistics, which I hate with all my heart . . . On the other hand, I'm very fond of snakes and rats," writes legendary director Luis Buñuel in his autobiography.[23] His aesthetics and surrealistic techniques seem applicable to Lynch's TV effort. When Laura Palmer's murderer was finally revealed, the concern for unraveling the crime was obviously not the heart of "Twin Peaks." Not only had Lynch carried television to a new level—he had guaranteed that possibility for television programming from his series forward. Because of the barrage of publicity, the attempts of the audience to reduce the series to hourly episodes with pat resolutions, and Lynch's tendency to push his postmodern aesthetic too far, early high ratings soon faded. Of course, the same season Michele, a tiny, saccharine tot with the largest vocabulary in her extended TV family, earned TV's highest rating on the extremely popular "Full House." But to lampoon the couch potato is too simplistic.

Art is not synonymous with popular audience reception. This is the case with literature, the plastic arts, music, and architecture. So too with cinema: jeering and stone throwing broke out in the first Paris audiences of Buñuel's films. But "Twin Peaks" opened doors. And some critics and some members of the audience—considering the size of television's audience, a great number of people—witnessed and appreciated that freedom. And the scene revealing Laura Palmer's murderer illustrates the achievements of the series in spite of ratings. Agent Dale Cooper sits in the roadhouse listening to Julie Cruise and her rendition of a haunting Lynch/Badalamenti song. Shots cut to the ominous traffic light and the wind-scored, deserted streets of the town drowning in night's darkness.

Cooper sees a giant on stage who moans, "It is happening again." Leland sees the grotesque Bob in his mirror and adjusts his plastic gloves. His wife collapses in her living room. A white stallion appears. Leland chokes Madeline with a blatant violence continuing without the respite of an expected TV cut in the jumpy, spinning sequence. Finally, he crashes her head into the glass of a framed poster of Missoula on his living-room wall.

The killer is revealed—now here come the questions in the answer: Is the dancing, show-tune-singing father hilarious or harrowing? Was Leland's white hair more Bob-like than first noticed? The giant is recognizable, but what's the horse? Is Mrs. Palmer dead, why did she faint, did she see the crime? Isn't Lynch from Missoula, Montana? And they go on. They extend far enough to include, did what just happened on the screen really happen?

The multiplicity of levels in this scene in "Twin Peaks" indicates the show's contributions to television. First, Lynch recognized that television could convey more than simple narrative lines. Lynch also raises the technical level of TV: the cinematography is splendid, the sound is exceptional, the editing is chilling, and the score is full-bodied and memorable.

Lynch has put his brand on TV. He has stretched again, this time from film to television. He continues that expansion regardless of critical bouquets garnered or awards lost, regardless of cancellation or glorification of the series. Unlike Andy Warhol, who also moved from plastic art into the world of film, Lynch must not falter into creating art not *from* but simply *of* his world. Warhol electrified pop art with his Day Glo paintings. Yet Warhol is more celebrated for his lifestyle. His classic statement about the fleeting moment that constitutes contemporary fame, that simultaneous media hype and overkill, telescopes our times, reaffirming Warhol's savvy, if it is uncomfortably applicable to his own fame. After his death, an auction of his effects demanded attention and enormous bids, even for his personal collection of cookie jars both campy and chic. Warhol's posthumously published diaries were also a sensation—glorifying and decimating forever the "artsy" circle in and on which he lived.

David Lynch's artistic creations include Lynch himself. He continues beyond precedent to display, to satirize, and to expand his contemporary aesthetic. Somewhere, of course, a line may be crossed and his balance knocked off center. Here, over the border, the artist wakes up to be merely an icon. This is the quagmire of twentieth-century celebrity. The significance of "Twin Peaks" may be obvious today, but the series's place in the context of Lynch's work—and its meaning for art tomorrow—remains open to speculation.

6

Lynch on the Road—*Wild at Heart*

> This has been the most complicated century in human history. I believe next century will be happier.
>
> —Dalai Lama

Lynch's next film meets with a wide range of critical responses. "Lynch's kinky fairy tale is a triumph of startling images and comic invention . . . Creating a bonfire of a movie that confirms his reputation as the most exciting and innovative filmmaker of his generation."[1] Seen by some critics as a savior, Lynch is seen by others as a celebrated charlatan. "*Wild at Heart* is a cul-de-sac of a road movie in which nothing leads anywhere or makes the barest minimum of sense."[2] Reception seems to vary depending on what side of the theater aisle one sits on. Thus, like its prize for best film at Cannes, *Wild at Heart* meets with the jeers and accolades which consistently, if contradictorily, greet Lynch's work.

When *Wild at Heart* opens in August 1990, it is Lynch's world, Lynch's year. An unresolved season finale has left TV viewers wondering about "Twin Peaks." Lynch has been a story, most often the cover story, in news, film, fashion, even decorating magazines during the preceding months. He has been featured in newspapers from *Soap Opera Digest* to the *New York Times*. A documentary about his filmmaking has been nationally screened at selected theaters. His new feature film, winner of the Palme d'Or, is launched in general release in the heat of the summer, traditionally the big-time/small-brained movie season.

The work of a young director (David Lynch has only four previous feature films to his name and is in his forties) is at a popular pinnacle seemingly impossible to duplicate, much less to surpass. Regardless of the critical abuse the film sometimes takes, Lynch's status as a director seems to be now firmly established. "David Lynch's *Wild at Heart* recalls something a friend said 20 years ago as we crawled out of Ken Russell's *The Music Lovers*. Something about how an ordinary bad movie can't match the whoppers we sometimes get from filmmakers who actually have talent."[3]

Of course, there is a lifetime of a career yet to unfold. But Lynch's tremendous early fame has made him an identifiable film stylist. His dual perspective, film consciousness, network of auditory and visual images, and sense of humor are eminently recognizable to his audience. But in this post-Warhol-generation America, celebrity comes big, hard, and deadly. The crowds that filled New York's Waverly Theater for the record-breaking nine months of *Eraserhead*'s initial run are a far different group than the first-day audiences at multi-theater shopping-mall complexes across the country. This larger, new audience is a different one to please.

Lynch attempts a cinematic hat trick—expanding his audience to incorporate the "see the movie, buy a snack, hit the parking lot" crowd of filmgoers without losing his audience from the midnight movies. Lynch more overtly includes romanticism, graphic violence, and comedy than in his previous films. Some members of the mixed audience judge Lynch's film successful. It stands to reason, though, that the amalgamation of expectations and Lynch's distinctive aesthetic philosophy mean *Wild at Heart* also disappoints members of either audience constituency.

No other filmmaker better blurs the distinction between film's necessary business considerations and film's artistic ability to fly. Suddenly a "serious" movie is playing down the street, not for a limited week's run in a gentrified urban theater near some college campus. Woody Allen had begun to lure this audience with his sophisticated comedies. But now the commercial audience is watching an avant-garde filmmaker at work. Regardless of audience response, Lynch's films become an artistic option to an audience that was previously labeled incapable of ever appreciating Buñuel's films—that is, if it would even see them.

And his isn't the evangelizing mission of an elitist. Lynch makes the transition through television. He goes where Palme d'Or winners previously feared to tread, surviving where even a Steven Spielberg series has faltered. Lynch has not lost his standing as a serious filmmaker to the "small screen." He has recognized the potential of using TV conventions to expand a medium of almost infinite possibilities, if heretofore with a slow track record in innovations. As did Alfred Hitchcock, Lynch succeeds in popularizing his work through television.

Lynch has also recognized the potential of the film audience to understand more than conventional film fare. *Wild at Heart* gives the audience an option; Lynch's option extends film's possibilities as an art form. "In the wider context, the whole phenomenon of the man and his mind bursting into the mainstream is worth watching. What he is doing is simple enough, but wildly at odds with the demands of the forms of big budget movies or primetime soaps."[4] Lynch seeks a whole new audience for twentieth-century film art.

As with other *auteurs,* Lynch has a definite sphere in which he is seen to operate. The midnight-movie maker turned general release is now saddled with a giant reputation: he makes "David Lynch films." His celebrity is inescapable. If Lynch makes a film like his previous works, he is offering another "David Lynch film." If Lynch makes a film completely different than any other he has ever made, he is seen as making a film nothing like a "David Lynch film." So in *Wild at Heart* Lynch is called to task both for straying from and staying with familiar material. For example, in yesteryear's slang, *Wild at Heart*'s comedy is seen as "just not his bag," while *Wild at Heart*'s violence is seen to be pulled from his "old bag of tricks."

But, far more important, audiences view *Wild at Heart* with expanded critical expectations. One can expect anything from his movies, goes the thinking, because they are "David Lynch films," operating beyond film's previous limitations. The breadth of his reputation in breaking new ground gives Lynch's new film both a prestigious critical award and TV recognizability at the box office.

His success on both levels is scrutinized. But his works' common denominator is the extremes of critical and popular reception. So it is in response to *Wild at Heart.* As Lynch is considered outrageous, he uses his reputation, recently embellished through his TV series, to extend the range of possibilities in his film. Free to break down, even annihilate, some of the barriers of film conventions, Lynch next turns around and invokes other movie conventions in *Wild at Heart,* employing them to his advantage.

Nonetheless, Lynch now operates straddling both avant-garde and commercial worlds. He puts the double ingress to productive use as a film innovator. He extends the province of film through his multiple interests and lack of bias. He challenges the audience to appreciate the extension.

Another component of *Wild at Heart*'s audience expectations relates to literature. Film conventionally adapts books, and there is a historical precedent for film to flounder in adapting literary sources. Anecdotes abound about 1940s producers attempting to solve adaptation problems by insisting that Washington Irving be hired to do his own film treatment or trying to do lunch with Robert Louis Stevenson.

The work of bringing a novel to the screen is hazardous; witness Lynch's difficulties in creating *Dune*. Films of works of fiction have a larger number of creator, critic, and audience biases to endure than original screenplays. Any book is an encumbrance to the filmmaker if the audience expects not to see a film—but the book—on the screen. With *Wild at Heart* Lynch again uses a novel as the basis of his film. Lynch, as director and screenplay writer, clearly sees cinematic possibilities in fiction. "'Movies are an incredible thing,' Lynch says. 'Because it's possible to say very abstract things with this medium and to give people feelings that are really thrilling and, you know, big feelings. It can be so magical. I'm always looking for the right kind of story to allow certain things that I think film can do to happen. That's one of the reasons I love *Wild at Heart*. It's got some kind of strange cinema going on in it. It feels different, it's a different way of telling a story'" (Campbell, 36).

In *Wild at Heart,* reputations have reversed audience expectations. No longer is an up-and-coming filmmaker approaching an underground classic of fiction; now it is David Lynch translating a book into a Lynch film. Additionally, he is not dealing with a cult classic of the page. And he is himself an icon.

This is adaptation reminiscent of Alfred Hitchcock's work with Daphne du Maurier or James Buchan. Hitchcock's choice of film adaptations suggests leaving a great novel where it works best—as a great novel—while bringing to film novels that work as great films. And *Wild at Heart* is a genre film—a road picture. Thus Lynch makes his film vision of a book; it does not not bring the novel to the screen. The confidence shows. And it's to his film's advantage.

Worth the price of admission is taking the trip with Lynch on the open road. The story of characters in passage was not invented in the last hundred years by the motion-picture camera. It roots in our earliest literature. Travelers' adventures have been part of fiction since

Homer's epic poetry. Odysseus faced sirens, a cyclops, sea storms, and a swine-oriented femme fatale before he found the road back home. Huck Finn was initiated into society's cruelties at every stop along the Mississippi in Twain's American classic. Kerouac penned the Beat Generation's travels across America. Lula Pace and Sailor Ripley are also literary characters on a journey in Barry Gifford's novel.

Yet when Lula and Sailor come to the screen, it is the tradition of the road film, not the heritage of literature, which is the forerunner. From early motion-picture history, some road pictures have historical or literary sources, others originate on the screen. But road films have developed conventions as a film genre in their own right. Many have achieved classic movie stature. In *Wild at Heart* Lynch once again exhibits his film consciousness.

A road film presents a rite of passage resolved through a journey. In 1934, Frank Capra's depression-era comedy *It Happened One Night* follows Peter (Clark Gable), an out-of-work reporter, and Ellie (Claudette Colbert), a runaway heiress, on their open-road adventures. The couple fights the lack of cash, hitchhiking delays, and traffic accidents, strange characters, including an operatic driver with Lynch film possibilities, and other impediments. The lovers are even exposed to sexual temptation, but corruption remains conversational in an exchange of witty double entendres. Thirties propriety is respected. Peter and Ellie continue on the highway, riding out the potholes of the depression, and realize their love.

As a result of the 1940s call to World War II and its aftermath, much of the audience was "on the road" or adjusting to or from being "on the road" during the war. Bing Crosby and Bob Hope took to the road on screen. Their journeys too involve scrapes and near disasters in places beyond a familiar environment. The movie pair meets new characters, passes unfamiliar road signs, and becomes entangled in episodes that the audience expects them to escape because they have each other. On exotic back-lot sets suggesting foreign destinations, they are assaulted by mystery and intrigue, and head home wiser by the final fade.

The following decade, Hitchcock's Roger Thornhill (Cary Grant) and Eve Kendall (Eva Marie Saint) in *North by Northwest* (1959) lace road-film couples with a tinge of the criminal. This road film employs a chase within a chase. Thornhill is pretending to be a fictional character whom he is chasing across the country while being chased by spies who think he is the fictional character. Eve is a counterspy. By the end of the film, Roger and Eve, having survived a plethora of road mishaps, modes of transportation, and sexual innuendos—even a chase across the Mount Rushmore monument—toss aside the façades given them by their pasts and hop a train into a bright future together.

Stanley Donen's *Two for the Road* follows Mark (Albert Finney) and Joanna (Audrey Hepburn) traveling European roads. Recalling youthful episodes from their hitchhiking free-spirit days, they battle the ennui, social conventions, and love of money that encumber the glamorous European social season. They salvage their love despite financial success. The lovers here don't face the class distinctions of the depression or the cultural differences of a postwar world community. They are chased not by spies but by phantoms of their youth: their nemesis is "selling out." This road film's release date is 1967.

Although road-film couples already contain elements of both predator and prey, criminals on the road glitter in Arthur Penn's allegory *Bonnie and Clyde* (1967). The love of Bonnie Parker (Faye Dunaway) and Clyde Barrow (Warren Beatty) whitewashes their violent spree across the open country until a graphic, bloody shoot-out with the law in the sultry heat of a Texas back road exterminates them. The criminal element in rural America continues on two wheels; flower-child hero (Dennis Hopper) and conservative southerner (Jack Nicholson) make a motorcycle road trip in *Easy Rider* (1969). Here a foreboding surfaces that the sixties' rationale of balance in nature is flawed by the intolerance of human nature. In *Badlands* (1974) alienated lovers are romanticized on another mass-murder joyride through America's heartland. Later crime couples graduate into big business, international espionage, even cosmic crusades, becoming comic-book superheroes by the decade's end.

The postnuclear-age foes of *Mad Max* (1979) are added to road tradition. Mad Max (Mel Gibson) travels with an innocent child into the parched wasteland on after-the-holocaust roads. He searches for sources of energy and signs of humanity. The journey into the desolate future requires complicated special effects. As the series continues into the next decade, Max still acts with love and courage, two conventional elements in the road film, but props and gimmicks of futurism begin to weigh more heavily.

The road film's tradition continues into the eighties with *Raiders of the Lost Ark* (1981). Extravagant adventures carry Indiana Jones and his love interest around the globe chasing and being chased by Nazis. Special effects propel him to sequels. Nostalgia of the open road re-

Laura Dern is Lulu Pace Fortune and Nicolas Cage plays Sailor Ripley in *Wild at Heart*. Courtesy of the Museum of Modern Art/Film Stills Archives.

places romance; action plays a growing role in an adventure-film series evoking 1930s film serials. The *Raiders,* like the *Mad Max* series, uses the road as a device to carry action and adventure.

Jonathan Demme's fine film *Something Wild* (1986) returns more closely to the spirit of the earlier road films. In Demme, a conservative white-collar worker involves himself with a heroine perhaps more mad than madcap and finds himself on a spree down the New Jersey turnpike. The couple encounters violence, lives out fantasies, and changes identities along the road back home.

The road film, then, is a genre with history. Is there a place for Lynch's film in this tradition? Or has it all been done by now? On the contrary, it is the conventions of the genre that give Lynch's film its rich texture. Adding and deleting from conventions, Lynch's changes reflect his style and techniques as well as his times. Fundamentally, he accomplishes this by borrowing some elements from different types of road films, from the earliest talkies to the most recent productions. But he also redefines conventions of the route traveled. Lynch generates elements of the road film. Thus—as Lynch has a distinctive style as scenarist and director, defines a new itinerary, creates hybrid character types, and amalgamates film history—Lynch fashions a film unique in the genre, the 1990s road film.

In Capra's classic hotel-room scene, with the makeshift wall of Jericho protecting the couple from each other, the thirties couple is exposed to sexual temptation. Peter threatens to disrobe in their first shared motel room, filling Ellie in on the secrets of his toilette and exposing himself; however, he only undresses as far as to bare his chest. Peter and Ellie, falling in love, go to sleep in twin beds on opposite sides of the blanket wall—confident of the promise of the future. In Lynch, Lula is already in the double bed they share when Sailor returns after a night of heavy drinking and crime planning with Bobby Peru. Casually, the hirsute Sailor strips down to his underwear and climbs into bed as he confides in the pregnant Lula. Sailor is apprehensive about risking everything tomorrow, but he is determined—if off base—to support the woman he loves. The characters, really in love, go to sleep dreaming of the future. The explicit sexual relationship of Lula and Sailor is a far cry from the sparks of attraction between Ellie and Peter in Capra's road film. But are the couples actually so different?

Lynch's characters, unlike Hitchcock's couple, are already in love and sexually, almost constantly, active. So there is no need for brilliant double entendres, no Freudian pulling of anyone into an upper berth on a train rushing into a tunnel in the final fade. Cool blonde ice goddess, Eve Kendall is the antithesis of Dern's wanton sex kitten, Peanut. And Nicholas Cage may do a mean Presley, but based on his role as Sailor Ripley, he won't get a call-back for the Cary Grant ministries biodrama. However, are there more telling similarities between the couples? Hitchcock's sophisticates are running for their lives, stopping only for innuendo, intrigue, and brilliant dialogue. The youthful, exuberant Sailor and Lula also must just keep running; these lovers do stop only for music, food, or intercourse.

Neither is Lula the convent schoolgirl nor Sailor a preppie doing Europe. Unlike the 1960s *Two for the Road* couple, they don't look headed toward becoming jaded, jet-set types. Bobby Peru won't be dropping in to their Relais suites in the south of France to urinate. Lula's eatable necklaces and Sailor's black bikini underpants suit the 1990s couple, without any ties to the haute couture of Mark and

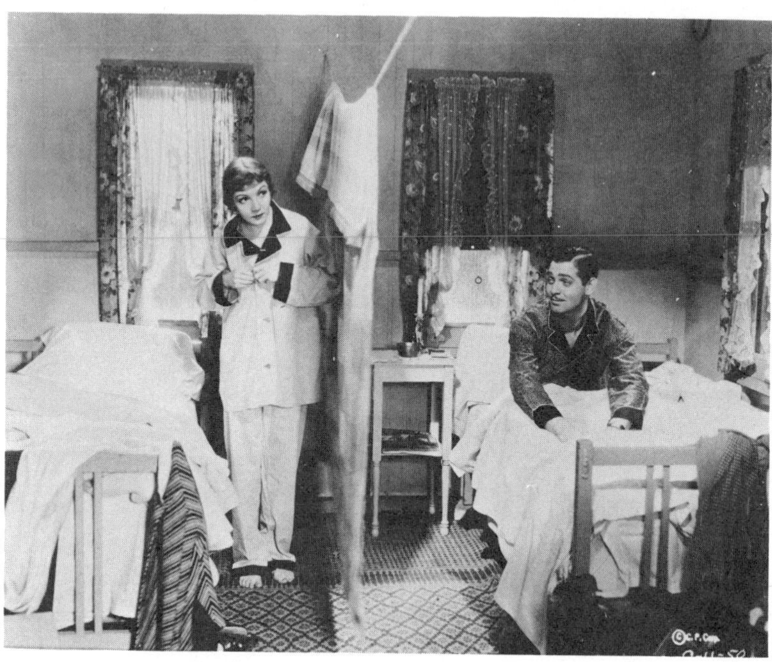

Claudette Colbert and Clark Gable separated by a sheet in Frank Capra's *It Happened One Night*. Courtesy of the Museum of Modern Art/Film Stills Archives.

Laura Dern is Lulu Pace Fortune and Nicolas Cage plays Sailor Ripley in *Wild at Heart*. Courtesy of the Museum of Modern Art/Film Stills Archives.

Joanna. Yet superficial differences mask similarities: Both films trace the struggles of lovers to maintain the passions of their youth. And both films romanticize love—especially commitment, family, and "the happily ever after."

Violence closely ties Lynch's couple to *Bonnie and Clyde*. Critical reception to Penn's film was as mixed as are reviews of Lynch's later works. In fact some of it seems appropriate to Sailor and Lula. "There are indeed a few moments where the gore goes too far," cautioned a critic of the sixties road trip. "And yet, precisely because *Bonnie and Clyde* combines these gratuitous crudities with scene after scene of dazzling artistry, precisely because it has the power both to enthrall and appall, it is an ideal laboratory for the study of violence, a subject in which we are all matriculating these days."[5]

But more important, Lynch alters the sixties couple: a depression Robin Hood and Maid Marian are nowhere to be found in his 1990 film. The qualities that lionize Bonnie and Clyde, elevating their road trip into an American fable, are annihilated. In an age of agoraphobia and cocooning, Lula and Sailor are concerned with themselves and only themselves. They generated no band of outcasts who bond together. Lynch's lovers neither seek nor gain the affection of growing hoards of the homeless who still wander the American landscape; no trip to a rustic Hooverville for Lynch. Sailor and Lula are lovers of the neoconservative generation.

Sailor and Lula's motel exploits satiate the longings of the previous couples on the road. Sailor and Lula are sex partners, but they are first in love. The affectionate companions depend on each other completely in an unfamiliar, hostile terrain, as did Hope and Crosby. Buddies have become lovers.

This is not a story that asks, Will boy get girl? This is a film in which the audience relies on the genuine bond between the man and woman. Lynch builds on that premise. "It's a love story where people start off being in love, which is kind of unusual. In a wild modern world, it's an indication of how it's cool to be in love. And Lula and Sailor have the perfect take on sex in the middle of a solid relationship. They are, like, so innocent and yet completely wild at the same time. It's like looking into the Garden of Eden before things went bad" (Campbell, 36).

Lynch's 1990s road film is more explicit than Capra's. His couple is more sexual than Bob and Bing. Gross and tasteless incidents bluntly separate them from Hitchcock's or Donen's sophisticated couples. But

Sailor and Lula are in many ways heirs of the earlier teams, if with Lynch's erotic twist. Lynch's sexy couple inherits comic sparks, a sense of danger, and rockbed loyalty. Mutual security in their union, romantic innocence, underlies the nineties couple's relationship, distinguishing them from the squalor and frenzy of their world. Actress Laura Dern recognizes Lynch's vision of the lovers. "The thing that is so great about Sailor and Lula is that it's sooo sexy because of the love. And that's the thing that's so beautiful about David. Here's this guy who's so weird and does things that are so terrifying to the psyche. And yet there's this purity in him and this belief in love that is almost cartoonlike and childlike."[6]

The openness of the 1990s in depicting sexual relations heightens the romanticism of Lynch's couple. Obviously different than their forerunners in explicit sexuality, these lovers actually evidence a more idealized, all-encompassing relationship. The relationship of Lula and Sailor is romantic: passionate, emotional, abiding, and wild. Lynch's lovers in the violent 1990s film even find a more upbeat, American Dream happy ending than those in previous road classics. In fact, Lynch's film is criticized for the excess of the film's happy ending. Friends, lovers, and parents, Peanut and her man wind up with a parole, a blonde, baby son, still-another eleventh-hour reprieve, an epiphany, and an Elvis Presley rock-musical Hollywood ending. Lynch insists that his film lovers have a happy ending.

As the century in America unravels, the American Dream as economic, political, social, and philosophic reality is seen facing annihilation. Lynch mourns the watershed of the American fifties, and his nineties road reflects this cultural fall from grace. *Wild at Heart* traces the country's spiral from a land of free-enterprise, new-frontier opportunity to a diminished new place in the world order and to domestic decadence. The unfulfilled promise—Go West, Young Man—of an earlier America is seen lost in hypocrisy, racism, revisionism, creeping censorship, witch-hunts, violence, neo-Puritanism, bureaucracy, and national mediocrity. The loosening center of the gyre abandons the last decade of the century in America's maelstrom.

The romantic streak of the ending then is essential to *Wild at Heart*. The exaggeration of the happiness Sailor and Lula find over the rainbow beckons to a disillusioned film audience that no longer sees the possibility that the nineties road leads to a resolution. This brutal indictment of the aimless society of turn-of-the-century U.S.A. fuels Lynch's flamboyant conclusion as the only kind of romantic closure his audience can buy. *Wild at Heart* is a road film for those who are romantic against all odds. Thus the film creates its virtual reality from fantasy. It validates the hyperbolic romanticism of the movies. David Lynch, questioned if he ultimately sold out to love and marriage as a balm for brutality, explains, "With the happy ending? No. It was even the reverse of that. I almost wanted to do a miserable ending just to show that I wasn't trying to be commercial. And that's wrong—doubly wrong. And so, like I said, it's got to feel honest, and if it does, that's what you have to do" (Breskin, 98).

His road film is unreservedly romantic. The lovers find infinite solace in a love that defeats all obstacles hampering their continued journey. In the thirties, classless love defeated economic distinctions of the Great Depression. In the 1960s, youthful love defeated aging and conformity. In Lynch's 1990s film, unexplained terror, self-defeat and abuse, absence of direction and depravity are annihilated by movie magic.

Lynch finds as much unfamiliar here as in previous road films; Hope and Crosby's roads from Singapore (1940) to Rio (1947) are no more foreign than the road to Big Tuna. But the changes in the 1990s itinerary are significant. First, unlike Crosby and Hope, Lula and Sailor never return safely home. These nomads are denied any home in a loveless landscape except in each other's arms. Thus Sailor and Lula have no safe geographical place from which to begin or to which to direct their journey. They must carry their home with them whenever they get back into bed together, no matter how seedy the motel, how transient the stop.

More important, Lynch denies the 1990s audience the comfort of distance. Lynch's landscape is neither the world of the international spy chased by a lethal crop duster nor the grandeur of the ancient Himalayas seen from Indiana Jones's nostalgic prop plane. The audience isn't shown how foreign things are on the other side of the world. There are no passports for Lynch's odyssey. The audience is not transported into a future devastated by environment changes from which they can still save themselves as they watch. The audience is accosted instead with the banality of their own environment. It travels without papers, using a map which defies rational explanation. It is today's brutal road that Sailor and Lula must navigate.

Lynch further diminishes the audience's comfort through redefining his foreign world. His world is America. But the states through which Sailor and Lula travel take the audience where no motor-club "triptik" routes a map. It is the frightening landscape just beyond the driver's window off the next turnpike cloverleaf that Lynch explores. "His eye for the absurd detail that thrusts a scene into shocking relief and his taste in risky, often grotesque material has made him, perhaps, Hollywood's most revered eccentric, sort of a psychopathic Norman Rockwell" (Woodward, 20). Lynch details the unknown lurking just around every unfamiliar corner. He shows the peculiar pervading every everyday contemporary scene. The lovers' itinerary is to cruise the bizarre along infinite interstates.

There is an adaptation of the chase-within-a-chase structure; the couple runs to and from—a chase within a chase—with only each other to trust. Like Hitchcock's Roger, Sailor neither knows his real crime nor can distinguish the good guys from the bad guys. Silver dollars dropping in mail slots on Reindeer's command and a sybil with bleached hair and stiletto heels controlling fate replace the international network of espionage stretching from the United Nations to a Dakota landing strip. And before the resolution, Sailor and Lula hang just as perilously on the edge of a precipice as Roger and Eve do.

But Lynch's chase expands to graft the imaginary onto an even more graphic narrative reality. This circular chase is witnessed by a photo of Lula's own treacherous mother. Marietta replaces the stone Mount Rushmore visages of the U.S. presidents and offers mute, uncaring testament to the nineties chase. Neither Eve nor Sailor can outrun the lies of their pasts. But while Roger is tricked by his metaphoric "fatherland," Lula is literally double-crossed by her mother. Sailor is chasing the limits of his parole while being chased by Farragut and Marrietta as Santos and the underworld pursue him. Sailor and Lula are running from threats of both physical and psychological violence. Reflective of Lynch's alteration, psychological baiting and emotional blackmail play a part in fueling the chase. In fact they are chasing and being chased by reality's limits: guilt, delusion, and dream.

Of course, further distinguishing the chases, Lynch shows whereas Hitchcock suggests. Graphic violence usurps suspense. Roger naively, calmly, almost comically, tries on suits from a Chicago hotel-room closet, not knowing he is beginning his chase. Sailor had set up his chase when he witnessed the incendiary crime, long before he commits violence in an exaggerated frenzy bordering on the comic in the opening shot of the film. Subtle gestures at art auctions carry another meaning for Thornhill. Beatings and maimings, vomit and rotten teeth are boldly featured in Sailor's brutal world.

Here is a film from a tradition that encompasses ballooning over India in *Around the World in 80 Days* (1956) and driving cross-country to Wallyworld with the cadaver of Aunt Edna in her rocker strapped to the station wagon's roof in *National Lampoon's Vacation* (1983). Lynch uses everyone from Fogg to Griswold to create his coterie of film types rooted in the dream and nightmare images of the motion-picture world. His bold techniques recall the rich tradition of the Hollywood road to illusion. Loyalty, love, and violence await the couple on the journey, juxtaposed with the fantastic brutality, comedy, romance, adventure, and fantasy of motion-picture history. *Wild at Heart* echoes the grandeur of the film epic while it approaches the bold, bright colors and gestures of the animated movie cartoon. Because of Lynch's film consciousness, his road film is not a remake, send-up, or merely this decade's phase in a tradition—*Wild at Heart* is a contemporary road film.

Borrowing from early road-film classics includes lifting more than a touch from Victor Fleming's universally recognized fantasy, *The Wizard of Oz* (1939). Dorothy travels from her restricted, black-and-white life in Kansas down the yellow brick road. She and some fellow travelers seek answers. Despite the misadventures of their technicolor journey through Oz, they finally defeat the witches and realize they have no need for a wizard's showmanship: the answers were always right in their own backyard. "*Wild At Heart* is *Blue Velvet* meets *The Wizard of Oz,* a surreal southern sortie into Lynchland. Lula, a vamped-up, punked-out Dorothy (down to the red shoes), and her Elvis-like ex-con boyfriend are on the run from Lula's weird, witchy mother, Marrietta, who has put her lover, gumshoe Johnnie Farragut (Harry Dean Stanton), on their trail. The couple cruises through the neon-lit hotels and speed-metal dives of the gothic South with a group of grotesques in hot pursuit. Willem Dafoe plays a demonic villain named Bobby Peru—even his teeth are bad. Isabella Rossellini is back as the evil dude's main squeeze, Perdita Durango, but this time she's a blond. And Crispin Glover plays Lula's bizarre cousin, who's got a but fetish that makes Kafka's Gregor Samsa look tame. It's a deeply deranged fairy tale" (Hoban, 89).

So many specific references are made throughout *Wild at Heart* to the classic that a critic suggests, "The myriad *Oz* references may be Lynch's attempt to lift his tale to a mythical level; instead they turn it into camp."[7] But the world of fantasy in the Oz journey incorporated by Lynch is fundamentally redefined in his road film. *Wild at Heart* is not simply Lynch's camp remake of the road-trip allegory. Sailor Ripley, albeit hairy, afraid to love, and not too bright, is no nineties lion, tin man, or scarecrow. Lula is not merely a sexually hyperactive Dorothy embodying a permissive nineties libido. This critical slant would reduce the film to nothing more than a campy remake of a remake of *Oz—The Wiz* but in punk neon and without the music.

If Lynch were that blatant, it would be extremely uncharacteristic. The director forces the audience to get the film's connection to *Oz,* not nudging with the blue-velvet gloves of suggestion but bludgeoning with a cinematic billy club. The occurrence of elements of fantasy from *The Wizard of Oz* is incontestable. In fact, Fleming's film is affectionately, almost reverentially, treated. Filmmaker Lynch is not a man drawn to camp as a point of view. Lynch reaffirms, "Camp is not only not creative, it is putting yourself above something else that has already been done and poking fun at it. To me that is a lower kind of humor" (Carlson, 22). *Wild at Heart* doesn't reuse *Oz*'s theme, but creates by building on familiarity with Fleming's film. The bridge is obvious, and is so to endow the *Oz* fantasy in Lynch with irony and the *Oz* irony in Lynch with fantasy.

As the world moved to war, Fleming offered his audience a promise that everything would work out. Happiness waited "right in your own backyard." That solace was the welcome product of the Hollywood dream factory. But the original audience are now grandparents who have made *The Wizard of Oz* a film classic. Lynch recognizes that his nineties audience grew up on *Oz* as film experience, screened and rescreened as holiday fare. Thus Lynch builds his nineties film by using his audience's familiarity with the classic Fleming road film and evoking movie connotations as a starting point. Images of *Oz* are not merely camp; they are the constant in Lynch's supersonically changing virtual reality. Lynch assumes that his audience knows the classic thirties film. Fleming's film is a given: prop, film device, common point of reference.

Lynch's 1990s road trip blatantly dismisses the distinctions between Fleming's black-and-white reality of Kansas and a technicolored world over the rainbow. *Wild at Heart* shimmers with nineties ambiguities like the illusion of a puddle ahead on hot asphalt pavement. Fantasy happens; reality is unbelievable. The lovers travel a dual world not from Kansas to Oz—but through Kansas and Oz, intermingled outside the speeding car's windows.

If the conclusion of the film, with the good witch (in the bubble) reigning and Marrietta, the wicked witch, defeated, is *Wild at Heart*'s message, Lynch has merely remade Fleming's film. That critical interpretation pigeonholes Lynch's film. But Lynch here again does not use film to preach a doctrine. He uses the *Oz* road conventions, but typically does not employ them to promote some message. Questioning the references to *Oz* as carrying Lynch's message, David Breskin asks, "At the end of the picture, the Good Witch in a bubble tells us repeatedly, 'Don't turn away from love.' Might one accuse David Lynch of going to Western Union to send a message?" Lynch answers, "No. That's the Good Witch talking" (Breskin, 98).

Sailor and Lula, in the tradition of the road genre, have been looking for answers in Victor Fleming's fantasy film, *The Wizard of Oz,* and *Wild at Heart*'s context in the road-film genre is important. "In *Wild at Heart*—as entertaining, bizarre, mesmerizing and occasionally stomach-churning a two hours at the movies as you are likely to encounter this year," writes a critic, "genre conventions whether included or deleted, play an important role. In fact the play on expectations and the distortion in the uses of the conventions is the basis of audience response to *Wild at Heart*" (Ryan, 5). The jolts in this film come not from a superficial intent to shock—although that is an element—but from the sabotage and arch subversion of our assumptions about genre movies and the world outside. The director's additions and alterations are as significant to the film's place in the road genre as are its adherence to that tradition.

Lynch typically combines eras in his road trip, crisscrossing styles and looks of different decades. But beyond his customary film consciousness and his eclectic use of grafted chronological settings, this film includes myriad film allusions. Critics debate the success of the grafting technique but not the existence of Lynch's fantastic allusions to other films. "Lynch fills his movie with cross-references to other movies besides his liberal use of quotations from *The Wizard of Oz*. The cumulative effect is to lull the viewer into a false sense of security that doubles the impact of the surprises and eerie turns" (Ryan, 5). Lynch makes his road film out of Hollywood's hundred-year cinematic movie trailer.

A recognition of Lynch's use of film reference, his film consciousness, is most important here: road travelers in *Wild at Heart* find their destination—their solution—in movie traditions. Lula and Sailor find their solution not in the cinematic conventions of the road film, specifically in the film fantasy of *Oz,* but in the conventional happy Hollywood musical ending. Thus music, love, and family security from the movies become their virtual reality after all. The fade-out's final fantasy embrace is screen and virtual reality.

Wild at Heart is both familiar and distinctive in its technical and artistic intensity. Lynch's film is a powerhouse of plot, images, sound, and pacing. The film ignites frenzy. Lynch's technical intensity highlights the charge of his dual perspective. But this film also illuminates Lynch at his most romantic. "Like 'Blue Velvet' and 'Twin Peaks,' 'Wild at Heart' deals with secrets, voyeurism, small-town evil, and the shadowy interface between sex and violence. Above all, though, Lynch's latest film is a paean to wildness, to following the dictates of your heart—whether it be a heart of darkness or of light."[8]

Lynch seeks a greater impact from the plot incidents of *Wild at Heart.* There is little argument that Lynch plots are ever models of subtlety. However, the plot now almost consistently incorporates acts of violence and passion. The film opens in Cape Fear, North Carolina, as Sailor bashes out the brains of a surly thug without his or the camera's flinching. The audience becomes a part of the narrative without being given any introductory exposition. In fact, the knowing looks of Marrietta and the altercation's immediate, frenzied presentation as the film's opening sequence compel the audience into the action, forcing them to move with the story if they hope to keep up.

Scenes are intense. In a flashback Lula's father staggers around the room on fire, igniting everything he comes near. Marrietta vomits into her toilet as she cosmetically bloodies her face with smeared lipstick in a scene reminiscent of the frustrated nun's toilette in Powell's *Black Narcissus* (1947). Impassioned dancing and anal sex fill the nights and days of Lula and Sailor. A holdup scene includes hayseed police, shotgun blasts, a severed body part, and a playful dog. Everyone is always on the run; and there is a porn movie being shot, a cockroach fetish, heads blown off, even dream sequences keeping the film moving.

The cinematography, again by Frederick Elmes, is graphic. Scenes are often shot in extreme close-up as are those of the lighted match that introduces scenes. Colors are vivid. The Texas landscape is shot in brilliant shades under the big, blue sky. Shots have the look of cartoons with their splashy color. If not consistently appreciated, the photography is always noted. "Lynch's gorgeously lurid style is superbly complemented by the photography of Frederick Elmes," raves *Rolling Stone* (Travers, 35). The *New York Times* review finds the composition of the photography and its subjects, in fact, unbalanced. "*Wild at Heart,* beautifully photographed by Mark Plummer, looks very modish. This time, though, Mr. Lynch's conceits are less often pleasurably disorienting than out of focus."[9]

Unlike "Twin Peaks," the immediately previous Lynch project, *Wild at Heart* is more hard hitting and feverish in each of its actions. But Lynch continues to include a great number of plot incidents, stringing together an almost relentless series of episodes, from Sailor Ripley's first violent crime to his final gang-fight-provoked musical number on a moving car's hood. Thus *Wild at Heart* is a dense, rich film in image and incident.

Lynch has an intuition about how to move movies along, and what he creates here is a cinematic missile. The film flashes. It appears that, once launched, no one—not the characters, not the audience, not even he—can stop it. He achieves intensity in no small degree by continuing to show actions as a barrage, without taking any film time to make them into message. "When he keeps his intuition under control, Lynch is funny, scary, and utterly riveting. His awareness of human queerness gives him acres of territory all to himself. His refusal to turn it into a statement means you can't outguess him. Even he seems not to know what happens next" (Sobran, 52).

The characters, like the plot actions, are intense in *Wild at Heart.* Marrietta Pace is a sexual, vengeful dynamo slithering in men's-room stalls. Cousin Dell is a gorgon of a Southern gentleman standing in his underwear and fondling roaches. Lula is relentlessly devoted to her passion for Sailor. The hirsute Sailor is a rock-and-roll poser par excellence. Customarily, Lynch characters are not shrinking violets, but none before these has spent so much time dancing, lovemaking, chasing, running, or smoking.

The image of striking a match is an epic exaggeration in sight and sound. Among an arsenal of spellbinding images, this one best conveys the tone of the film. As in Lynch's other excessive images, the superintensity of the flames conveys passion, while its exaggeration suggests humor. And Lynch repeats the image to heighten its intensity.

The audience has been warned by the cliché: do not play with matches or you'll get burned. The contradictory pleasure found in gazing into the magic of a fire mesmerizes on screen. Further, the image insinuates itself into the film on the narrative level. Lula and Sailor are chain-smokers, striking match upon match. Lula's dad, a victim of arson, was set aflame by the striking of matches. Symbolic and metaphoric suggestions of the image further intensify its uses in the film.

For example, scenes are introduced by an explosion of flame that engulfs the screen. The editing technique of focusing on the repeated striking of matches symbolically ignites and engulfs passions in the heat of torrid sex. This recognizable image sparks both film narrative and visual context. The metaphor of striking a match "to light up" the situation is visualized. In other words, the audience sees fire as a symbol of passion, and the explosion and smoldering of fire also look like passion exploding and seething on the screen.

Flames are used to bring each scene to light. They literally illuminate the feel of passion, whereas narrative events are presented as dark and murky interludes. Ignition visualizes that feelings, not events, are the film's reality, while suggesting the irony in the transitory power of passion's explosion. Thus flames illuminate the flammable, non-narrative context of Lynch's story.

Hot and burning is the image to follow. The film, in fact, always has the torrid rhythm of sex, the sweaty, intense wonder of youthful sexual frenzy—the bold, brash rapidly changing pictures of a world aroused. "Regarding sexuality, Lynch often draws upon his naughty adolescent urge, based more on lust or kink than romance. When Laura Dern, as Lula in *Wild at Heart,* flounces in the front seat of her boyfriend Sailor's T-Bird, dressed in a lacy teddy, you can almost hear Lynch coaching her: 'Ride that car as if you were having sex.'"[10] And the film looks and moves toward visual, sexual climax.

Lynch's films are musical. Badalamenti's lush scoring has become an expected treat in Lynch's films. The wildness of the title carries into the soundtrack as well. Although silences in Lynch again have their place, *Wild at Heart* is a rock-and-roll film. As in *Blue Velvet,* Lynch gives new connotations to pop hits, and the inclusion here of a haunting instrumental of Chris Isaak is no surprise. And in *Wild at Heart,* two Presley classics, already rock anthems, become both narrative and visual devices employed to keep the story moving.

The throbbing musical score is made obvious; the rock sound in the dialogue is as noteworthy. Lynch screenplays exhibit a fine ear for the spoken word—as it sounds to its speaker. Refreshingly, characters speak with a halting drama rare in casual speech or a combustion unreached in daily conversations. The lurid twang of Lula is constantly musical. Sailor manages to word the rock beat.

The language is lyrical, often drawling in southern rhythms and patterns. Dialogue borders on musical lyric. Characters often repeat colorful catch phrases like rock songs' pulsating refrains. In Sailor's mind, as he poses to "Rocking good news" rolling from his lips, he is the coolest, sexiest, hippest Elvis around. And Lynch sees and hears Sailor as Sailor looks and sounds to himself.

Dialogue, background noise, background music, and musical numbers commingle. The soundtrack propels the plot, giving *Wild at Heart* its wildness. Visual and auditory images create an intensity true to Lynch's world. "The structure emphasizes the Lynch method of composition: he assembles imagery around a plot and relies entirely on his own imaginative instincts to ensure they are 'right'" (Appleyard, 57).

What Lynch does is to combine aural and visual elements of his structure with the speed of their delivery. Most intensity in *Wild at Heart* is created by the pacing. Lynch is a master at presenting scenes before the camera at his own pace. If other Lynch films focus longer than expected on a pained face, if even *Wild at Heart* takes its sweet time lingering over vomit on a motel-room rug, it is the lightning speed of sights and sounds in the film that prevails in determining its intense feel.

The film gyrates, throbbing with its youthfully exuberant sexual rhythm. This rhythm drives the pace of most of the scenes. For example, Lula's frenzied thrashing of cotton balls on the motel-room bed is continued feverishly in the cut to the frantic dancing of Lula and Sailor on the crowded dance floor. The pacing is recognizable again in the shots of the convertible's hood swallowing the yellow lines of the highway as the lovers make their escape.

The tremendous range of the film, from the comic to the grotesque, includes scenes of the comically grotesque. Humor is an important element in Lynch; his sense of humor is most obvious in *Wild at Heart* of all his films. Its humor ranges from ribald to black, but the film's humor rests in the absurd. The intensity of the characters is often funny, as is the excess of their violence. Literal epigrams become screen images. Like "don't play with matches" or "lighting up the screen," "beating someone's brains out" becomes a visualized cliché. The film is often burlesque—exaggerating the already bizarre. "The movie is Lynch's try at comedy, if you can use that term to describe a movie with exploding heads, voodoo murder and auto fatalities" (Gary Thompson, 37).

There is cinematic precedent for this grisly funny bone. Tony Richardson's film adaptation of Waugh's *The Loved One* (1961) tackles death with a similar sly humor. Some fun with gritty sex surfaces in Alex Cox's fine film biography *Sid and Nancy* (1986). Some of the quirky youthful exuberance is found in Rob Reiner's *The Sure Thing*. Pedro Almodovar in *Tie Me Up, Tie Me Down* (1990) perhaps comes closest to blending violence and love, terror and laughter. Yet Almodovar's films are essentially suggestive, avoiding graphic presentation and romanticizing eroticism.

Lynch's particularly stinging sense of humor, on the other hand, does more than just include pain; laughter at the cruel and vile is pivotal in his film style. The brittle, black humor, graphic violence, and explicit sex in Lynch's film may have roots in absurd theater, particularly in the plays of Joe Orton.

Orton's irreverent stage humor includes cross-dressing, crime, manipulation, sexual deviancy, rape, and body snatching. His plays—like his biography—operate at a manic clip, juggling the mundane and the absurd. Orton's life experience includes his much-publicized defacing of Islington Library books, using his recently buried mother's false teeth as a stage prop, and the final blending of his ashes with those of the homosexual lovers who had bludgeoned him to death in a rage. In the excellent film based on his biography, *Prick Up Your Ears* (1987), screenwriter Alan Bennet and director Stephen Frears transfer Orton's style and brand of humor to the screen. *Entertaining Mr. Sloane* (1970) and *Loot* (1972), two of Orton's plays, have themselves been adapted to film. Nonetheless, although this kind of screen humor occurs in Orton as well as in other films before and corollary to Lynch's *Wild at Heart,* Lynch's rare breed of joke-making separates his film style from that of most other mainstream filmmakers.

The comedy techniques that pepper Lynch's films can best be illustrated in an analysis of a specific film sequence, the story of Dell, Lula's cousin. The vignette visualizes Lula's bedroom confidence to Sailor as she narrates the rise and fall of her cousin to illustrate how one can be led astray by bad thoughts.

Cousin Dell lives with his mother. First seen in the sweltering heat, in the back of a squad car, Dell becomes hysterical when his mother tells him of the six-month wait until Yuletide festivities. Because he loves Christmas, he often dresses in a Santa Claus suit. In fact, Lula confides, Dell so loved Christmas that he was called Christmas-Dell.

Dell would also stay up all night preparing lunches. He is pictured during a night of sandwich-making frenzy in the kitchen with tens of sandwiches before him in stages of preparation. When his mother asks what he is doing, bread knife still in hand, Dell replies with biting agitation. He finds her question ridiculous in the face of his totally rational actions. He resents the disturbance of his herculean culinary chore. He answers in a curt, no-nonsense manner what everyone in the audience sees: "I'm making my lunch."

Dell begins to fear being kidnapped by gloved aliens and purports many theories about the environmental and emotional havoc that space invaders reek on the earth. Dell likes to play with roaches, putting them down into his jockey shorts, trying to put them on his anus. He spends much of his time in his underwear poking with a stick at a black rubber glove on the floor of his room. Lula concludes Dell's story with his disappearance from home. The callow, handsome youth is last seen in an uncomfortable dance outside his home.

This is truly one of those jokes where the audience has to be there; in Lynch, they even have to *see* there. Certainly the pathetic incidents of Dell's madness are not comic. But seeing the extent of Dell's madness prohibits any serious understanding. The extreme cruelty of "The Three Stooges" or the absolute misery of the Little Tramp must be comic because they cannot be serious. Such humor may not be politically correct: it ridicules physical abuse, advocates maiming, condones mirth at the plight of the homeless. But laughter at pain and misfortune is a standard comic tool. To pity the pain is to prick humor's balloon. Lynch gives Dell's story humor in a film context. Humor in the sequence works only as a cinematic joke, in its cinematic context.

Exaggeration is taken to hyperbole—convoluted with Santa suits, sandwiches, black rubber gloves, and aliens, giving way to galactic conspiracies and abhorrent uses for repugnant insects. The movie blatantly depicts Dell's actions and objectively shows them as pathetic and sickening. But the audience sees juxtaposed in the same shot what Dell sees and its antithesis, what is shown. It is utterly preposterous; it is utterly ridiculous. And therefore the episode is funny.

Humor is further supported by Lynch's structuring of the sequence and its narration in the film. Sailor and Lula talk in bed. Dell as Santa disembarks from a squad car. Lynch cuts to the post-intercourse faces of Sailor and Lula. Lula makes a point; Sailor deadpan reacts. The film cuts back to Dell acting out the next, more bizarre scene of Lula's narration on screen. The film cuts back to Sailor's grimace in reaction to the bugs in Dell's pubic hair. Lula's story, Sailor's response, and Dell's actions become more preposterous.

The audience laughs as Dell's story continues to top and top itself again. Sailor's hangdog reactions and Lula's sincerity of delivery become more amusing. The audience sees the distance between the preposterous fable of Dell and its narrative context. Dell's story is left without closure. He stands waiting before his fence. The camera returns to Lula and Sailor in bed, Dell is gone from *Wild at Heart* as quickly as he intruded. The film cuts back to Sailor, who bemoans the cruelty of fate that Dell didn't seek a solution from the Wizard of Oz.

The film actually includes Dell as a story. It is not part of the virtual reality of the film. It is an anecdote of a character inserted into the plot. A tale. Lula tells the tale to Sailor and to the audience. Second, and more important, the camera mirrors Lula's deadly earnest point of view. She tells the story about her peculiar cousin as seriously as if she were talking about a cousin who took a class trip to Disneyworld. Her delivery and the film's presentation of the ridiculous material, inserted into the story in a clear, straight manner, elevate the episode to absurdity.

Typical of the dual tone of Lynch's humor, laughing at Dell's rationale that an alien invasion threatens our world is as funny—and no funnier—than Sailor and Lula's moronic choice of Dell's escapades as pillow talk. Rapid cuts replace Lula's anecdote with shots of the cannibalizing Marrietta on the phone and then of beasts on Farragut's hotel-room TV devouring each other. The laughter changes gears. The audience can still hear itself laughing derisively at Dell while it is alarmed and repelled by another, but no more pitiful act of violence.

Humor continues in tandem with violence. After a robbery, a victim searches around a crime scene for his hand, which has just been shot off. A coworker counsels him to keep looking, as nowadays doctors can sew body parts back on. Outside a cop's head is blown off by a shotgun blast in the parking lot. The hand is spotted being carried onto the lot in the mouth of a large dog. David Lynch explains,

"Laughs are a weird thing. They do pop out in strange places. The violence wasn't intended to be funny. Some of it is a hair absurd, and some of it is so violent that it enters into an area where, well, the laughter isn't really that strange . . ." (Gary Thompson, 37).

Laughter often greets the grotesque as a defense mechanism. When scenes are uncomfortable enough, there is often no other response but nervous laughter. In the 1990s the unprovoked, random violence of the times may necessitate a darker sense of humor in order to survive. Lynch taps into that dark humor. Some scenes present comedy in the film through the incongruous, peculiar, and ridiculous, while others find humor in violence.

Wild at Heart is also a film of extreme vileness and violence for its own sake. This is Lynch's backyard and some critics feel that *Wild at Heart*'s idiosyncratic mining of the subconscious is already becoming tired. "While a number of French critics see it, *naturellement,* as a profound critique of violent America, it's nothing of the kind. It's yet another journey inside Lynch's seething subconscious, an exciting place to visit but one that is beginning to show its limitations."[11]

But graphic subjects do play a role in contemporary times, and Lynch's inclusion of violence is seen by other critics as a statement of that condition. The film finds humor in its milieu in order to laugh and perhaps in order to survive. Lynch expands the arena for screen humor, again breaking new ground. "But Lynch has a knack for heightened reality that keeps us attuned to the pleasures of the unexpected. 'This whole world is weird on top and wild at heart,' says Lula. And who better to chart such a world than David Lynch? Even over the rainbow, he finds his own kind of truth" (Travers, 35).

It is certain that this violent film reaches for the sickening in searching for the truth. Blowing off a head, beating out a brain, and shooting off a hand are examples of explicit violence in the film. And the sickening? At the Pennsylvania Academy of the Fine Arts in his early years, Lynch's student film was a series of exploding, vomiting heads. *Wild at Heart,* over 20 years later, also has a vomit-inclined script.

The vomit scenes of Marrietta and Lula are different in all ways save that both are difficult for the squeamish to endure. Marrietta vomits in one of the film's lengthiest and most dramatic scenes, intercut first with Marrietta talking to Farragut on the phone, and then with Sailor and Lula talking in bed. Finally, smeared with her own lipstick war paint, Marrietta vomits into her toilet, writhing on her bathroom floor; the sequence ends in a final fade of her pointed, witchy red slippers, her body huddled under her toilet as the witch in Fleming's *Oz* is crushed by a falling house.

Her daughter Lula has her own vomiting style. Indiscreet in her throwing up, she fails to reach the toilet and vomits near her bed on the rug. The accident provides fly-infested shots of vomit lingering on the carpet. The frequent references to its stench reach the audience's imagination.

The sympathetic, or more appropriately "a-sympathetic" vomiting of Marrietta corresponds to Lula's morning sickness, Marrietta's worst fear realized. Lula's vomiting is a sign of her pregnancy. Film mother and daughter (the actresses are really mother and daughter) vomit as they live; Marrietta is covert while Lula is uninterested in hiding, much less cleaning up, the debris.

The scenes cause a disgusted stir. They are given critical attention and popular scrutiny. But a film character's getting sick to the stomach needs a rationale no more than does any other element of the plot. People do get sick to their stomachs. Pregnant women, like Lula, do experience morning sickness. No one is incensed that Lynch shows Sailor driving a car or Lula dancing. Including both of these voluntary actions is accepted without question.

Filming vomiting breaks a taboo. Lynch shows a shard of life's ugliness; the scenes are ugly. But the vomiting scenes are labeled more offensive than scenes of a young girl's abortion, a skull-crushing murder, or an attempted rape. These scenes depict unnatural, criminal acts. Lynch's vomiting scenes and the reaction to them indicate a disproportionate sensitivity to what looks ugly compared to the truly ugly as depicted. Far more reprehensible acts come before the camera and are accepted: squeamishness at seeing nausea seems a stronger reaction than outrage at viewing the nauseating. David Breskin asks about vomit's inclusion in the film: "There are not many movies where you get to see both a mother and a daughter throw up!" And director Lynch replies, "Yeah, it's a real thrill (laughs). That alone is worth the price of a ticket" (Breskin, 98).

Romance is also important in Lynch's films. Here Lynch is romantic in several senses of the term. *Wild at Heart* is romantic in that it idealizes marriage and family; romantic too in its recollection of the movies. Lynch is also in the romantic tradition. He glorifies nature. He courts the supernatural. He is flamboyant. Romantic, in this sense, is not only a descriptor—it is a philosophy. Lynch employs the romantic

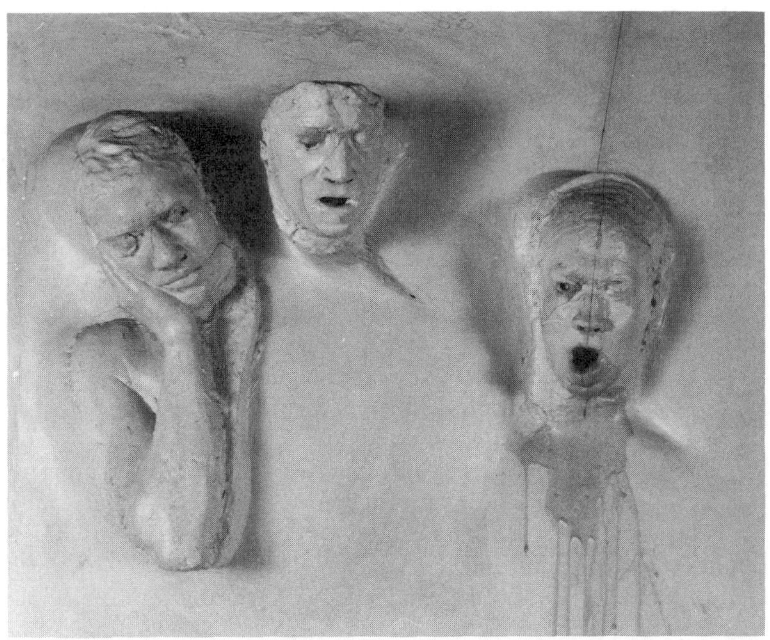

"Six Men Getting Sick." Sculpture screen (detail) by David Lynch. Courtesy of Rodger La Pelle and Christine McGinnis.

code. Lynch's intensity galvanizes the look and feel of the film. His passion flashes uninhibited. Lynch mythologizes the pop-rock culture of the American road.

The landscape is geographically beautiful as Sailor and Lula drive across the country. The road stretches out to the horizon as they pass farm fields. The open country, promise, and love are as unbounded as the Texas sky. The ominous, black, empty sky swallows the horizon as they pass scattered debris near a car wreck. Litter, violence, and depravity also ride the highway. The natural wonders of the landscape share footage with the sleazy highway society in which the film takes place. And the shots of seedy, ramshackle small towns festering along the roadway are as strangely beautiful as those of golden fields. It is a world of glorious marvels, from Sailor's first victim's brain oozing on the steps to Sailor's son's flaxen hair under his father's palm.

Lynch's film again uses the world as subject without a preordained social or cinematic system that determines acceptable and appropriate subjects. It is Lynch's romanticism that finds vomit and car wrecks as beautiful and mysterious as starless nights and sunsets. Lynch features the beautiful and the reprehensible without censure. Thus the dense film's virtual reality is romantic.

"Every work of art is a vision and a legend of reality, all art replaces actual life with a Utopia, but in romanticism the Utopian character of art is expressed more purely and more fully than elsewhere."[12] Lynch does not evaluate the beautiful and ugly of a landscape: his composition melds contemporary contradictions. Lynch shows the audience his world with unreserved exuberance—"warts and all." Lynch's romanticism motivates him to view his whole world, regardless of the multifaceted, contradictory, sometimes repugnant view.

And Lynch's cinematic world is our world: *The Wizard of Oz* and Elvis Presley, the king of rock and roll. It includes the immediacy, hype, and decay of today's disposable society. Media measure time, create reality, and crown royalty. *In* becomes *out, out* becomes *camp,* and *camp* becomes *retro*. Encores are programmed and rehearsed. Last night's standing ovation is tonight's jeers. In pop America, yesterday's status symbol is today's joke. And in Lynch's world, tomorrow's symbol is today's taboo.

Ironically, the real film, that is the film being shot within the virtual reality of the movie, is a porno film. But in the bedroom or speeding down the highway, Sailor and Lula identify not with their tawdry narrative but with the memory of a children's movie classic. Lula tries to click her red heels out of Bobby Peru's aggression. Sailor knowns that the highway holds the answer if he continues to follow the yellow brick road. Both Sailor and Lula adopt pop fantasy as their reality to escape the horrific virtual reality of the film. Lula sees Marrietta as the Wicked Witch, and her mother's destruction is that of *Oz*'s witch: she disintegrates. After Sailor is beaten by a street gang, Glinda, the Good Witch, appears in her bubble and gives him still another last chance to wise up. Sailor and Lula both seek and fear the world of fantasy. They evoke the 1939 film in a virtual reality more somber than its Kansas, more technicolor than its scenery over the rainbow. The irony that their virtual reality in the film is both more dreadful and more fantastic than Fleming's escapes them.

It is in movies, not in reality, that Sailor and Lula find substance. The characters live in a fantasy world. *Oz* is misinterpreted by the lovers not as film but as media guidebook, a celluloid 900 telephone number spouting guidance for how to deal with problems, even how to dress. Sailor's jacket is, by his own pseudocomic definition, a sign of his individuality. "Though not mentioned in the original script, the jacket has since become a key prop in *Wild at Heart,* taking on the status of a minor character or subplot, as props often do in Lynch's films" (Rugoff, 82). The jacket is a pop symbol to Sailor, who grabs himself like still another rebel hero. Evoking for the audience the melancholy plumage of another midnight cowboy, the snakeskin jacket attains satiric, sarcastic, and pathetic connotations.

Sailor's "individuality" is neither his nor is it individual. The jacket screams origins of stock equipment in the hyped persona wardrobe of every rock-and-roll rebel. It is distributed through outlet racks in shopping malls. The mass-produced costumes of rock fantasy, like the hyped sounds of rock, determine Sailor's reality.

"David is a huge lover of music and he wanted me to sing two Elvis songs," explains Cage in answer to questions about his singing performance.[13] Lynch's decision to include Elvis Presley hits in the score develops the film's continuity. Sailor's association with Presley's songs is Lynch's most overt tie to the mythology of pop culture.

Elvis embodies rock-and-roll America. The heavy-set, middle-aged performer, even the dead man, cannot displace the hip-swinging icon who lives in rock mythology. From humble beginnings to fame, Elvis, like his music, is rooted in the American Dream. Few faces in the twentieth century are more easily identified worldwide than the king of rock and roll. Elvis's fame, however, has elevated him beyond even his legendary recording career or his biography. There are probably more annual sightings of Elvis than of Nessie, alien spacecrafts, and all religious personages combined. Elvis is a pop-culture phenomenon with a life all its own.

Sailor is the genuine pop article—like "100% synthetic" products. He is honestly an Elvis impersonator. Sailor's truest feelings in the film are expressed through copying Elvis's rock-and-roll songs and performance style. It is the revered litany of Presley's lyrics that he will not compromise. Singing Elvis's song seals Sailor's vows, appropriately made atop another pop-culture symbol, the convertible, to a pop-culture childhood sweetheart and his son and heir.

Accidents, street gangs, movie characters, and rock legends collide in the film's final frame. "But this sensory overload all comes across as alienating and enigmatic, right down to the closing shot of two people who start twirling around, in carousel fashion, even though they're supposed to be standing still on the roof of a car."[14] Lynch takes on representing pop culture in all its aspects; he adopts reverence and ridicule, awe and loathing toward the contemporary U.S.A.

The film is not a tribute to pop society, nor, from Lynch's perspective, is it a condemnation of it. Lynch plainly recognizes that turn-of-the-century U.S. society trivializes anything and overkills everything. All issues are reduced to disposable, digestible media segments. All causes are potential trends. What was previously unthinkable is as suddenly tiresome through its media repetition. As with the terrifying, the pathetic is instantly typed, exposed, confessed, televised, hyped, and trivialized in 30-second promos. Today's burning concern is also yesterday's mundane TV talk-show topic. This is the self-devouring oxymoron of Lynch's film and contemporary America. Lynch's pacing and plot incidents in his film echo the brutal barrage.

A good example occurs when car radio stations announce disasters from around the globe. The pain of all mankind is instantly shared worldwide and integrated as broadcast epigrams introduced into the film's virtual reality through modern communication. An electronic volcano spews the incessant perversions, tricks of fate, cruelties, and miseries of the world. As surely repugnant, it sounds funny to the audience—it has to sound funny: avalanche of horrors—pathetic—ridiculous—so real. On screen Lula survives by turning off the radio. Without media communication, disasters half-way around the world are no problem. Why should she care? They are not happening here, to her. She and her Elvis leap from the car and strike a rock-and-roll pose in the amber fields of grain.

The film, it has been seen, met some critical and popular disapproval just as Lynch has achieved stature in the pop culture he depicts that is both blessing and liability. The film's most unfavorable reviews generally included comparison of the film to other Lynch films and to the reputation of the director. "*Wild at Heart* is a sorry spectacle. It's not pleasant to watch a brilliant filmmaker flailing around like this—especially when the horse he's whipping so furiously was dead before he got on it. The picture is one startling lapse of taste after another; we gaze in disbelief as the original error in judgment—the choice of material—metastasizes on the screen."[15]

If Lynch in *Wild at Heart* is seen as stagnating by his critics, he is also deified by his followers. Pop culture has awarded the Cannes prize as much to its celebrated creator as to his film. "Each Thursday night during the festival, the American Pavilion threw a Twin Peaks party (serving pie and a good cup of black coffee) for crowds of Peaks addicts who, ignoring the hundreds of new movies unreeling around them, preferred to huddle in front of TV monitors watching tapes of the latest episode from the United States. The first screening of *Wild At Heart*—at 8:30 in the morning—was so eagerly anticipated that the 2,400 seat Grand Auditorium Lumiere was half full of sleepy souls by 8. When the film ended, with the Elvis-like Nicolas Cage atop a car crooning "Love Me Tender" to Laura Dern, the audience broke into wild cheering. After a steady diet of lugubrious and sometimes immobile films from around the world, Lynch's lurid comic melodrama was a blast of freshly fetid American air" (Ansen, June 1990, 81).

It is interesting to note the enthusiastic world response compared to that of American critics. American culture has become part of the twentieth-century global culture. It is both national and worldwide. French critics are effusive that Lynch's vision is the quintessential violent American milieu. Lynch is seen abroad as boldly visualizing images of America. In America, on the other hand, he is seen as depraved and artificial at worst and as a surreal visionary at best. Far from labeling his perspective as faulty or accurate, the diversity of his critical reception suggests his philosophical and aesthetic presentation of so many contradictory elements of the American scene that critics from all segments of the contemporary world audience find scenes to bless—and to damn—in Lynch's screen world.

The international critical vantage point is further illustrated in Japanese reaction to Lynch. *Wild at Heart* is released in Japan in the same year that the Touku Museum of Contemporary Art mounts an exhibit of Lynch's paintings: "David Lynch exhibition caused a great sensation in Japan . . . They are fascinated by his world."[16] The film is seen in an American light in the context of nineties international art and cinema. "To be more precise, I would say America has begun to enter its fin de siecle. That would mean that America is acquiring the potential to produce an art which is properly decadent. As a film of American fin de siecle art, *Wild At Heart* was a powerful shock."[17]

Thus both friend and foe, audience and critics, actually sing a similar refrain. Critical and popular response to Lynch illustrates the lack of a separation between fame and art in the twentieth century's last decade. This overlapping is especially obvious in reaction to movies and to Hollywood, America's dream factory—which are the material that twentieth-century dreams are made of, including the frayed status of nineties celebrity: contemporary American fame. The contemporary scene is a labyrinth: fads, scientific miracles, trends, televised history, ins and outs, violence, racism, deadly viral epidemics, and economics weave pop culture. To some, fantasy becomes the only reality. The range of *Wild at Heart*'s reviews, the adulation and the derision, may prove the most startling vindication of Lynch's film style and Lynch's vision.

This is not a rationalization of the failings of some of *Wild at Heart*'s film elements. Reliance on a slight story in a strong frame weakens the film. Limitations in characterization are sometimes detrimental to the film. Mixed signals in tone sometimes inconsistently tinge events with stilted, coy humor. It runs to the self-indulgent. Some images on screen are already tried and self-conscious "Lynch" images.

Yet even images branded tired are well founded and unique to Lynch. Some are startlingly new in cinema's evolution while others are aware of—even function because of—genre conventions. Lynch parades the twentieth century before the camera with reverence and revulsion—amusement, ridicule, and terror commingle. *Wild at Heart* breaks ground to create an audience for the movies that has heretofore never been assembled.

Wild at Heart is a mixed bag of a film. There are no steps forward without some shaking. Lynch is on the move. The film is part of the evolving process of the filmmaker. Its production flashes "like lightning with a script that Lynch proceeded to rewrite substantially as he shot. And not only that, he shot a lot. He brought in a first cut that was some four hours long. After the early marketing screening (which quite a number of shocked folk walked out on), for which the film had been trimmed to about two hours and a half, he cut more scenes and then went out and shot more footage. 'I don't think anything's finished till it's finished,' he says" (Campbell, 81). The film's place in the progression of Lynch's style is obvious. But the film's role in that cinematic evolution is still an unknown. Assessing the risks, potential, and significance of *Wild at Heart* is unfinished.

A telling review of the film sees its effect as a genesis rather than a closure. "One comes out of the theatre feeling as if the mind has begun to melt" (Canby 1990, C6). Einstein's nuclear age is filled with "meltdowns." Technology has become so lethal that its success and collapse equally threaten annihilation. Fantasy becomes reality as reality expands to include previous generations' dreams. Reality becomes fantasy as it realizes every generation's nightmares.

Lynch remains on that cutting edge if sometimes as innovator and others merely as icon. As always, reception to Lynch seems to vary depending on what side of the theater aisle one sits on. Thus, as was *Wild at Heart*'s Best Film prize at the Cannes Festival, *Fire Walk with Me*'s festival screening in 1992, this time labeled a mega-failure, is also met with jeers and outrage. "Also strong, but for all the wrong reasons, was the disastrous *Twin Peaks: Fire Walk With Me,* David Lynch's much-vaunted prequel to his successful television series. It was hard to say whether the film played worse to "Twin Peaks" fans, who already knew more than enough about the death of Laura Palmer, or to anyone happening onto this inpenetrable material for the first time. Either way, Mr. Lynch's taste for brain-dead grotesque has lost its novelty, and it now appears more pathologically unpleasant than cinematically bold."[18]

When the film opens first in Japan the following month, Lynch inspires a rash of Laura Palmer wakes as the spring season's "in" party theme. The film does brisk box office business. *Twin Peaks: Fire Walk With Me*'s premiere in Tokyo is covered in the U.S. papers where the movie will open that August.

Lynch's other project in the spring of 1992 was a dark comedy. The frenetic, half hour situation comedy "On the Air" debuted in June. The show, set in the days of live television, was a change from Lynch's usual brooding work and a break from "Twin Peaks" continual continuations. It received some respectable if quiet notices and very slight popular attention. Thus David Lynch mirrors and creates the meltdown of the twentieth-century filmmaker. Lynch's celebrity is Lynch's notoriety. If times past had been labeled "a-changing," living our times may best be labeled messy. As are Lynch films. Society grapples with a new order—so too must art.

NOTES AND REFERENCES

Preface

1. Richard B. Woodward, "A Dark Lens on America," *New York Times Magazine,* 14 January 1990, sec. 6, p. 30; hereafter cited in text.

Chapter One

1. David Chute, "Out to Lynch," *Film Comment,* October 1986, 22:32; hereafter cited in text.
2. David Breskin, "The Rolling Stone Interview with David Lynch," *Rolling Stone Magazine,* 6 September 1990, 60; hereafter cited in text.
3. Larry Rohter, "David Lynch Pushes America to the Edge," *New York Times,* 12 August 1990, II: 19.
4. Richard Corliss, "Czar of Bizarre," *Time,* 1 October 1990, 136:86; hereafter cited in text.
5. Makoto Takimoto, "A Rough Sketch for Lynch," trans. Charles Worthen, exhibit program, Touku Museum of Contemporary Art, Tokyo, Japan, January 1991, 28.
6. Nan Robertson, "The All-American Guy behind Blue Velvet," *New York Times,* 11 October 1986, 11:1; hereafter cited in text.
7. David Ansen, "The Kid from Mars," *Newsweek,* 9 April 1990, 115:68; hereafter cited in text.
8. Robert Henri, *The Art Spirit* (New York: Harper & Row, 1984), 90; hereafter cited in text.
9. John Francis Marion, *Famous and Curious Cemeteries* (New York: Crown Publishers, 1977), 71.
10. Rodger La Pelle, interview with author, Philadelphia, 14 July 1990.
11. Gary Thompson, "Philly Was the Lynch-Pin for His Creativity," *Philadelphia Daily News,* 15 August 1990, 33; hereafter cited in text.
12. J. Hoberman and Jonathan Rosenbaum, *Midnight Movies* (New York: Harper & Row, 1988), 223–24; hereafter cited in text.
13. Katherine Heller, "To Lynch, This Is Sick City," *Philadelphia Inquirer,* 21 August 1990, 7D.
14. Winthrop Neilson, letter to Mr. and Mrs. R. Barclay Scull, son-in-law and daughter of Dr. William S. Biddle Cadwalader, who founded the Cadwalader Memorial Prize, 25 May 1967, Archives of the Pennsylvania Academy of the Fine Arts, with PAFA permission.

15. Eileen Fisher, "Classics in His Closet," *Applause,* May 1989, 15:10.

16. Rodger La Pelle, interview with author, Philadelphia, 23 June 1990.

17. Jim Jerome, "Bio," *People,* 3 September 1990, 34:82; hereafter cited in text.

18. Paul Mandelbaum, "Kinkmeister," *New York Times Magazine,* 7 April 1991, 34.

19. Joseph Gelmis, "One of the Most Original American Films," *Newsday,* 17 October 1980, 2:7.

20. Archer Winsten, "Review of *Elephant Man,*" *New York Post,* 18 October 1980, 15, in *Film Review Annual,* ed. Jerome Ozer (Englewood, New Jersey: Film Review Publications), 28.

21. Susanne K. Langer, *Feeling and Form* (New York: Scribner's, 1953). 95.

22. Howard Rheingold, *Virtual Reality* (New York: Summit Books, 1991).

23. Virginia Campbell, "Something Really Wild," *Movieline,* September 1990, 35; hereafter cited in text.

24. Lloyd Rose, "Tumoresque: The Films of David Lynch," *Atlantic,* October 1984, 254:108.

25. James Monaco, *American Film Now* (New York: Oxford Press, 1979), 280.

Chapter Two

1. David Nunn, interview with author, London Hospital Medical Museum, London, England, 29 May 1991.

2. David Steritt, "Review of *Elephant Man,*" *Christian Science Monitor,* 9 October 1980, 18, in *Film Review Annual,* ed. Jerome Ozer (Englewood, New Jersey: Film Review Publications), 28; hereafter cited in text.

3. Henry Baker, "Review of *Elephant Man,*" *Cineaste,* Spring 1981:28, in *Film Review Annual,* ed. Jerome Ozer (Englewood, New Jersey: Film Review Publications), 28.

4. Pauline Kael, "The Frog Who Turned into a Prince, the Prince Who Turned into a Frog," *New Yorker,* 27 October 1987, 56:179; hereafter cited in text.

5. Diane Jacobs, "Films: The Freak and the Pariah," *Horizon,* November 1980, 23:70; hereafter cited in text.

6. Michael Norman, "Always in Character," *New York Times Magazine,* 2 December 1990, 55; hereafter cited in text.

7. Roger Ebert, *Movie Home Companion* (New York: Andrews & McMeel, 1990), 227.

8. Bruce Kawin, "Review of *Elephant Man,*" *Film Quarterly,* Summer 1981:21, in *Film Review Annual,* ed. Jerome Ozer (Englewood, New Jersey: Film Review Publications), 256.

9. Jack Kroll, "Odd Man Out," *Newsweek,* 6 October 1980, 96:72; hereafter cited in text.

10. Vincent Canby, "*The Elephant Man,* Study in Genteelness," *New York Times,* 3 October 1980, C8.

11. Judith Crist, "A Disappearing *Elephant Man,*" *Saturday Review,* October 1980, 7:92.

Chapter Three

1. David Ansen, "Stranger Than Paradise," *Newsweek,* 10 December 1984, 103:94; hereafter cited in text.

2. Desmond Ryan, "A Jolting Road Movie from David Lynch of 'Twin Peaks'," *Philadelphia Inquirer,* 17 August 1990, 5; hereafter cited in text.

3. Jeff Griswold, "*Dune*: $52 Million, David Lynch interviewed by Jeff Griswold," *Film Comment,* January–February 1985, 21:55; hereafter cited in text.

4. John J. O'Conner, "TV's Film Editors Both Giveth and Taketh," *New York Times,* 12 June 1988, H37.

5. Leonard B. Meyer, *Music, the Arts, and Ideas* (Chicago: University of Chicago Press, 1973), 207.

6. Pauline Kael, "David and Goliath," *New Yorker,* 24 December 1984, 60:74; hereafter cited in text.

7. K.R. Hey, "*Dune* Review," *USA Today,* March 1985, 113:97; hereafter cited in text.

8. Vincent Canby, "Seen in 1984, the Future Looks Bleak," *New York Times,* 23 December 1984, II:19:1; hereafter cited in text.

9. John Clark, "Filmographies," *Premiere,* September 1990, 4:124; hereafter cited in text.

10. "David Lynch," *Toronto Globe and Mail,* 19 September 1986, in *Current Biography Yearbook 1987,* ed. Charles Moritz (New York: H. W. Wilson Publishers), 378.

11. T. O'Brien, "*Dune* Review," *Commonweal,* 11 January 1985, 112:18.

12. Richard Corliss, "The Fantasy Film as Final Exam," *Time,* 17 December 1984, 124:99.

13. Janet Maslin, "War of the Worms," *New York Times,* 14 December 1984, C18:4; hereafter cited in text.

14. Tom O'Hanlon, "The First Billion Dollar Flick?" *Forbes,* November 1984, 134:64–66.

Chapter Four

1. Stephen Schiff, *Vanity Fair,* September 1986, 50:87.

2. Terrence Rafferty, "*Blue Velvet* Review," *Nation,* 18 October 1986, 243:383; hereafter cited in text.

3. André Bazin, *What Is Cinema?*, vol, 1, trans. Hugh Gray (Berkeley: University of California Press, 1967).

4. "NC Artist Made Blue Velvet Grisly," *Wilmington Star,* 2 November 1986, 10.

5. Janet Maslin, "Blue Velvet Comedy of the Eccentric," *New York Times,* 19 September 1986, III:12:5.

6. Sergei Eisenstein, *Film Form,* ed. and trans. Jay Leda (New York: Harcourt, Brace, 1969).

7. Tracy Biga, *Film Quarterly,* Fall 1987, 41:46.

8. Pauline Kael, "Out There and in Here," *New Yorker,* 22 September 1985, 52:99; hereafter cited in text.

9. Cathleen McGuigan with Janet Huck, "Black and Blue is Beautiful?" *Newsweek,* 27 October 1986, 108:104.

10. David Ansen, "Stranger Than Paradise," *Newsweek,* 15 September 1986, 108:69.

11. Roger Ebert, *Movie Home Companion* (New York: Andrews & McMeel, 1989), 85.

12. Gina White, "Film Was Welcome Houseguest," *Wilmington Star,* 9 October 1986, 1D.

13. Janet Maslin, "New Films Rethink the Small Town," *New York Times,* 21 December 1986, 2:1.

14. Richard Corliss, "Our Town," *Film Comment,* November–December 1986, 22:17; hereafter cited in text.

15. Susanne K. Langer, *Feeling and Form* (New York: Scribner's, 1953), 412.

16. David Thompson, "Beyond Norman Rockwell," *California Magazine,* September 1986, vol. 11, no. 9, p. 43.

17. John Powers, "Last Tangȯ in Lumberton," *LA Weekly,* 12 September 1986, 8:42.

18. James M. Wall, "The Best Film of 1986: Probing the Depths of Evil," *Christian Century,* 7–14 January 1987, vol. 104, no. 1, p. 9.

19. "Maybe You Didn't Like Blue Velvet, But Somebody Did," *Wilmington Star,* 1 November 1986, 12.

20. Ben Steelman, "*Blue Velvet*: A Walk on the Dark Side," *Wilmington Star,* 26 September 1986, 10.

21. Miriam Horn, "Dark Visitors of the Silver Screen," *U.S. News and World Report,* 30 March 1987, 102:75.

Chapter Five

1. Vincent Canby, "*Zelly and Me* Review," *New York Times,* 15 April 1988, C4:4.

2. Charles Leershen with Lynda Wright, "Psychic Moms And Cherry Pie," *Newsweek,* 7 May 1990, 115:58; hereafter cited in text.

3. Terrence Rafferty, "One Thing After Another—or Why This Idyllic Setting Fills Us With Such Apprehension," *New Yorker,* 9 April 1990, 66:87; hereafter cited in text.

4. John Rockwell, "The Music That Haunts 'Twin Peaks'," *New York Times,* 1 July 1990, II:20:3; hereafter cited in text.

5. Northrop Frye, *Anatomy of Criticism* (Princeton, New Jersey: Princeton University Press, 1973), 78.

6. Timothy Egan, "Northwest Noir: The Art of the Seriously Goofy," *New York Times,* 14 July 1991, H1.

7. R. Zoglin, "Like Nothing on Earth," *Time,* 9 April 1990, 135:96; hereafter cited in text.

8. Jonathan Storm, "The Peaks Experience: The Eerie Fascination with 'Twin Peaks'," *Philadelphia Inquirer,* 24 May 1990, D10; hereafter cited in text.

9. "Twin Peaks Speaks: Behind the Scenes," *Soap Opera Weekly,* 16 October 1990, vol. 1, no. 48, p. 15.

10. "Twin Peaks," *Electronic Media,* 26 March 1990.

11. Rodger La Pelle, unpublished article.

12. Joseph Sobran, "Weird America," *National Review,* 10 October 1990, 42:40; hereafter cited in text.

13. T. Carlson, "Welcome to the Weird New World of Twin Peaks," *TV Guide,* 7 April 1990, 38:22; hereafter cited in text.

14. Jonathan Storm, "*Twin Peaks,* Art to Behold," *Philadelphia Inquirer,* 8 April 1990, 10L; hereafter cited in text.

15. Gary Thompson, "At the Peak of His Form," *Philadelphia Daily News,* 15 August 1990, 33; hereafter cited in text.

16. Walter Goodman, "One More Thing, Diane: Buy Me Some Insurance," *New York Times,* 25 May 1990, C26:5.

17. Jack Evans, *Little Histories: North Bend–Snoqualmie Washington* (Seattle: SCW Publications, 1990), 2; hereafter cited in text.

18. Jim Knipfel, "Slackjaw," *Welcomat,* 18 April 1990, 19:39.

19. Susan Schindehette et al., "Cryptic Dreams, Dead Prom Queens, Dwarf Back-Talk: Here at Last Is a Guide to What Twin Peaks Is All About," *People,* 14 May 1990, 33:85.

20. Craig R. Whitney, "In Britain, It's All Just Beginning," *New York Times,* 7 November 1990, C21.

21. "Place Your Bets: Emmy Nominations," *Charlotte Observer,* 3 August 1990.

22. Mitchell Fink, "Insider—No Peaking," *People,* 9 October 1990, 34:43.

23. Luis Buñuel, *My Last Sigh* (New York: Knopf, 1983), 226.

Chapter Six

1. Peter Travers, "The Wizard of Odd," *Rolling Stone Magazine,* 6 September 1990, 35; hereafter cited in text.
2. John Simon, "Droopy Loves Drippy," *National Review,* October 1990, 42:46.
3. Mike Clark, "Wild, a bad joke from Lynch," *USA Today,* 17 August 1990, D4. col. 2.
4. Bryan Appleyard, "Lynch Fever," *British Vogue,* September 1990, 55; hereafter cited in text.
5. Joseph Morgenstern, "A Thin Red Line," in *Film,* ed. Richard Schikel and John Simon (New York: Simon & Schuster, 1968), 67–68.
6. Phoebe Hoban, "Childhood's End," *Premiere,* September 1990, 4:86; hereafter cited in text.
7. David Ansen, "David Lynch's *Wild Kingdom*: Southern-fried Freaks," *Newsweek,* 27 August 1990, 116;61.
8. Ralph Rugoff, "Wild at Heart," *Premiere,* September 1990, 4:80; hereafter cited in text.
9. Vincent Canby, "In the Eerie Cosmos of David Lynch, Reality is Reeling," *New York Times,* 17 August 1990, C6; hereafter cited in text.
10. "Culture Club—Getting Lynched," *Harper's Bazaar,* October 1990, 123:130.
11. David Ansen, "David Lynch's New Peak: Sex, Violence, and Rock and Roll Wins at Cannes," *Newsweek,* 4 June 1990, 115:81; hereafter cited in text.
12. Arnold Hauser, *The Social History of Art,* vol. 3, trans. with Stanley Godman (New York: Vintage Books), 176.
13. Terry Gross, "Outrageous Cage," *Applause,* October 1990, 16:13.
14. Ralph Novak, "Picks and Pans," *People,* 27 May 1990, 34:10.
15. Terrence Rafferty, "End of the Road," *New Yorker,* 27 August 1990, 66:291.
16. Rumi Miura, letter to author, 1 October 1991, Touku Museum of Contemporary Art, Tokyo, Japan.
17. Noi Sawaragi, "Leather, Slash, Splatter: Three Stigmata for the Hell's Angels," trans. Lewis Cook, exhibit program, Touku Museum of Contemporary Art, Tokyo, Japan, January 1991, 15.
18. Janet Maslin, "Lament at Cannes: Rarities are Rare," *New York Times,* 18 May 1992, C13.

SELECTED BIBLIOGRAPHY

Books

Buñuel, Luis. *My Last Sigh*. New York: Knopf, 1983.

Drimmer, Frederick. *The Elephant Man*. New York: Putnam, 1985.

Eco, Umberto. *Travels in Hyper-Reality*. Translated by William Weaver. New York: Harcourt Brace Jovanovich, 1986.

Gifford, Barry. *Wild at Heart*. New York: Vintage, 1990.

Henri, Robert. *The Art Spirit*. New York: Harper & Row, 1984.

Herbert, Frank. *Dune*. New York: Putnam, 1984.

Hoberman, J., and Jonathan Rosenbaum. *Midnight Movies*. New York: Harper & Row, 1988.

Howell, Michael, and Peter Ford. *The True History of the Elephant Man*. Harmondsworth, England: Penguin, 1992.

Knicklebine, Scott. *Welcome to Twin Peaks*. Lincolnwood, Ill.: Publications International, 1990.

Langer, Suzanne K. *Feeling and Form*. New York: Scribner's, 1953; New York: Macmillan, 1977.

Lynch, David, Mark Frost, and Richard Saul Wurman. *Welcome to Twin Peaks: Access Guide to the Town*. Twin Peaks Production and Access Press, 1991.

Lynch, Jennifer. *The Secret Diary of Laura Palmer.* New York: Pocket Books, 1990.

Montagu, Ashley. *The Elephant Man: A Study in Human Dignity*. New York: Dutton, 1979.

Norman, Tom, and [with additional writings by his son] George Norman. *The Penny Showman: The Memoirs of Tom Norman "Silver King."* London: Privately published, 1985.

Articles

Breskin, David. "The *Rolling Stone* Interview with David Lynch." *Rolling Stone,* 6 September 1990, 58–60.

Chute, David. "Out to Lynch." *Film Comment* (October 1986): 22, 32–35.

Corliss, Richard. "Czar of Bizarre." *Time,* 1 October 1990, 84–86.

Egan, Timothy. "Northwest Noir: The Art of the Seriously Goofy." *New York Times,* 14 July 1991, H1.

Jameson, Frederic. "On Magic Realism in Film." *Critical Inquiry* 12(1986): 301–25.

Kruger, Barbara. "What's High, What's Low—and Who Cares?" *New York Times,* 9 September 1990, H43.

Woodward, Richard B. "A Dark Lens on America." *New York Times Magazine,* 14 January 1990, 6, 19.

FILMOGRAPHY

The Alphabet (H. Barton Wasserman Production, 1967)
Written, directed, and filmed by David Lynch
Cast: Peggy Lynch (Girl)

The Grandmother (1970)
Financed by an American Film Institute Grant
Written, directed, filmed, and animated by David Lynch
Assistant Script Consultants: Margaret Lynch, C. K. Williams
Still Photography: Doug Randall
Music, Music Effects: Tractor
Sound Editing and Mixing: Alan Splet
Sound Effects: David Lynch, Margaret Lynch, Robert Chadwick, Alan Splet
Cast: Richard White (Boy), Dorothy McGinnis (Grandmother), Virginia Maitland (Mother), Robert Chadwick (Father)

Eraserhead (Columbia Pictures, 1977)
Ben Barenholtz presents a Libra Film
Producer: David Lynch with the assistance of the American Film Institute Center for Advanced Film Studies
Direction, Screenplay: David Lynch
Assistant to the Director: Catherine Coulson
Camera, Lighting: Frederick Elmes, Herbert Cardwell
Special Effects Photography: Frederick Elmes
Assistant Camera: Catherine Coulson
Picture Editing: David Lynch
Location Sound, Rerecording: Alan R. Splet
Sound Editing: Alan R. Splet
Sound Effects: David Lynch, Alan R. Splet
"Lady in the Radiator" song composed and sung by Peter Ivers
Pipe Organ by "Fats" Waller
Production Design, Special Effects: David Lynch
Production Manager: Doreen G. Small
Crew: Jeanne Field, Michael Groody, Stephen Groody, Toby Keeler, Roger Lundy, John Lynch, Dennis Nance, Anatol Pacanowsky, Carol Schreder
Special Thanks to Ron Barth, Ron Culbertson, Frank Daniel, Richard Einfeld, Jack Fisk, Ken Fix, Andre Guttfreund, Marvin Goodwin,

M.D., Randy Hart, Roman Hart, George T. Hutchinson, David Khasky, Jim King, Margit Fellegi Laszlo, Paul Leimbach, David Lunney, Mr. and Mrs. David W. Lynch, Peggy Lynch, Sarah Pillsbury, Sidney P. Solow, Sissy Spacek, George Stevens, Jr., Antonio Vellani

Cast: John Nance (Henry Spencer), Charlotte Stewart (Mary X), Allen Joseph (Mr. X), Jeanne Bates (Mrs. X)), Judith Anna Roberts (Beautiful Girl across the Hall), Laurel Near (Lady in the Radiator), V. Phipps-Wilson (Landlady), Jack Fisk (Man in the Planet), Jean Lange (Grandmother), Thomas Coulson (Boy), John Monez (Bum), Darwin Joston (Paul), Neil Moran (Boss), Hal Landon, Jr., (Pencil Machine Operator), Jennifer Lynch (Little Girl), Brad Keeler (Little Boy), Peggy Lynch, Doddie Keeler (People Digging in the Alley), Gill Dennis (Man with Cigar), Toby Keeler (Man Fighting), Raymond Walsh (Mr. Roundheels)

Running Time: 89 minutes

The Elephant Man (Paramount, 1980)

Producer: Jonathan Sanger

Director: David Lynch

Assistant Directors: Anthony Waye, Gerry Cavigan

Screenplay: Christopher De Vore, Eric Bergren, David Lynch (based on *The Elephant Man and Other Reminiscences* by Sir Frederick Treves and *The Elephant Man: A Study in Human Dignity* by Ashley Montagu)

Photography: Freddie Francis

Editor: Anne V. Coates

Music: John Morris

Costumes: Patricia Norris

Design: Stuart Craig

Art Director: Bob Cartwright

Cast: Anthony Hopkins (Frederick Treves), John Hurt (John Merrick), Anne Bancroft (Mrs. Kendal), John Gielgud (Carr Gomm), Wendy Hiller (Mothershead), Freddie Jones (Bytes), Michael Elphick (Night Porter), Hannah Gordon (Mrs. Treves), Helen Ryan (Princess Alex), John Standing (Fox), Dexter Fletcher (Bytes' Boy), Lesley Dunlop (Nora), Phoebe Nicholls (Merrick's Mother), Pat Gorman (Fairground Bobby), Claire Davenport (Fat Lady), Orla Pederson (Skeleton Man), Patsy Smart (Distraught Woman), Frederick Treves (Alderman), Stromboli (Fire Eater), Richard Hunter (Hodges), James Cormack (Pierce), Robert Bush (Messenger), Roy Evans (Cabbie), Joan Rhodes (Cook), Nula Conwell (Nurse), Tony London (Porter), Alfie Curtis (Milkman), Bernadette Milnes, Brenda Kempner (Fighting Women), Carole Harrison (Tart), Hugh Manning, Dennis Burgess, Fanny Carby, Morgan Sheppard, Kathleen Byron, Gerald Case, David Ryall, Dierdre Costello, Pauline Quirke, Kenny Baker, Chris Greener, Marcus Powell,

Gilda Cohen, Lisa Scoble, Teri Scoble, Eiji Kusuhara, Robert Day, Patricia Hodge, Tommy Wright, Peter Davidson, John Rapley
Black and white, Panavision, Dolby Stereo
Running Time: 125 minutes
Rating: PG

Dune (Universal, 1984)
Producer: Raffaella De Laurentis
Director: David Lynch
Assistant Director, Associate Producer: Jose Lopez Rodero
Screenplay: David Lynch, based on the novel by Frank Herbert
Photography: Freddie Francis
Editor: Antony Gibbs
Music: Toto
Costumes: Bob Ringwood
Special Effects: Kit West, Albert J. Whitlock, Charles L. Finance, Barry Nolan
Designer: Anthony Masters
Production Coordinator: Golda Offenheim
Art Directors: Pierluigi Basile, Benjamin Fernandez
Cast: Francesca Annis (Lady Jessica), Leonardo Cimino (Baron's Doctor), Brad Dourif (Piter de Vries), Jose Ferrer (Padishah Emperor Shaddam IV), Linda Hunt (Shadout Mapes), Freddie Jones (Thufir Hawat), Richard Jordan (Duncan Idaho), Kyle MacLachlan (Paul Atreides), Virginia Madsen (Princess Irulan), Silvana Mangano (Rev. Mother Ramallo), Everett McGill (Stilgar), Kenneth McMillan (Baron Vladimir Harkonnen), Sian Phillips (Rev. Mother Gaius Helen Mohiam), Jurgen Prochnow (Duke Leto Atreides), Paul Smith (The Beast Rabban), Patrick Stewart (Gurney Halleck), Sting (Feyd-Rautha), Dean Stockwell (Dr. Wellington Yueh), Max von Sydow (Dr. Kynes), Alicia Rosanne Wit (Alia), Sean Young (Chani)
Todd AO and Technicolor
Running Time: 140 minutes
Rating: PG-13
Soundtrack: Polydor Records

Blue Velvet (De Laurentis Entertainment Group, 1986)
Executive Producer: Richard Roth
Direction, Screenplay: David Lynch
Assistant Directors: Ellen Rauch, Ian Woolf
Photography: Frederick Elmes
Editor: Duwayne Dunham
Music: Angelo Badalamenti

Songs by various artists
Sound: Alan Splet, Ann Kroeber
Sound Effects: Richard Hyams
Special Effects: Greg Hull, George Hill
Special Effects Makeup: Dean Jones
Designer: Patricia Norris
Production Supervisor: Gail M. Kearns
Cast: Kyle MacLachlan (Jeffrey Beaumont), Isabella Rossellini (Dorothy Vallens), Dennis Hopper (Frank Booth), Laura Dern (Sandy Williams), Hope Lange (Mrs. Williams), Dean Stockwell (Ben), George Dickerson (Detective Williams), Priscilla Pointer (Mrs. Beaumont), Frances Bay (Aunt Barbara), Jack Harvey (Mr. Beaumont), Ken Stovitz (Mike), Brad Dourif (Raymond), Jack Nance (Paul), J. Michael Hunter (Hunter), Dick Green (Don Vallens), Fred Pickler (Yellow Man), Philip Markert (Dr. Gynde), Leonard Watkins (Double Ed), Moses Gibson (Double Ed), Selden Smith (Nurse Cindy), Peter Carew (Coroner), Jon Jon Snipes (Little Donny), Andy Badale (Piano Player), Jean Pierre Viale (Master of Ceremonies), Donald Moore (Desk Sergeant), A. Michelle Depland, Michelle Sasser, Katie Reid (Party Girls)
Dolby Stereo
Running Time: 120 minutes
Rating: R
Soundtrack: Varese-Sarabande Records

Zelly and Me (Columbia Pictures, 1988)

Cypress Films and Mark/Jett Production
Executive Producers: Tina Rathborne, Elliott Lewitt
Producers: Sue Jett, Tony Mark
Associate Producer: Helena M. Consuegra
Direction, Screenplay: Tina Rathborne
Assistant Directors: Dick Feury, Chitra Mojtabai
Photography: Mikael Salomon
Editor: Cindy Kaplan Rooney
Music: Pino Donaggio
Songs: Leo Trombetta, Edward Mann, Michael Trombetta, Jeremiah Clarke
Conductor: Natale Massara
Sound: Scott Breindel
Costumes: Kathleen Detoro
Hair/Makeup Design: Hiram Ortiz
Designer: David Morong
Production Manager: Eva Fryer
Production Coordinator: Anne Nevin
Art Director: Dianna Freas
Casting: Barbara Shapiro

Cast: Alexandra Johnes (Phoebe), Isabella Rossellini (Mademoiselle), Glynis Johns (Co-Co), Kaiulani Lee (Nora), David Lynch (Willie), Joe Morton (Earl), Courtney Vickery (Dora), Lindsay Dickon (Kitty), Jason McCall (Alexander), Aaron Boone (David), Lee Lively (Elegant Gentleman), John Raynes (Bus Driver), Lynne Hallowell (Waitress), Michael Stanton Kennedy (Taxi Driver), Rick Warner (Policeman), Julia Beale Williams (Maid), Terrance Afer-Anderson (Chauffeur), Lee Lively (Joan of Arc Record Narration), Jason Allen, Haley Curvin, Justin Grant, Andy Grimes, Jennifer Lee Harvey, Melissa Klein, Matt Laffler, Stephanie Malara, Sharon May, Katie McGinty, Kris Monson, David Norris, Abby Parker, Erika Riter, Woody Sullender, Curtis Worth, Amy Young
Deluxe Color
Running Time: 97 minutes
Rating: PG
Soundtrack: Varese-Sarabande Records

Wild at Heart (Samuel Goldwyn, 1990)
Executive Producer: Michael Kuhn
Producers: Monty Montgomery, Steve Golin, Joni Sighvatsson
Director: David Lynch
Screenplay: David Lynch, based on the novel by Barry Gifford
Cinematography: Frederick Elmes
Editor: Duwayne Dunham
Music: Angelo Badalamenti
Designer: Patricia Norris
Casting: Johanna Ray
Cast: Nicolas Cage (Sailor Ripley), Laura Dern (Lula Pace-Fortune), Diane Ladd (Marrietta Fortune), Willem Dafoe (Bobby Peru), Isabella Rossellini (Perdita Durango), Harry Dean Stanton (Johnnie Farragut), Crispin Glover (Dell), Grace Zabriskie (Juana), Jack Nance (O. O. Spool), J. E. Freeman (Marcello Santos), W. Morgan Sheppard (Mr. Reindeer), David Patrick Kelly (Dropshadow), John Lurie (Sparky), Calvin Lockhart (Reginald Sula), Marvin Kaplan (Uncle Pooch), Freddie Jones (George Kovich), Sherilyn Fenn (Girl in Accident), Sheryl Lee (Good Witch), Pruitt Taylor Vince (Buddy), Gregg Dandridge (Bob Ray Lemon), Glenn Walker Harrison (Paçe Roscoe), Frances Bay (Madam), Blair Bruce Bever (Hotel Custodian), Peter Bromilow (Hotel Manager), Lisa Ann Cabasa (Reindeer Dancer), Frank A. Caruso (Old Bum), Frank Collison (Timmy Thompson), Eddy Dixon (Rex), Brent Fraser (Idiot Punk), Cage S. Johnson (Man at Shell Station), Valli Leigh, Mia M. Ruiz (Mr. Reindeer's Valets), Nick Love (Man in Wheelchair), Daniel Quinn (Young Cowboy), Charlie Spradling (Irma), Billy Swann (Himself), Koko Taylor (Singer at

Zanzibar), Ed Wright (Desk Clerk), Darrell Zwerling (Singer's Manager), Sally Boyle (Aunt Rootie)
Running Time: 124 minutes
Distributor: Samuel Goldwyn Company

Hollywood Mavericks: Top Directors Talk about Filmmaking (American Film Institute/NHK Enterprises, 1990)

Director: Florence Dauman
Writers: Todd McCarthy, Michael Henry Wilson
With: Martin Scorsese, Paul Schrader, Peter Bogdanovich, Francis Coppola, David Lynch
Running Time: 90 minutes
Distributor: Roxie Releasing

Twin Peaks Premiere Episode (Lynch/Frost Productions, 1990)

Producer: David J. Latt
Director: David Lynch
Writers: David Lynch, Mark Frost
Photography: Ron Garcia
Editor: Duwayne Dunham
Composer, Conductor: Angelo Badalamenti
Costumes: Patricia Norris
Production Design: Patricia Norris
Selected Series Directors: Duwayne Dunham, Tina Rathborne, Tim Hunter, Lesli Linka Glatter, Caleb Deschanel, Mark Frost, Todd Holland, Graeme Clifford
Selected Series Writers: Harley Peyton, Robert Engels, Jerry Stahl, Barry Pullman, Scott Frost
Selected Series Cast: Kyle MacLachlan (Dale Cooper), Michael Ontkean (Sheriff Harry S. Truman), Piper Laurie (Catherine Martell), Joan Chen (Jocelyn Packard), Madchen Amick (Shelly Johnson), Dana Ashbrook (Bobby Briggs), Richard Beymer (Benjamin Horne), Lara Flynn Boyle (Donna Hayward), Sherilyn Fenn (Audrey Horne), Warren Frost (Dr. William Hayward), Peggy Lipton (Norma Jennings), James Marshall (James Hurley), Ed Hurley (Everett McGill), Jack Nance (Pete Martell), Ray Wise (Leland Palmer), Russ Tamblyn (Dr. Lawrence Jacoby), Eric De Ra (Leo Johnson), Harry Goaz (Deputy Andy Brennan), Michael Horse (Tommy "The Hawk" Hill), Sheryl Lee (Laura Palmer/Madeline Ferguson), Chris Mulkey (Hank Jennings), Walter Olkewicz (Jacques Renault), Victoria Catlin (Blackie O'Reilly), Wendy Robie (Nadine Hurley), Kimmy Robertson (Lucy Moran), Grace Zabriskie (Sarah Palmer), David Patrick Kelly (Jerry Horne), Gary Hershberger (Mike Nelson), Miguel Ferrer (Albert Rosenfield),

Don Davis (Major Briggs), Catherine E. Coulson (Margaret, The Log Lady), Mary Jo Deschanel (Eileen Hayward), Jan D'Arcy (Sylvia Horne), Jane Greer (M. T. Wentz [Vivien]), Al Strobel (Philip "Michael" Gerard), Frank Silva (Bob), David Lynch (Gordon Cole), Ian Buchanan (Richard Trelaine), Lenny Van Dohlen (Harold Smith), Michael Parks (Jean Renault), Phoebe Augustine (Ronette Pulaski)

INDEX

THE AUTHOR

Ken Kaleta moved to the east coast from Chicago to attend Villanova University in suburban Philadelphia. He took his Ph. D. at New York University. His dissertation is a study of the prose of F. Scott Fitzgerald in translation to film. Now residing in South Jersey, Dr. Kaleta is a member of the Communications Department at Rowan College of New Jersey. In addition to being an avid filmgoer, Ken Kaleta is a member of the University Film and Video Association and an experienced traveler.